THE Extreme OLD TESTAMENT BIBLE TRIVIA Challenge

TROY SCHMIDT

BroadStreet
PUBLISHING

BroadStreet Publishing Group, LLC
Racine, Wisconsin, USA
BroadStreetPublishing.com

The Extreme Old Testament Bible Trivia Challenge

ISBN-13: 978-1-4245-5238-2 (softcover)
ISBN-13: 978-1-4245-5272-6 (e-book)

Stock or custom editions of BroadStreet Publishing titles may be purchased in bulk for educational, business, ministry, fundraising, or sales promotional use. For information, please e-mail info@broadstreetpublishing.com.

Cover design by Chris Garborg at www.garborgdesign.com
Typesetting by Katherine Lloyd at www.theDESKonline.com

Printed in the United States of America

16 17 18 19 20 5 4 3 2 1

Contents

PART 1: THE QUESTIONS

Genesis 7
Exodus 31
Leviticus 46
Numbers 52
Deuteronomy 61
Joshua 68
Judges 74
Ruth 83
1 Samuel 85
2 Samuel 95
1 Kings 104
2 Kings 115
1 Chronicles 126
2 Chronicles 132
Ezra 141
Nehemiah 144
Esther 147
Job 151
Psalms 158
Proverbs 173
Ecclesiastes 183
Song of Songs 187
Isaiah 190
Jeremiah 201
Lamentations 211
Ezekiel 213
Daniel 221
Hosea 227
Joel 229
Amos 230
Obadiah 232
Jonah 233
Micah 235
Nahum 237
Habakkuk 238
Zephaniah 239
Haggai 240
Zechariah 241
Malachi 244

PART 2: THE ANSWERS

Genesis 247
Exodus 255
Leviticus 261
Numbers 262
Deuteronomy 265
Joshua 268
Judges 270
Ruth 273
1 Samuel 274
2 Samuel 278
1 Kings 281
2 Kings 284
1 Chronicles 288
2 Chronicles 290
Ezra 293
Nehemiah 294
Esther 295
Job 296
Psalms 298
Proverbs 303
Ecclesiastes 306
Song of Songs 307
Isaiah 308
Jeremiah 312
Lamentations 315
Ezekiel 315
Daniel 317
Hosea 320
Joel 320
Amos 321
Obadiah 321
Jonah 321
Micah 322
Nahum 322
Habakkuk 322
Zephaniah 323
Haggai 323
Zechariah 323
Malachi 324

Keep Score 325
Group Quiz Score Card 348
About the Author 351

PART ONE

THE QUESTIONS

Genesis

1. What are the first three words that start the book of Genesis?
2. When the earth was created, what hovered over the waters?
3. What were the first words spoken by God in the Bible?
4. What was the first thing God created by saying, "Let there be ..."?
5. What did God separate light from?
6. What did God create on the first day?
7. What did God create on the second day?
8. On what day did God create land and sea?
9. On what day did God create vegetation (plants/trees)?
10. On what day did God create stars?
11. On what day did God create the sun and the moon (called "the greater light" in the day and "the lesser light" in the night)?
12. On what day did God create sea creatures and birds?
13. On what day did God create land creatures?
14. On what day did God create humans?
15. Of all the creations, which one did God create in his own image?
16. God told Adam and Eve to be fruitful and do what?
17. What was the first thing God gave Adam and Eve for food?

18. What did God first offer to the beasts of the earth for food?

19. On what day did God say all of his creation was "very good"?

20. On what day did God rest from all this work?

21. Which day of creation did God make holy?

22. How did God water the earth in Genesis 2?

23. What did God form Adam out of?

24. Into what part of Adam did God breathe the breath of life?

25. In what direction—north, south, east, or west—was the garden located?

26. What was the location of the garden called?

27. What were the names of the two trees God put in the middle of the garden?

28. Name the four rivers flowing from the garden of Eden.

29. Which of the four rivers flowed to a land rich in gold?

30. Which of the four rivers flowed to the land of Cush?

31. Which tree did God say would cause Adam and Eve to die if they ate from it?

32. During creation, what was the first thing God said was not good?

33. Why did God bring the animals to Adam?

34. From what part of Adam's body did God form Eve?

35. Because of the union of a man and woman, what would they leave to be united with each other?

36. In Genesis 2, God said that when a man is united with his wife, they become one what?

37. What animal was craftier than any of the wild animals God made?

38. Where in the garden was the tree that God told Eve not to eat from?

39. What did Eve tell the serpent would happen if they ate from the tree of knowledge of good and evil?

40. What happened to Adam and Eve's eyes when they ate the fruit?

41. What did Adam and Eve sew together after they realized they were naked?

42. According to Genesis 3, what was the temperature in the garden when God was walking through?

43. Why did Adam say he was afraid when he heard God coming?

44. Whom did Adam blame for the fruit-eating incident?

45. Whom did Eve blame for the fruit-eating incident?

46. Because of the deception, God told the serpent he would eat what from then on?

47. Because of the sin of Adam and Eve, Eve's pain would increase during what event?

48. Because of the garden deception, what two horticultural problems would grow from the ground?

49. When Adam died, to what would he return, since from it he was taken?

50. Who named Eve?

51. What kind of garments did God make for Adam and Eve?

52. What did God place on the east side of the garden to guard the tree of life?

53. Who was the first recorded child born in the Bible?

54. Who was the second recorded child born in the Bible?

55. What occupation did Abel take up?

56. What occupation did Cain take up?

57. What kind of offering did Cain bring?

58. What kind of offering did Abel bring?

59. Whose offering did God look at with favor—Cain's or Abel's?

60. Whom was God talking to the first time the word *sin* was used?

61. Who was the first murderer in the Bible?

62. Who said, "Am I my brother's keeper?"

63. According to God, whose blood cried out from the ground?

64. Who did God say would be a restless wanderer on the earth?

65. According to God, how many times over would someone suffer vengeance if he killed Cain?

66. What did God put on Cain so nobody would kill him?

67. What land did Cain move to?

68. What was the Land of Nod east of?

69. Who is the first recorded grandchild of Adam and Eve?

70. What did Cain name after his son Enoch?

71. What was the name of the first recorded city in the Bible?

72. Who was the first herdsman that lived in a tent?

73. Who was the first musician mentioned (he played the harp, flute/stringed instruments, and pipes)?

74. What did Tubal-Cain forge out of bronze and iron?

75. According to the Bible, who was the third son born to Adam and Eve?

76. Who was Seth's son?

77. According to Genesis 4, what did people first start doing during the lifetime of Enosh?

78. Who lived longest—Adam, Seth, or Enosh?

79. How many years did Adam live?

80. In Genesis 5, who was the second oldest person to live?

81. Whom in Genesis did God "take away"?

82. Who was the oldest person to live in the Bible?

83. How old was Methuselah when he died?

84. Who was Noah's father?

85. How old was Noah when he became a father?

86. What were the names of Noah's three sons?

87. In Genesis 6, to what age did God limit human life?

88. Who were called the heroes of old, the men of renown?

89. The Nephilim came about when the heroes of old went to the daughters of whom?

90. What was God sorry he had made?

91. In Genesis 6, who was the one person that found favor in God's eyes?

92. What kind of wood was the ark made of?

93. What was the ark coated with, inside and out?

94. How many decks did the ark have?

95. How many of each living creature would be called to the ark?

96. How many pairs of every kind of clean animal did God tell Noah to take on the ark?

97. How many kinds of unclean animals did God tell Noah to take on the ark?
98. Of what species did God specifically tell Noah to bring seven of every kind?
99. How many days passed from the moment God talked to Noah in Genesis 7 to when the rains came?
100. How many days did God say he would allow it to rain?
101. How old was Noah when the floodwaters came on the earth?
102. How many humans were on the ark?
103. How much higher did the waters rise above the mountains?
104. How many days after the rain did the flood waters cover the earth?
105. How many days after the flood stopped did the ark rest on a mountain?
106. On what mountains did the ark rest?
107. What did Noah first open to let a bird fly out?
108. What kind of bird did Noah send out first?
109. What bird did Noah send out the second time?
110. How many days did Noah wait before he sent out the dove a second time?
111. What was in the beak of the dove when it returned to the ark?
112. How many total times did Noah send out the dove?
113. What happened to the dove after it went out the last time?
114. How old was Noah when he lifted off the cover to the ark to see if the water had dried up?
115. What was the first recorded thing Noah that did when he got off the ark?

116. Who smelled the sacrifice and was pleased?

117. In Genesis 9, what did God tell Noah to eat when he got off the ark?

118. What did God tell Noah must not be in the meat when he ate it?

119. What did God promise not to destroy the earth with in Genesis 9?

120. What did God reveal in the sky as a sign of the covenant between God and every living creature?

121. Which of Noah's sons was the father of Canaan?

122. What did Noah plant when he got off the ark?

123. Where was Noah lying when he passed out drunk?

124. Who saw his father's nakedness and then told his brothers about it?

125. What did the other two brothers do when they heard their father was naked?

126. Whose descendants did Noah curse because of what Ham did?

127. How many years after the flood did Noah live?

128. How many total years did Noah live?

129. Who grew to be a mighty hunter and warrior on the earth?

130. In what book of the Bible do we first hear about the areas of Babylon, Assyria, and Nineveh?

131. Who first built Nineveh?

132. What two notorious cities, later destroyed by God, did the Canaanites build?

133. On what eastern plain did the men of earth settle after Noah?

134. Instead of stone, what did the people use to build the Tower of Babel?

135. What did the people use for mortar when building the Tower of Babel?

136. In addition to a tower, what else did the builders of Babel construct?

137. To inhibit the people's progress, what did God confuse?

138. What was the place called because of what was confused that day?

139. Who was Abram's father?

140. Who were Abram's brothers?

141. What was the name of Haran's son (and Abram's nephew)?

142. Who was Abram's wife?

143. Who was Nahor's wife?

144. What city did Terah, Abram, Sarai, and Lot leave from?

145. Where were they headed?

146. Where did they settle instead (the place where Terah eventually died)?

147. How old was Abram when he set out from Harran to Canaan?

148. From what region did Abram leave to go to the Promised Land?

149. What two people went with Abram to Canaan?

150. During the famine in Genesis 12, to where did Abram and Sarai travel for help?

151. Fearing Pharaoh would kill him to take Sarai as his wife, how did Abram describe his relationship with Sarai?

152. Which group in Egypt saw Sarai and praised her beauty to Pharaoh?

153. What animals did Pharaoh give Abram in return for Sarai?

154. Because Pharaoh took Sarai as his wife, the Lord inflicted diseases on whom?

155. What group of Abram's and Lot's workers began quarreling?

156. What plain did Lot choose when he and Abram split up?

157. What two infamous cities were in the area Lot chose to live?

158. Like what particle, too numerous to count, did God promise Abram that his descendants would number?

159. After Lot departed, Abram moved his tents to live near the great trees of what?

160. The Valley of Siddim contained what sea?

161. What gooey ecological obstacle was the Valley of Siddim full of (that people fell into)?

162. Which of Abram's relatives was taken prisoner during the war?

163. Who was first called a Hebrew in the Bible?

164. How many fighting men did Abram take with him to rescue Lot?

165. What title besides king did Melchizedek hold?

166. What was Melchizedek the king of?

167. What food did Melchizedek bring Abram?

168. What fraction of an offering did Abram give the priest Melchizedek?

169. What payment did Abram want from the king of Sodom for his help in defeating the enemies?

170. If Abram didn't produce an offspring, who would inherit all his property?

171. To understand how many descendants Abram would have, what did God tell him to look up and count?

172. When Abram believed God, what was he credited with?

173. What five animals did God ask Abram to sacrifice for the covenant in Genesis 15?

174. What came down and tried to eat Abram's sacrifice in Genesis 15?

175. God foretold that the Israelites would be strangers in a country for how many years (talking about Egypt)?

176. In Genesis 5, what passed between the pieces of sacrifice Abram offered God?

177. What was the name of Sarai's maidservant?

178. Where was Sarai's maidservant from?

179. Who comforted Hagar at the desert spring after she ran away?

180. Who would be called a wild donkey of a man?

181. What did Hagar call the well where God met and comforted her?

182. How old was Abram when Ishmael was born?

183. God changed Abram's name to Abraham because he would be the father of many what?

184. In Genesis 17:10, what new covenant did God establish with Abraham that every male needed to keep?

185. At what age were boys to be circumcised?

186. God changed Sarai's name to Sarah because she be the mother of all what?

187. Who gave Abraham's son Isaac his name?

188. Isaac's name means "he _______" because that's what Abraham did when he heard he would be a father at a hundred years old.

189. How many rulers/princes would be born to Ishmael?

190. How old was Abraham when he was circumcised?

191. How old was Ishmael when he was circumcised?

192. In what location were the great trees where Abraham pitched his tents?

193. How many men visited Abraham in that location?

194. What did Abraham ask Sarah to make for the visitors?

195. Where was Sarah when she heard the news that she would have a child in one year?

196. What did Sarah deny doing when accused by the Lord of having done it?

197. What two cities did Abraham bargain with the Lord to save?

198. To save Sodom, how many righteous people did Abraham first bargain for?

199. What was the final number that ended Abraham's bargaining for Sodom?

200. At what time during the day did the angels arrive in Sodom?

201. Where was Lot sitting when the angels arrived in Sodom?

202. What did the men of Sodom want to do with the visiting angels?

203. Whom did Lot offer to the men of the city instead of the angels?

204. What physical condition did the angels strike the Sodom mob with to help with Lot's escape?

205. Who thought Lot was joking when he pleaded with them to leave Sodom?

206. Who were the four people that originally got out of Sodom safely?

207. To what town did Lot want to flee?

208. What rained down on Sodom and Gomorrah?

209. In addition to the people and the two cities, what two other things does Genesis 19 say God destroyed that day?

210. Who disobeyed the angels and looked back at the destruction?

211. What did Lot's wife become when she looked back at the destruction of Sodom?

212. Whom did Lot's oldest daughter give birth to?

213. Whom did Lot's younger daughter give birth to?

214. What two future enemies of Israel were sons of Lot?

215. What was the name of the king of Gerar that Abraham lied to, saying that Sarah was his sister?

216. How did God communicate to the king of Gerar to stay away from Sarah?

217. According to Abraham, how was Sarah related to him outside of marriage?

218. What did God close up in Abimelech's household because of the incident with Sarah?

219. How old was Abraham when Isaac was born?

220. Besides a son, what did Sarah say that God had brought her?

221. In what desert did Hagar and Ishmael find themselves?

222. When God opened Hagar's eyes, what did he show her?

223. What skill did Ishmael perfect in the desert?

224. From what country did Hagar find a wife for Ishmael?

225. What did Abraham's servants and Abimelech's servants argue over in the desert?

226. What kind of a tree did Abraham plant in Beersheba?

227. To what region did God tell Abraham to take his son Isaac?

228. What kind of an offering did God want Isaac to be?

229. What animal did Abraham take with him to Mount Moriah?

230. How many servants went with them on the journey?

231. After how many days of traveling did Abraham see the place where the sacrifice would occur?

232. What did Isaac carry up the mountain for the sacrifice?

233. What two items did Abraham carry up the mountain?

234. What did Isaac believe they had forgotten for the sacrifice?

235. What part of Abraham's body did the angel grab to stop the sacrifice?

236. What animal did they see caught in the bushes?

237. What did Abraham call the place where God stopped the sacrifice of Isaac?

238. In Genesis 22, God promised Abraham that he would make him as numerous as what two things?

239. How old was Sarah when she died?

240. Where did Sarah die?

241. What was the place where Sarah was buried?

242. Who owned the field where Abraham buried Sarah?

243. What did the land cost Abraham?

244. Whom did Abraham send to find a wife for his son Isaac?

245. From what people group did Abraham specifically say he did not want Isaac to marry?

246. How many camels did Abraham's servant take with him to find a wife for Isaac?

247. To what town did the servant travel to find a wife for Isaac?

248. Near what did the servant stop and wait for Isaac's wife to come by?

249. As a sign that Abraham's servant had found the right wife for Isaac, what did he pray the woman would offer to give a drink to?

250. While the servant prayed, who walked up with her water jug?

251. Who was Rebekah's father?

252. What jewelry did Abraham's servant give Rebekah when they first met?

253. Who was Rebekah's brother?

254. How many more days did Laban and her mother want Rebekah to stay before the servant took her away?

255. Who was Abraham's wife after Sarah died?

256. To whom did Abraham leave everything he owned?

257. How old was Abraham when he died?

258. Where was Abraham buried when he died?

259. Who was the firstborn son of Ishmael?

260. How many sons did Ishmael have?

261. Near what border did the sons of Ishmael live?

262. How old was Isaac when he married Rebekah?

263. What did the Lord tell Rebekah there were two of in her womb?

264. What did God say would be the relationship between the twins inside Rebekah's womb?

265. What color was Esau when he was born?

266. Who got his name because he was red and hairy?

267. How does the Bible describe Esau's whole body?

268. When Jacob was born, what was he grasping?

269. How old was Isaac when Rebekah gave birth?

270. What was Esau skilled in?

271. While Esau loved the open country, where did Jacob prefer to stay?

272. Which son did Isaac love more?

273. Which son did Rebekah love more?

274. What color was the stew Esau desired?

275. Why was Esau called Edom?

276. What did Jacob want in return for the stew?

277. What did Esau sell to Jacob?

278. What kind of stew did Jacob make?

279. What did Esau despise after that day?

280. What so severely struck the land that it caused Isaac to move?

281. Where did Isaac move to?

282. Where did God tell Isaac not to move to?

283. How did Isaac tell the men of Gerar that Rebekah was related to him?

284. What was the name of the king that Isaac lied to about his wife Rebekah?

285. What were the four things called Esek, Sitnah, Rehoboth, and Shibah?

286. What does the name Rehoboth mean?

287. What two women did Esau first marry?

288. What kind of dinner did Isaac want Esau to prepare for him?

289. What did Jacob put on his arm to make it seem hairy like Esau's?

290. What one quality almost gave away Jacob's deception of Isaac (that he was actually Esau)?

291. Where did Rebekah tell Jacob to stay while Esau cooled down?

292. In what region did Laban live?

293. Jacob went to Paddan Aram to find a wife among the daughters of whom?

294. When Esau heard that Isaac went to Paddan Aram to find a wife from his own family line, to whose family line did he go to find another wife?

295. What was the name of the third wife Esau married?

296. What did Jacob use as a pillow before he saw the stairway in a dream?

297. Who was ascending and descending the stairway to heaven in Jacob's dream?

298. What did Jacob call the place where he saw the stairway to heaven?

299. What was this city, which Jacob renamed, formerly called?

300. What was Rachel's occupation?

301. What was Jacob's relationship to Rachel?

302. What was Jacob standing by when he first saw Rachel?

303. How were Leah's eyes described?

304. How long did Jacob offer to serve Laban for the hand of Rachel?

305. Who was the servant that Laban gave to Leah?

306. Whom did Jacob wake up with on his first wedding night?

307. How many more years did Laban want Jacob to work for Rachel?

308. How long did Jacob wait to marry Rachel after marrying Leah?

309. Why did God bless Leah and give her sons?

310. Who was the first son born to Jacob?

311. Which of Jacob and Leah's sons' names means "he has seen my misery"?

312. Which of Jacob and Leah's sons' names means "he heard me"?

313. Which of Jacob and Leah's sons' names means "attached to me"?

314. Which of Jacob and Leah's sons' names means "praise the Lord"?

315. Who were Jacob and Leah's sons?

316. Who were Jacob and Rachel's servant Bilhah's sons?

317. Which of Jacob and Bilhah's sons' names means "he has vindicated"?

318. Which of Jacob and Bilhah's sons' names means "my struggle"?

319. Who were Jacob and Leah's servant Zilpah's sons?

320. Which of Jacob and Zilpah's sons' names means "good fortune"?

321. Which of Jacob and Zilpah's sons' names means "happy"?

322. What plant did Rachel and Leah argue over?

323. Which of Jacob and Leah's sons' names means "rewarded"?

324. Which of Jacob and Zilpah's sons' names means "honored"?

325. What was Jacob's only daughter's name?

326. Who were Jacob and Rachel's sons?

327. Which of Jacob and Rachel's sons' names means "added"?

328. What two livestock became the center of the negotiation to divide the flocks of Isaac and Laban?

329. What kind of tree branches did Jacob use to cause the newborn goats to have spots and speckles?

330. When Jacob ran away from Laban, what did Rachel steal from her father?

331. Whom did God warn Laban in a dream not to harm?

332. How many total years did Jacob serve Laban?

333. What did Jacob call the stone pile covenant between him and Laban?

334. What did Jacob name the place where he saw the angel camp?

335. How many men were with Esau when he came to meet Jacob?

336. Where on Jacob's body did the angel touch during their wrestling match?

337. What new name did the angel give Jacob after the wrestling match?

338. What does Jacob's new name mean?

339. What did Jacob name the place where he claimed he saw God face-to-face?

340. Because of Jacob's hip injury, typically what don't Jews eat today?

341. After Jacob left his meeting with Esau, he set up shelters in a place called what (which actually means "shelters")?

342. Who was the Hivite leader that violated Dinah, then fell in love with her?

343. Name the father of the Hivite that tried to negotiate with Jacob for Dinah.

344. What Jewish custom did the brothers of Dinah ask the Hivites to perform before they could intermarry?

345. Which two sons of Jacob retaliated against the Hivites for the rape of their sister?

346. Before going to Bethel, what did Jacob tell his household to get rid of?

347. Rachel died after giving birth to which son?

348. What did Rachel originally name Benjamin before Jacob changed it?

349. Rachel was buried on the way to what city?

350. Which of Jacob's sons slept with Bilhah, Jacob's concubine?

351. Genesis 36 gives the genealogy of what man that lost his birthright?

352. Whose daughter was Basemath, a woman Esau married?

353. Esau and his family moved to the hill country of what area?

354. How old was Joseph when he tattled on his brothers to Jacob?

355. Why did Jacob love Joseph more than all his brothers?

356. What gift did Jacob give Joseph?

357. Joseph's first dream involved sheaves of what bowing to another sheaf?

358. Joseph's second dream involved what three objects in space?

359. What nickname did Joseph's brothers give him when they saw him approaching them in the field?

360. What did Joseph's brothers throw him into?

361. Which brother first defended Joseph and kept the others from killing him?

362. To whom did Joseph's brothers sell him?

363. To what country were these traders headed?

364. Which brother suggested selling him to the traders?

365. For how much did Joseph's brothers sell him?

366. Which brother returned to the cistern too late and found Joseph gone?

367. What animal's blood did they put on Joseph's robe?

368. What did Jacob think happened to his son Joseph?

369. Whom did the Midianites sell Joseph to in Egypt?

370. What was Potiphar's job?

371. Who were Judah's two wicked sons?

372. Why did God put them to death?

373. What did Onan spill on the ground, refusing to have a child with his brother's wife?

374. Who was Judah's third son that he didn't give Tamar as his wife?

375. Who disguised herself as a prostitute and slept with her father-in-law Judah to have children by him?

376. What three items did Tamar take as a pledge from Judah?

377. When the twins were born, what did the midwife tie on the wrist of the one that stuck his arm out first?

378. Who were the twin sons born of Judah and Tamar?

379. Which one stuck his arm out first?

380. Who was Potiphar's boss?

381. What clothing evidence did Joseph leave in Potiphar's wife's hands?

382. What did Potiphar's wife accuse Joseph of?

383. Whom did Joseph immediately find favor with while in jail?

384. What two Egyptian officials did Joseph meet in prison?

385. To whom did Joseph say all dream interpretations belong?

386. Who had the dream in prison of vines and grapes?

387. Who had a dream in prison of three baskets of bread?

388. What in the baker's dream kept stealing the bread from the basket?

389. In both dreams, what did the three items (branches and baskets) mean?

390. During what occasion did Pharaoh restore the cupbearer to his position?

391. What happened to the baker?

392. How long after the cupbearer's release did Pharaoh have a dream about cows?

393. On what river bank was Pharaoh standing in his dream?

394. In Pharaoh's dream, what did the seven skinny cows do to the seven fat cows?

395. In Pharaoh's dream, seven healthy heads of what were eaten by seven sickly heads?

396. What two groups of people could not interpret Pharaoh's dream in Genesis 41?

397. Who told Pharaoh about Joseph's ability to interpret dreams?

398. What two things did Joseph do to look presentable before he met with Pharaoh?

399. In both of Pharaoh's dreams, what did the seven stand for?

400. What did Joseph interpret the seven fat cows to mean?

401. What did Joseph interpret the seven skinny cows to mean?

402. What percentage of crops did Joseph suggest should be collected and stored for the lean years?

403. What three items did Pharaoh give Joseph after interpreting the dream?

404. Whom did Pharaoh rename Zaphenath-Paneah?

405. What was the name of the daughter that Pharaoh gave to Joseph?

406. How old was Joseph when he started serving Pharaoh?

407. Name Joseph's two sons.

408. Which of Joseph's sons was named because God helped Joseph forget his troubles?

409. Which of Joseph's sons was named because God made him fruitful?

410. How many of Joseph's brothers went to Egypt during the first trip to buy grain?

411. Which son was Jacob reluctant to send to Egypt to buy grain?

412. What did Joseph accuse the brothers of being when he first met them?

413. Which brother stayed behind in Egypt while the other brothers returned to Jacob?

414. What did Joseph secretly return to his brothers in their pouches on the first trip back to Israel?

415. Which two brothers promised Jacob that they would make sure Benjamin returned home safely?

416. According to Genesis 43, what did the Egyptians consider to be a detestable thing to do with Hebrews?

417. How much bigger was Benjamin's food portion compared to his brothers' when served a meal while in Egypt?

418. What item did Joseph have planted in his brothers' sacks and then accuse them of stealing?

419. What did Joseph's steward say Joseph used the cup for?

420. In the sack of which of Joseph's brothers was the silver cup found?

421. Which brother made a desperate plea to Joseph when Joseph told them he would imprison Benjamin?

422. When Joseph revealed himself to his brothers, what was the first question he asked?

423. Why did Joseph feel he needed to be sent to Egypt?

424. In what area did Joseph tell his brothers they would live in Egypt?

425. While every brother got a set of new clothes, how many sets of clothes did Benjamin get?

426. Who did God say would close Joseph's eyes at death?

427. How many people in all traveled from Israel's home to Egypt, not counting the wives?

428. What occupation was detestable to Egyptians?

429. What occupation did Joseph want his brothers to tell Pharaoh they did so they would be allowed to settle in Goshen?

430. How old did Jacob tell Pharaoh he was?

431. Before Jacob left Pharaoh, what did he do to him?

432. After the Egyptians ran out of money buying food, what two things did they exchange for food?

433. According to Joseph's plan, what fraction of all produce was given back to the Egyptian government?

434. Before he died, how long had Jacob lived in Egypt?

435. How old was Jacob when he died?

436. Where did Jacob not want to be buried?

437. Who switched his father's hands, thinking Jacob was blessing the grandsons in the wrong order?

438. Which of Joseph's sons was younger but got the older son's blessing?

439. Which son did Jacob not bless because he had defiled his father's bed?

440. Which two sons did Jacob call, before his death, men/weapons of violence?

441. Which of his sons did Jacob compare to a lion?

442. What did Jacob say would not depart from Judah?

443. What two animals did Jacob prophesy about Judah that Jesus would later ride when coming into Jerusalem?

444. Which of his sons did Jacob call a rawboned donkey?

445. Which of his sons did Jacob say would provide justice and be called a serpent by the roadside?

446. Which son did Jacob say would be a fruitful vine?

447. Which son did Jacob call a ravenous wolf?

448. In what cave did Jacob asked to be buried?

449. Who else was buried in the cave Jacob asked to be buried in?

450. How many days did it take to embalm Jacob?

451. Before he died, where did Joseph ask to be buried?

452. What of his did Jacob want carried there?

453. How old was Joseph when he died?

454. Of all of Jacob's sons, the Bible gives an age at death for only one. What was his name?

Exodus

455. According to Exodus 1, how many in Jacob's family went to Egypt?

456. To make their lives bitter, what did the Egyptian slave masters force the Israelites to build?

457. What two Egyptian cities does Exodus 1 say the Israelite slaves built?

458. With what two items did the Egyptians make the Israelites build?

459. In addition to on building sites, where else were the Israelites treated harshly?

460. What job did the Hebrew women Shiphrah and Puah have in Egypt?

461. Which gender of Israelite baby—boy or girl—did the king of Egypt ask the midwives to kill?

462. What did the midwives tell the king of Egypt that the Hebrew women did before they arrived?

463. Because the midwives feared God and did not carry out Pharaoh's orders, what did God give them?

464. Into what did the king of Egypt want all the Hebrew boys thrown?

465. From what tribe were Moses' parents?

466. For how long did Moses' mother hide him after he was born?

467. From what kind of reed was baby Moses' floating basket made?

468. What was baby Moses' basket covered with?

469. What member of baby Moses' family watched him float down the Nile?

470. Who found the basket with baby Moses inside?

471. Who was hired to nurse baby Moses?

472. Who named Moses?

473. What does Moses' name mean?

474. Whom did Moses see an Egyptian beating?

475. Where did Moses hide the Egyptian he killed?

476. When he heard Moses killed an Egyptian, who wanted to kill Moses?

477. In what region did Moses hide when Pharaoh wanted to kill him for the murder of an Egyptian?

478. From what did the shepherds drive the women away but Moses came to their rescue?

479. What was the spiritual title of the man whose daughters Moses saved?

480. How many daughters did the man have?

481. What was the name of the man from Midian that took Moses in?

482. Who became Moses' wife?

483. What was the name of Moses' first son?

484. What did his son's name mean?

485. What was another name for Reuel, Moses' father-in-law?

486. Whose flocks were Moses tending to when the burning bush appeared?

487. On what mountain did the burning bush appear?

488. What were God's first two words to Moses?

489. What did God ask Moses to remove before he stepped closer to the burning bush?

490. God told Moses the land he stood on was what kind of ground?
491. God promised to take the Israelites to a land flowing with what?
492. When Moses asked what God's name was, how did God answer?
493. What did Moses' staff turn into when thrown to the ground?
494. When Moses grabbed the staff by the tail, what did the snake turn into?
495. When Moses put his hand into his cloak, what disease covered it?
496. What third miracle did God tell Moses to do if the Egyptians did not believe the first two?
497. What did Moses say he was slow in?
498. Who did God suggest could be Moses' mouthpiece?
499. When Moses returned to Egypt, whom did he take with him?
500. Why was God going to kill Moses?
501. Who circumcised Moses' son?
502. What kind of a cutting instrument was used to circumcise Moses' son?
503. What was that cutting instrument made of?
504. Where did the Lord tell Aaron to meet Moses?
505. For how many days did Moses ask Pharaoh to release the Israelites to worship God in the wilderness?
506. Angry at the Israelites, what did the Egyptian slave drivers make the Israelites gather for themselves to make bricks?
507. Who was the father of Gershom, Kohath, and Merari?
508. Who was Moses' father?
509. What was the name of Moses' mother?
510. How old was Moses when the plagues began?

511. How old was Aaron when the plagues began?

512. Whose staff turned into a snake in front of Pharaoh?

513. What three groups in Pharaoh's court were able to reproduce some of Moses' miracles?

514. What did Aaron's snake/staff do to the magician's staff that had turned into snake?

515. What did God say he would turn into blood?

516. Because the Nile turned to blood, what died and stunk up Egypt?

517. Which three plagues happened as a direct result of Aaron's staff?

518. Who stretched his hand and staff over the waters and caused the frogs to cover Egypt?

519. What was the first plague the Egyptian magicians could not replicate?

520. What was the fifth plague?

521. After which two plagues did Pharaoh ask that Moses pray for him?

522. What did the sixth plague sicken?

523. Though the livestock of the Egyptians got sick, whose livestock did not get sick?

524. What did Moses toss into the air that triggered the plague of boils?

525. In addition to the hail, what two other weather phenomena occurred at the same time?

526. What two crops were destroyed when the plague of hail hit Egypt?

527. Which two crops were not destroyed when the plague of hail hit Egypt because they ripen later?

528. What was the eighth plague Egypt faced in the book of Exodus?

529. Which two plagues occurred when Moses lifted his staff?

530. What drove the locusts away?

531. Where were the locusts carried away to?

532. How many days did the plague of darkness blackout Egypt?

533. When the Israelites left after the final plague, God told them to ask their neighbors for articles made of what two elements?

534. At what time in the day was every firstborn in Egypt prophesied to die?

535. During the plague on the firstborn, what did Moses say a dog wouldn't even do?

536. The month of Passover was the first month of what?

537. On what day of that month did the man choose the lamb?

538. How old did the Passover animals need to be?

539. The Passover animal needed to be which gender—male or female?

540. What two animals could be used as Passover sacrifices?

541. On what day of the month were the people to sacrifice their Passover animal?

542. At what time of the day were the people to sacrifice their Passover animal?

543. What two places on the doorframes were the people told to put the Passover blood?

544. How should the Passover lamb be cooked?

545. What two other items were the people to eat with the Passover animal?

546. What were the Israelites instructed to do with the meat if any was left the morning after Passover?

547. How were the Israelites instructed to dress as they ate the Passover meal?

548. In addition to people, what other group would also lose their firstborn that Passover night?

549. What would God see on the houses and "pass over" it?

550. How many days were they told to eat bread without yeast during the Passover?

551. What happened to a person that ate bread with yeast?

552. What kind of branch did the Israelites use to apply the Passover blood to the doorframes?

553. What passed over the household when there was blood on the doorframe?

554. At what time did the firstborn die in Egypt?

555. Exodus 12 says that everybody from the firstborn of Pharaoh to what other person would be affected by death?

556. What three items did the Israelites ask the Egyptians for as they left?

557. How many Israelite men traveled out of Egypt after the Passover?

558. How many years did the Israelites live in Egypt prior to the Passover?

559. When the Israelites left Egypt, whose bones did they take with them?

560. God led the Israelites out of Egypt by day with a pillar of what?

561. God led the Israelites out of Egypt by night with a pillar of what?

562. How many chariots pursued the Israelites out of Egypt?

563. What did God keep doing to Pharaoh's heart?

564. What did the Israelites say there were none of in Egypt so Moses had brought them out to the desert to die?

565. What two things did Moses raise and stretch out to divide the Red Sea?

566. From what direction did the wind blow to turn the sea-soaked land dry?

567. In Exodus 14, God looked down from the pillar of fire and confused whom?

568. What did God do to the chariots of the Egyptians that pursued the Israelites through the Red Sea?

569. How many of Pharaoh's army survived the Red Sea incident?

570. Exodus 15 says ________ and the Israelites sang a song after the Red Sea incident.

571. Who led the Israelite women in song after the Red Sea incident?

572. What instrument did she play?

573. Why did the Israelites call the desert place Marah?

574. What did Moses throw into the waters of Marah so it would become fit to drink?

575. How much time had passed since they came out of Egypt when the Israelites grumbled over the food?

576. What did the Israelites say they had pots of in Egypt?

577. How much manna were the people told to gather for five mornings?

578. How much manna were the people told to gather on the sixth day?

579. In Exodus 16, what did God provide for them to eat at twilight?

580. What did the people say when they saw the manna?

581. What specific weight of manna could each person could take daily?

582. If the Israelites kept any manna until morning, what infested the batch?

583. On the sixth day, how many omers of manna were collected?

584. What color was the manna?

585. The manna was the same color as what kind of seed?

586. The manna tasted like wafers made with what?

587. Moses had the manna put in the jar so who could see it?

588. For how many years did the Israelites eat manna?

589. What fraction of an ephah is an omer?

590. In what area was the rock that Moses struck in Exodus 17, causing water to come out?

591. Why was the place of the first water-from-rock miracle called Massah?

592. Why was the place of the first water-from-rock miracle also called Meribah?

593. Who were the first enemies to attack the Israelites in the desert?

594. Who led the first battle against the Amalekites in the Egyptian desert?

595. What did God instruct Moses to do during the battle with the Amalekites?

596. What did Moses sit on when he got tired?

597. Who held up Moses' hands during the battle when he got tired?

598. When the Israelites defeated the Amalekites, what did Moses call the altar?

599. In addition to being Moses' father-in-law, what religious role did Jethro hold in Midian?

600. What was the name of Moses' second son?

601. What does Eliezer mean?

602. Which family member visited Moses in the desert and gave him some leadership advice?

603. What did Jethro suggest Moses should appoint to help lead the people?

604. What was the name of the mountain Moses climbed to receive the Ten Commandments?

605. What were the Israelites told to wash before the Lord visited Mount Sinai?

606. What were the Israelites told not to touch (or they would be killed) when the Lord visited Mount Sinai?

607. If anyone touched the mountain, they were to be stoned or shot with a what?

608. While Moses was on Mount Sinai, what were the people told to abstain from on the third day?

609. Whom did Moses take with him when he climbed Mount Sinai to meet God?

610. According to the first commandment, what should we not have?

611. In the second commandment, God said we should not make an image in the form of anything found in what three places?

612. In the second commandment, God said he was jealous and punished children for the sin of the parents to what two generations?

613. According to the third commandment, what should we not misuse?

614. What day did the fourth commandment say God blessed and made holy?

615. What reason did God give that the Israelites should work six days and rest on the seventh?

616. According to the fifth commandment, what two people should we honor so that we will live long in the land God gave us?

617. What is the sixth commandment?

618. What is the seventh commandment?

619. What is the eighth commandment?

620. According to the ninth commandment, what kind of testimony should we not give against our neighbor?

621. Which animals did the tenth commandment specifically say we should not covet?

622. How long did a Hebrew servant serve before being set free?

623. If a slave wished to remain with his master for life, what was pierced as a sign of his desire?

624. What tool would do the piercing?

625. What was the penalty for attacking a father or mother?

626. What was the penalty for kidnapping?

627. What was the penalty for cursing a father or mother?

628. If someone quarreled and injured someone, confining them to bed, what did the guilty party pay for?

629. What was the punishment for beating a slave to death?

630. What two other parts of the body came after the statement about an eye for an eye and a tooth for a tooth?

631. A slave could go free if the owner knocked out what two parts of a slave's body?

632. According to the Mosaic law, what must happen to a bull that gored someone for the first time?

633. According to Mosaic law, what must happen to a bull that gored people repeatedly and to the owner because the warnings were not heeded?

634. Why could the owner of a bull be put to the death if the bull killed another person?

635. If a man dug a pit and a donkey fell in, what must the owner do?

636. If a man seduced a virgin before they were pledged to be married, what must the man do?

637. In Exodus 22, whom did God say the Israelites should not mistreat because they were once ones in Egypt?

638. In Exodus 22, what two groups of people, if taken advantage of, would arouse God's anger?

639. In Exodus 22, God said that if money was lent to one of his people, what could not be charged?

640. According to Mosaic law, if a cloak was borrowed as a pledge, when must it be returned?

641. What must be done if someone saw their enemy's ox wandering around loose?

642. What must be done if someone saw their enemy's donkey fall down?

643. An Israelite must not oppress an alien because they were once aliens where?

644. According to Exodus 23, what four things would benefit from a Sabbath rest?

645. During the Festival of Unleavened Bread, how many days did the Israelites eat bread without yeast?

646. How many times a year did a man need to appear before the Lord?

647. What must a young goat not be cooked in?

648. What insect did God say (figuratively) that he would send ahead to drive out the enemies?

649. In Exodus 24, what was the name of the book Moses wrote after his first meeting with God on the mountain?

650. When Moses and the others saw God, the bright blue material under God's feet looked like what?

651. In Exodus 24, how many days and nights did Moses spend on the mountain alone with God?

652. From what kind of wood was the ark of the covenant made?

653. What was inserted into the rings and used to carry the ark?

654. What two figures sat on top of the ark, facing each other?

655. According to Exodus 25, what were the first two items to be put in the ark?

656. What was inserted into the rings and used to carry the table?

657. What five items were put on the table that became part of the tabernacle?

658. How many lamps were in the tabernacle?

659. What part of the tabernacle was made of fine linen and blue, purple, and scarlet yarn?

660. The hair of what animals was used to make the tabernacle curtains?

661. From what kind of wood were the frames and crossbars of the tabernacle made?

662. From what material were the bases of the tabernacle's frame made?

663. The curtain surrounding the ark separated the Holy Place from what?

664. The altar built by the Israelites in the desert was made of what kind of wood?

665. What stuck out of each of the four corners of the altar?

666. What kind of oil must be used in the lamps?

667. The priests had to keep the lamps lit from when to when?

668. In Exodus 28, the priestly garments were made for Aaron and whom else?

669. The priest's ephod had two stones with whose names written on them?

670. In what order were they written?

671. The priest's breastplate had four rows of twelves stones that represented what?

672. Over what part of Aaron's body was the Urim and Thummim placed?

673. What did the Urim and Thummim help Aaron make?

674. What two items were alternately sewn into the hem of the priestly robe?

675. What instruments were built into the priestly garments to make a sound, so the priest would not die when he entered the Holy Place?

676. What words were engraved on a gold plate fastened to Aaron's forehead?

677. From what were the priests' undergarments made?

678. When the priests were anointed, what part of their body was the oil poured on?

679. When the priests were consecrated, what was placed on their right ear lobe, right thumb, and right big toe?

680. At what two times of the day did the priest offer fragrant incense on the altar?

681. What three gifts mentioned in the Gospels are found in Exodus 30?

682. When the census was taken, each person twenty years and older had to pay how much?

683. From what material was the wash basin made?

684. Who were the only people that could be anointed with the anointing oil?

685. Who were the two craftsmen that received God's Spirit to design the tabernacle?

686. What did God inscribe the first tablets of testimony with?

687. What piece of jewelry did the Israelites donate to the idol they made at the foot of Mount Sinai?

688. Who made the golden idol in Exodus 32?

689. In what image was the idol made?

690. In Exodus 32, what did Moses keep God from doing to the Israelites?

691. How were the words inscribed on the first set of tablets that Moses brought down from the mountain?

692. After Moses saw the idol, what did he do to it?

693. What did Aaron say happened after he threw the gold into the fire?

694. Which tribe carried out the death sentence on the people with swords?

695. How many people died by the sword as a result of the golden calf incident?

696. Because of the golden calf incident, what did God strike the Israelites with?

697. When the pillar of cloud stood at the entrance to the tent of meeting, what did all the Israelites do?

698. Exodus 33:11 says the Lord spoke to Moses as a man speaks to whom?

699. When Moses wanted to see God's glory, God told Moses he could not see what part of God's body and live?

700. Where did God put Moses as he passed by so Moses would not die if he saw God?

701. When God passed by Moses, what part of himself did he cover Moses with?

702. God did not allow Moses to see his face but what instead?

703. Who carved the second set of stone tablet commandments?

704. What did God tell the Israelites not to make with any of the tribes living in the Promised Land?

705. What didn't Moses consume for forty days and forty nights while on the mountain with God?

706. After being with God for forty days, how was Moses' face described?

707. What did Moses put over his face to cover the radiance he reflected?

708. What three colors were the yarn that the people gave to the tabernacle construction?

709. During the construction of the tabernacle, what were the people restrained from doing?

710. Of all the items for the tabernacle listed in Exodus 37, which one did not require poles to carry it?

711. Every article for the table listed in Exodus 37 was made from what precious metal?

712. In Exodus 38, the altar of the burnt offerings, the wash basin, and the courtyard materials all shared what precious metal in common?

713. What part of the tabernacle was one hundred cubits long and fifty cubits wide?

714. How many cubits long were the curtains around the tabernacle?

715. In all, what three precious metals were used to make the tabernacle according to Exodus 38?

716. How many rows of precious stones were on the priest's breastplate?

717. What did the twelve stones on the breastplate represent?

718. What fruit was fashioned out of blue, purple, and scarlet yarn and attached to the hem of the priest's robe?

719. What was the inscription written on the sacred emblem found on the priest's garment?

720. What covered the tent of meeting, preventing Moses from entering it?

Leviticus

721. Every burnt offering needed to be a male without what?
722. According to Leviticus, whose sons were responsible for the sacrifices?
723. What kind of oil was mixed with the grain offering?
724. Every grain offering brought to God had to be made without what?
725. What was every grain offering seasoned with?
726. According to the lasting ordinance in Leviticus 3:17, the Israelites were not to eat what two parts of an animal?
727. If an anointed priest sinned, what kind of animal without defect must he present?
728. A priest dipped his finger in the blood of the sacrifice and put it on what part of the altar?
729. What kind of animal was offered as a sin offering for the unintentional sin of the whole community?
730. What kind of animal was offered as a sin offering for the unintentional sin of a leader?
731. If a person could not afford a goat as a sin offering, what were they told to bring instead?
732. If a person could not afford a pigeon as a sin offering, what were they told to bring instead?

733. If a person stole from a neighbor, they must make full restitution and add what fraction of the value when paying them back?

734. What two parts of the animals could the priests eat with a fellowship offering?

735. What were the five offerings described in the first seven chapters of Leviticus?

736. What seven clothing items mentioned in Leviticus 8 did Aaron wear during his ordination?

737. How many times did Moses sprinkle the altar with oil?

738. When anointing the priests, Moses put ram's blood on them in what three places?

739. How many of loaves of bread did Moses offer as a sacrifice during the first tabernacle ceremony?

740. What part of the ram did Moses wave as a wave offering?

741. What two liquids did Moses ordain and sprinkle Aaron and his sons with?

742. How many days did Aaron and his sons have to remain at the tent of meeting after the ordination ceremony?

743. If the priests left before that time, what would happen to them?

744. As Aaron performed the first sacrifice, what came out from the presence of the Lord and consumed the burnt offering?

745. Name Aaron's sons that were consumed by fire when they made an inappropriate fire offering.

746. What could the Levites not drink before entering the tent of meeting?

747. What two qualities of an animal that walked on all fours, outlined in Leviticus 11 (with exceptions), made it acceptable for the Israelites to eat it?

748. What four animals with a split hoof and that chewed the cud were not acceptable to eat?

749. What qualities of a sea creature made it permissible to eat?

750. According to Leviticus 11, what four insects were permissible to eat?

751. If an unclean animal touched a clay pot, what must a person do to that pot according to Leviticus 11?

752. How many days after giving birth to a son was a woman ceremonially unclean?

753. At what age was an Israelite boy to be circumcised?

754. How many days after giving birth to a daughter was a woman ceremonially unclean?

755. According to Leviticus 13, who had to examine every swelling or rash?

756. If the person had a skin disease, how many days did they initially need to be isolated?

757. What color did the flesh and sores need to turn to in order to be called clean?

758. What part of the skin did the priests check to see if it had turned white, black, or yellow?

759. Once someone was declared clean, what did they need to wash?

760. If a person was bald, was he considered ceremonially unclean?

761. If someone had a defiling disease, what must they do to their clothes?

762. What must the defiled person cry out if someone came near?

763. What three types of materials could be infected by mildew and, if so, needed to be thrown out?

764. If a fabric had mold that was spreading, what must the priest do to it?

765. According to Leviticus 14, anyone with a defiling skin disease needed to be brought to whom in order to determine whether they were clean?

766. How many times did the priest sprinkle the one cleansed of the defiling disease?

767. Which three parts on the right side of an infected person did the priest apply blood to cleanse them?

768. What two birds were regularly part of the sacrifices?

769. What kind of defiling disease could spread throughout a house, requiring the owner to tell a priest?

770. What specific kitchen utensil must be broken if it came in contact with a man with an unhealthy discharge?

771. What was the name of the day when the scapegoat was released?

772. What was the name of the animal that ceremonially carried the sins of Israel away from the camp once a year?

773. What part of the animal made atonement for the people?

774. How many days was a woman considered unclean during her monthly period?

775. According to Leviticus 18:6, who could not be approached for sexual relations?

776. In Leviticus 18, what was the name of the god that the Israelites were told not to sacrifice their children to?

777. When harvesting, what were Israelites told to leave behind for the poor and foreigners?

778. Leviticus 19 warned people of taking advantage of individuals with what two handicaps?

779. In Leviticus 19:19, what three things were Israelites told not to mix?

780. What grooming rules did Leviticus 19 offer for men's faces?

781. What were people told to do when in the presence of an aged person?

782. What was the punishment for the adulterer and adulteress in Levitical law?

783. What was the punishment for a medium or spiritist according to Levitical law?

784. According to Leviticus 21, what one quality was most important for a priest's wife?

785. According to Leviticus 21, name three kinds of women a priest could not marry.

786. What was the youngest an animal could be when it became a food offering?

787. What was the seventh day of rest called?

788. What feast began at twilight on the fourteenth day of the first month?

789. What feast began on the fifteenth day of the first month?

790. What holiday didn't start until the Israelites arrived in the Promised Land and harvested their first crops?

791. What feast began fifty days, or seven weeks, after the seventh Sabbath?

792. Name the feast that had to do with the blast of a certain musical instrument.

793. What feast began on the tenth day of the seventh month, with strict orders not to do any work?

794. What was the name of the festival during which the Israelites lived in tents outside the camp?

795. How many loaves of bread were baked and set on the golden bread table in the tabernacle?

796. According to Leviticus 25, what was the land given every seventh year?

797. What was the fiftieth year, when no crops were planted, called?

798. Who was set free on the Year of Jubilee?

799. How many times over would God multiply afflictions if the people remained hostile to him and refused to listen to him?

800. On what mountain did God decree and establish the laws found in Leviticus between himself and Israel?

801. When dedicating a field or house, what additional fraction of the value had to be added to the price if the owner redeemed it back?

Numbers

802. The book of Numbers got its name because it begins with what?

803. The book of Numbers was written how many years after the Israelites came out of Egypt?

804. During the census in Numbers, at what age and older were the men that were counted?

805. Those that were counted in the census in Numbers were able to serve where?

806. Of all the tribes, which was the largest?

807. How many hundred thousand men were counted during the census in Numbers?

808. Which tribe was in charge of taking down and setting up the tabernacle?

809. What did the tribes of Israel set up their tents around?

810. What did each tribe camp underneath?

811. What were the three Levite clans that helped to maintain the tabernacle?

812. Which of the three Levite clans was responsible for the care of the tabernacle curtains and the tent?

813. Which of the three Levite clans was responsible for the care of the articles in the sanctuary, including the ark?

814. Which of the three Levite clans was responsible for the frames, crossbars, and posts of the tabernacle?

815. Between what ages were men eligible to serve in the tabernacle?

816. A jealous husband that accused his wife of unfaithfulness could have a priest mix a bitter water drink that would curse her and cause her to be what if she were guilty?

817. What drink did a Nazarite abstain from?

818. What food did a Nazarite not eat?

819. What grooming instrument did a Nazarite need to stay away from?

820. What kind of people did a Nazarite need to stay away from?

821. After a Nazirite shaved his head as a symbol of dedication, what was he to do with his hair?

822. Which of the three divisions of Levites did not get carts to carry the parts of the tabernacle because they were required to carry the objects on their shoulders?

823. When Moses entered the tabernacle to speak to the Lord, from where did he hear the Lord's voice speak to him?

824. What age range did the Levite men need to be in, to serve in the tent of meeting?

825. At what age did a Levite need to retire from serving?

826. After retirement, what duty could a Levite perform at the tabernacle?

827. If an Israelite was ceremonially unclean and missed Passover, how much later could they celebrate it?

828. What instrument called the Israelites together for general assemblies, festivals, and calls to war?

829. What was that instrument made of?

830. When the instrument was sounded once, who was to gather?

831. Who were the only ones that could blow the trumpets?

832. When the Israelites moved from their desert camp, which tribe went first?

833. When the Israelites moved from their desert camp, which tribe went last?

834. Who was Moses' brother-in-law?

835. In regards to the camp, where were the complainers that were burned to death located?

836. What was the place called where the fire came down and burned the camp after the Israelites complained?

837. While complaining about the lack of food in the desert, the Israelites remembered what five foods from Egypt?

838. What was the manna ground and crushed in?

839. What did the manna taste like it was made with?

840. How long did God say he would give them all the quail they could stand?

841. God said he would give them quail until it came out of the people's what?

842. How many elders gathered with Moses at the tent of meeting in Numbers 11?

843. What two men began to prophesy in the Israelite camp, making Joshua concerned?

844. What bird did the wind blow in from the sea to the feed the Israelites?

845. How many feet deep were the quail God sent to the camp of the Israelites in the wilderness?

846. While the Israelites ate the quail, God's anger burned and he struck the people with what?

847. What was the name of the place where the Israelites suffered the plague for eating quail?

848. Why did Miriam and Aaron begin to grumble about Moses?

849. What quality does Numbers 12 say Moses had more of than anyone else on the face of the earth?

850. Because of her grumbling, what was Miriam inflicted with?

851. How many days did Miriam have to spend outside the camp?

852. How many spies were sent into the Promised Land of Canaan by Moses?

853. From what tribe was Caleb the spy?

854. As one of the spies of the Promised Land, what tribe did Joshua represent?

855. What did the spies carry on a pole when they returned from the Promised Land?

856. What else did the spies return with?

857. For how many days did the spies explore the Promised Land?

858. What intimidating descendants did the spies claim they saw in the Promised Land?

859. What two spies gave a positive report that they could defeat the enemies of the Promised Land?

860. What pre-Noah group did the Israelite spies think they saw in the Promised Land?

861. What insect did the spies compare themselves to when standing up against the enemies in the Promised Land?

862. Because of Joshua and Caleb's positive report, what did the people want to do to them?

863. What caused God to bar one generation from seeing the Promised Land?

864. How many years did God say the Israelites' children would suffer for their sins in the desert?

865. Every Israelite of what age and older could not enter the Promised Land because of their grumbling?

866. Why did God decide that the number of years the Israelites would wander the desert would be forty?

867. How were the ten spies that gave a negative report about the Promised Land killed?

868. What was the Sabbath lawbreaker doing when he was discovered working in Numbers 15?

869. What were the blue tassels on the Israelites' garments meant to remind them of?

870. Who were the three main leaders that caused the rebellion?

871. How many Israelites rose up against Moses?

872. What did Moses tell Korah to put fire and incense in?

873. Which two men refused Moses' challenge to come to the tent of meeting?

874. Whose tents did Moses warn others to stay away from?

875. What opened up and swallowed Korah and his household?

876. What consumed the men offering the incense?

877. How many men that offered incense died?

878. Who was instructed to take the censers that the dead men were holding?

879. After the leftover censers were hammered into sheets, what did they overlay?

880. What began to spread once the people grumbled about Korah and the other men dying?

881. How many died from the plague in Numbers 16?

882. How many staffs did God tell Moses to collect?

883. From which member of the tribe were the staffs collected in Numbers 17?

884. What was written on each staff?

885. What did they place the staffs in front of?

886. Whose staff budded and produced almonds?

887. Of all the tribes, which one did not get a land inheritance?

888. What percent of the tithe were the Levites expected to tithe?

889. What color heifer, whose blood Eleazar sprinkled toward the tent of meeting, was killed and burned?

890. How many days was someone considered unclean if they touched a dead body?

891. Instead of speaking to the rock to get water from it, Moses did what instead?

892. As a result of Moses striking the rock instead of speaking to it, what was the consequence he faced?

893. What was the name of the place where Moses disobeyed God over the water from the rock?

894. What was the first country that would not allow the Israelites to pass through?

895. On what mountain did Aaron die?

896. Before Aaron died, what of his was given to his son Eleazar?

897. What did God send to attack the Israelites after they complained in Numbers 21?

898. What was the snake that Moses fashioned onto a pole made of?

899. If someone was bitten by a snake, what did they need to do to live?

900. Who was the king of the Amorites that would not allow the Israelites to pass through his country?

901. What was the name of the Amorite king's city?

902. Who was the king of Basham, defeated by the Israelites in Numbers 21?

903. Who was the son of Zippor?

904. In Numbers 22, what country was filled with dread because of the Israelites?

905. What country was Balak the king of?

906. Who was the prophet hired by Balak to curse the Israelites?

907. Whom was Balaam the son of?

908. Who told Balaam not to curse the Israelites?

909. What did Balaam refuse to take from Balak?

910. How many servants traveled with Balaam while he rode his donkey?

911. What stood in the road blocking Balaam from traveling with his donkey?

912. What did the angel have in his hand?

913. By pressing close to the wall, what part of Balaam's body did the donkey crush?

914. How many times did Balaam beat the donkey?

915. What did Balaam wish he had in his hand?

916. What did the angel threaten to do to Balaam if the donkey had not intervened?

917. What was the name of the place that Balak took Balaam to the top of to see the Israelite camp?

918. How many altars did Balaam tell Balak to build the first time?

919. How many times did Balaam build seven altars?

920. How many times did Balaam bless the Israelites instead of cursing them, before Balak kicked him out?

921. What did Balaam say would come out of Jacob and was probably the verse the wise men read?

922. What god did the Israelites begin to worship in Numbers 25 as a result of being seduced by the Moabite women?

923. Who killed the Israelite man that proudly brought another woman to his family right in front of Moses?

924. What did Phinehas kill the adulterous man and the foreign woman with?

925. After Phinehas killed the adulterous man and the foreign woman, what happened to the plague?

926. How many people died from the plague in Numbers 25?

927. In Numbers 26, of all the tribes counted in the second census, which was largest?

928. Was the number greater or less during the second census compared to the first census?

929. Whose daughters came to Moses about being overlooked in the inheritance because their father had no sons?

930. Who succeeded Moses in leading the Israelites into the Promised Land?

931. Which priest witnessed the commissioning of this new leader?

932. On what day during the first month was Passover held?

933. All three sacred assemblies—Festival of Trumpets, Day of Atonement, and Festival of Tabernacles—occur during which number month?

934. According to Numbers 30, if a woman made a vow, who could nullify it?

935. How many Israelites fought against the Midianites in Numbers 31?

936. How many Midianite kings died when the Israelites attacked in Numbers 31?

937. With what kind of weapon was Balaam killed?

938. What three tribes saw the lands of Jazer and Gilead, east of the Jordan, suitable for livestock and wanted to live there?

939. What did the Reubenites and Gadites agree to do before they settled in their land east of the Jordan?

940. How old was Aaron when he died on Mount Hor?

941. What was to be Israel's western boundary?

942. What mountain would be Israel's northernmost point?

943. What river would be Israel's eastern boundary?

944. If a person killed someone accidentally, they could flee to a city and not be avenged. What was that type of city called?

945. How many total towns did the Levites receive?

946. How many witnesses were needed to put someone to death for murder?

947. As the book of Numbers closed, the Israelites were on the plains of Jordan across from what city?

Deuteronomy

948. What book of the Bible means "second law"?

949. How many days should it have taken the Israelites to travel from Mount Horeb to Kadesh Barnea?

950. During what number year in the desert did Moses proclaim the words of Deuteronomy to the people?

951. The Emites were as strong and as numerous as what other tribe?

952. Both the Emites and the Anakites were also referred to by what other name?

953. The Zamzummites were as numerous and as powerful as what other tribe?

954. When the Israelites defeated Og of Bashan, how many cities did they take?

955. Whose bed was made of iron, fourteen feet long and six feet wide?

956. What other name was the Sea of Arabah known by?

957. Whom did God tell Moses to commission to lead the people into the new land?

958. According to Deuteronomy 4, no other god had ever tried to form what through signs, wonders, and war?

959. What did Deuteronomy 5 repeat that was also found in Exodus 20?

960. According to Deuteronomy 5, God said he could punish the children for the sins of the parents up to what generations?

961. What two animals, specifically mentioned by name, did God say needed to rest on the Sabbath?

962. Deuteronomy 6:4–5 contains the verses that Jesus called what?

963. To what two places on the body did the law suggest people should tie the commandments as symbols?

964. What two places did the law suggest people should write the commandments in their homes?

965. In Deuteronomy 7, God wanted the poles of what god torn down?

966. What wasn't a reason why God chose the nation of Israel, according to Deuteronomy 7?

967. Deuteronomy 8 says man does not live on bread alone, but on what?

968. What two things did not wear out during the Israelites' trip through the desert?

969. What part of the Israelites' body did not swell up during their trip through the desert?

970. What two metals would be abundant in the Promised Land?

971. According to Deuteronomy 9, what enemy in the Promised Land was a people strong and tall?

972. How many forty day/night periods did Moses spend on Mount Sinai?

973. Besides Mount Sinai, what four places did the Israelites make God angry, according to Deuteronomy 9?

974. After God told Moses to make two more stone tablets, what did he ask Moses to put them into?

975. Which of the twelve tribes carried the ark?

976. In Deuteronomy 11, what did God promise to send the Israelites if they obeyed his commands in the Promised Land?

977. In Deuteronomy 11, God promised to expand the land they set their foot on from what river to what sea?

978. What did the other nations burn in their fires as sacrifices, an act that was detestable to God?

979. What had to happen to a prophet that told the people to follow other gods?

980. What had to happen if a brother, son, daughter, wife, or close friend asked someone to worship other gods?

981. According to Deuteronomy 14, what two qualities of a land mammal made it acceptable to eat?

982. Which four animals were called unclean even though they had a divided hoof, even they did not chew the cud?

983. What two qualities of a marine animal made it permissible to eat?

984. What young animal could not be cooked in its mother's milk?

985. The word *tithe* means what mathematical fraction?

986. What did a creditor do have to do, every seven years, with a loan to a fellow Hebrew?

987. How many nations did God say Israel could borrow from?

988. What did a master have to do to a fellow Hebrew slave after he had served for six years?

989. If a servant wanted to serve his master for life, where on his body was he pierced to show his decision?

990. With what kind of tool was the servant pierced?

991. During the Passover celebration, for how many days did they eat bread without yeast?

992. At what time of day did they sacrifice the Passover?

993. After eating unleavened bread for six days during Passover, what did God ask the Israelites to do on the seventh day?

994. How many weeks after the beginning of the grain harvest did the Festival of Weeks start?

995. How many days after the produce was gathered from the threshing floor did the Feast of Tabernacles begin?

996. Each person was urged to bring a gift to the Lord in proportion to what?

997. If someone was accused of worshiping another god, who threw the first stone at the person's stoning?

998. In Deuteronomy 17, what three things did God say a king should not acquire a great number of?

999. What must a king entering office make a copy of?

1000. What was the sign of a true prophet?

1001. Deuteronomy 19 gave an example of an unintentional death involving the swinging of what tool?

1002. In Deuteronomy 20, who had to first address an army before going into battle?

1003. Before attacking a city, what did God tell the Israelites they must offer first?

1004. What three living things did God specifically say could be taken as plunder when attacking a city?

1005. When attacking a city, what kind of natural vegetation should not be destroyed?

1006. If a person was found slain in a field and the murderer was unknown, which town must offer a sacrifice for the sin?

1007. How much more of the inheritance did the firstborn son customarily receive?

1008. What punishment could the parents of a stubborn, rebellious, and drunk son have given to him by the elders of the town?

1009. If a person was hung on a tree, what did the law of Deuteronomy say people must do to the body before nightfall?

1010. In Deuteronomy 22, what three animals should be returned if they are found wandering around?

1011. What article of lost clothing does the passage instruct people to return if found?

1012. What kind of clothes must a woman not wear?

1013. When building a new house, what must a person put on the roof to keep people from falling off?

1014. According to Deuteronomy 22, what two animals should not plow together?

1015. According to Deuteronomy 22, what two fabrics should not be woven together?

1016. What should appear on the four corners of a cloak?

1017. If a man suspected that his wife was not a virgin, who gathered to hear this case?

1018. What should the parents display to prove her virginity?

1019. What was the fine for a wrongful accusation of promiscuity?

1020. If the charge was correct, what happened to the woman?

1021. Where did the stoning of a promiscuous daughter occur?

1022. In Deuteronomy 23, what two nations could not be included in the Israelite assembly?

1023. What two nations of people did Deuteronomy 23 say not to abhor?

1024. Where were the bathrooms designated to be in the Israelite camp while in the wilderness?

1025. When entering a neighbor's grain field, kernels could be picked with the hand but not by using what?

1026. A recently married man could not be sent where for one year?

1027. What was the maximum number of lashes allowed by law?

1028. While an ox treaded grain, what weren't the Israelites allowed to do?

1029. If a wife tried to rescue her husband from a fight and her hand accidentally touch the assailant's private parts, what happened to her hand?

1030. Name four groups of people that received a tenth of a person's crop as a tithe.

1031. Moses commanded the tribes to write these laws on stones covered with what?

1032. After the Israelites crossed the Jordan, on what mountain did Moses tell them to display the law written on rocks?

1033. In Deuteronomy 28, what two kitchen items would be cursed if the people were disobedient?

1034. If the people were disobedient, God threatened that swarms of what insect would destroy their crops?

1035. In Deuteronomy 28, Moses said that times could get so bad during an enemy siege that a woman could secretly intend to eat what disgusting thing?

1036. In Deuteronomy 29, what beverage did the people did not drink while in the desert for forty years?

1037. Which tribes received the land taken from Sihon, king of Heshbon, and Og, king of Bashan?

1038. According to Deuteronomy 29, what happened to the names of the disobedient and rebellious?

1039. In Deuteronomy 30, Moses said obeying God's commands was not as hard as reaching across what two faraway places?

1040. At what age did Moses realize he was too old to lead?

1041. In Deuteronomy 31, whom did Moses summon and tell to be strong and courageous?

1042. The Lord asked the Israelites to assemble and read aloud the law every how many years?

1043. During what festival was it read?

1044. In Deuteronomy 32, the grapes of the enemies were filled with what?

1045. On what mountain did Moses die?

1046. Moses' brother Aaron also died on a mountain. Which one?

1047. In Deuteronomy 33, when Moses blessed the tribes, which tribe was left out?

1048. In Deuteronomy 33, when Moses blessed the tribes, which tribe was described as wild ox that gored the nations?

1049. In Deuteronomy 33, when Moses blessed the tribes, which tribe was described as a lion's cub?

1050. Who buried Moses?

1051. Where was Moses buried?

1052. How old was Moses when he died?

1053. Which of Moses' senses never grew weak during his life?

1054. How many days did the Israelites mourn Moses' death?

1055. Joshua was filled with wisdom because Moses did what to him before he died?

Joshua

1056. As the newly appointed leader, what was Joshua supposed to cross with all the people?

1057. What four-word statement of encouragement was repeated four times in Joshua 1?

1058. What did God tell Joshua to keep always on his lips?

1059. How many spies did Joshua secretly send to check out the land?

1060. What was the name of the prostitute that let the spies stay at her home in Jericho?

1061. Where did Rahab hide the spies?

1062. In what part of the city did Rahab live?

1063. What marker did Rahab put on her windows so the Israelites would know to spare her family?

1064. Who was designated to carry the ark of the covenant?

1065. How much distance was kept between the people and the ark of the covenant when it marched ahead of them?

1066. When the Israelites marched into the Jordan River, what went first?

1067. When the priests touched the Jordan River as they crossed into the Promised Land, what happened to the water?

1068. As the Jordan River stopped up to allow the Israelites to cross, at what town upstream did the waters pile up?

1069. Where did the priests that carried the ark stand while the people crossed the Jordan?

1070. What did twelve members of each tribe use to create a memorial?

1071. How many men armed for battle crossed over to go to war?

1072. Where did Joshua set up the twelve stones as a memorial?

1073. After crossing the Jordan and before invading Jericho, what did every male do?

1074. What holiday did the Israelites celebrate before they attacked Jericho?

1075. After the Israelites ate the food from the Promised Land, what stopped appearing every morning?

1076. When Joshua asked the man with a sword whose side he was on, which side did the man indicate?

1077. What was the man's (angel's) rank?

1078. For the first six days, how many times did the Israelites march around Jericho?

1079. How many total days did the Lord tell Joshua to march around Jericho?

1080. What did the priests that marched in front of the ark carry?

1081. On the seventh day, how many times did the Israelites march around Jericho?

1082. How many priests marched in front of the ark?

1083. On the seventh day, what sounds did they make while marching around Jericho that they didn't make the other six days?

1084. What did God tell the people not to take from Jericho?

1085. What metals were the men told to take from Jericho and put into God's treasury?

1086. What three types of animals did the invading army also kill?

1087. Which of Rahab's family members were spared?

1088. Joshua pronounced a curse on anyone that tried to do what to Jericho?

1089. What did Joshua say would happen to whomever rebuilt Jericho?

1090. Who took some of the "devoted things" from Jericho and hid them for himself?

1091. From what tribe was Achan?

1092. What city did the Israelites lose to after their victory at Jericho?

1093. How many men went to fight against Ai and lost?

1094. How many died?

1095. What nation of people lived in Ai?

1096. What did Achan steal that caused God's disfavor?

1097. Where was the robe originally made?

1098. How many shekels of silver did Achan take?

1099. How many shekels did the bar of gold weigh?

1100. Where did Achan have these items buried?

1101. Where did all of Israel take Achan and his family to kill them?

1102. How did the Israelites kill Achan and his family?

1103. What did God tell the Israelites they could keep when they attacked Ai (but couldn't keep when the attacked Jericho)?

1104. What did Joshua hold in his hand until all of Ai was destroyed?

1105. Who was the only person from Ai that survived the battle but was later executed?

1106. After the victory against Ai, what did Joshua copy on stones?

1107. What nation tricked the Israelites into thinking they were from a distant nation and into signing a peace treaty?

1108. What dry and moldy food item did they present to the Israelites as proof that they traveled from afar?

1109. What did the Israelites forget to do, when dealing with the Gibeonites, that caused them to be deceived?

1110. Joshua cursed the Gibeonites and gave them what two jobs?

1111. During Joshua's campaign into the Promised Land, what did God hurl at the Amorites?

1112. What did God do to the sun during the attack on the Amorites?

1113. In Joshua 10, how many Amorite kings fled from Joshua and hid?

1114. Where did those Amorite kings try to hide?

1115. When Joshua defeated the five northern kings, what did God tell him to hamstring?

1116. And what did God tell him to burn?

1117. How many defeated kings are listed in Joshua 12?

1118. In chapter 13, God told Joshua there was still a lot of land to defeat but Joshua was getting very what?

1119. How many tribes took possession of the land west of the Jordan?

1120. How many tribes took possession of the land east of the Jordan?

1121. Which tribe received no land inheritance, only towns and food offerings?

1122. How old did Caleb say he was when he first spied on the land for Moses?

1123. How old was Caleb when he finally took possession of his land inheritance?

1124. What feared people lived in the area that Caleb attacked?

1125. What area did Caleb take possession of as an inheritance?

1126. Who was Caleb's daughter?

1127. Who attacked and captured Kiriath Sepher by Caleb's request and received his daughter as a reward?

1128. In Joshua 15, which town could Judah not dislodge?

1129. What people lived in that town?

1130. What was the other name for the town of Bethel?

1131. Who was Manasseh's firstborn son?

1132. According to Joshua 17, which group did the Israelites subject to forced labor because they did not drive them out completely?

1133. How many men from each tribe were appointed to survey the land for the remaining seven tribes?

1134. How did Joshua decide which of the remaining tribes got what tract of land?

1135. What tribe took possession of the land that included Jericho and Jerusalem?

1136. Which tribes' land inheritance lay within the land of Judah?

1137. What did Joshua receive from the Israelites as an inheritance?

1138. Before a person entered a city of refuge, to whom did he have to state his case?

1139. How many total towns were the Levites given in Joshua 21?

1140. What did the Reubenites, Gadites, and the half tribe of Manasseh build that nearly caused the other tribes to go to war with them?

1141. What did the Reubenites, Gadites, and the half tribe of Manasseh say that the altar would not be used for?

1142. What did the Reubenites and Gadites call "a witness between us that the Lord is God"?

1143. Before he died, Joshua warned the tribes that the other nations would be like whips on their backs and what in their eyes?

1144. Joshua told the Israelites to decide whom they would serve, but as far as Joshua was concerned, who would serve the Lord?

1145. How old was Joshua when he died?

1146. Whose bones were finally buried in Shechem?

Judges

1147. What two parts of King Adoni-Bezek's body were cut off when he was captured?

1148. What tribe attacked Jerusalem and took it over in Judges 1?

1149. Who advanced against the Kiriath Arba and received Caleb's daughter in marriage?

1150. In the book of Judges, the city of Bethel was also known by what other name?

1151. What does Judges 1 point out as the failure of all the tribes when they conquered a region?

1152. In Judges 2, where did the angel of the Lord meet the Israelites and deliver bad news?

1153. According to Judges 2, what two gods did the Israelites worship?

1154. What happened to the people after a judge died?

1155. Who was Othniel's uncle?

1156. In Judges 3, what town did King Eglon take possession of?

1157. Eglon was the king of what nation?

1158. What made Ehud physically distinct?

1159. From what tribe was Ehud?

1160. Where did Ehud strap his double-edged sword?

1161. What physical characteristic defined King Eglon?

1162. What did Ehud say to Eglon to get him alone in the room?

1163. Where did Ehud plunge the sword into Eglon?

1164. What did the servants think Eglon was doing so they delayed checking on him?

1165. Ehud led a charge against the Moabites that killed how many of them?

1166. Shamgar killed six hundred Philistines with what tool?

1167. Who was the king of Canaan during the time of Deborah?

1168. Who was the commander of the Canaanite army during the time of Deborah?

1169. What military equipment did Sisera have nine hundred of?

1170. Who was Deborah's husband?

1171. Who was the commander that Deborah called to defeat the enemy?

1172. To whose tent did Sisera flee?

1173. What was her husband's name?

1174. What drink did Jael serve Sisera?

1175. While Sisera slept, what did Jael drive into his temple?

1176. Whom did Deborah sing a song with in Judges 5?

1177. When were the Midianites more likely to invade the Israelites?

1178. Who was Gideon's father?

1179. Where was Gideon threshing wheat to hide it from the enemy?

1180. What clan was Gideon from (which he called the weakest)?

1181. Who was the first enemy terrorizing Israel that Gideon was called to defeat?

1182. What kind of animal did Gideon give as an offering to the angel?

1183. What did the angel do to Gideon's offering?

1184. What was the angel carrying?

1185. What was the name of the altar Gideon built to commemorate his first meeting with an angel?

1186. Gideon's first attack was on what god's altar?

1187. What god's pole did Gideon tear down?

1188. Who defended Gideon when the hostile crowd came to get him?

1189. Because of this attack on the altar, what was Gideon's new nickname?

1190. In what valley did the Midianites join forces to invade Israel?

1191. What did Gideon use to summon the Abiezrites to battle?

1192. What item did Gideon put on the threshing floor to test God's call?

1193. Using the wool fleece, what did Gideon first ask for dew to appear on—the fleece or the ground?

1194. When Gideon squeezed out the fleece, how much water came out?

1195. What was the first test on Gideon's army that caused 22,000 men to leave?

1196. Gideon took which men—those that brought the water to their mouths or those that knelt down to drink?

1197. How many men made the final cut of Gideon's army?

1198. Who was Gideon's servant?

1199. Gideon was encouraged to attack the Midianites after hearing of a man's dream of what tumbling into the enemies' camp?

1200. Gideon's army attacked the Midianites using what three items?

1201. Who were the first two Midianite leaders Gideon captured?

1202. The leaders of what town first refused to feed Gideon's army?

1203. What two Midianite leaders did Gideon pursue in Judges 8?

1204. What did Gideon threaten to torture the people of that town with since they refused to help?

1205. What was the second town that refused to feed Gideon's army?

1206. What did he threaten to tear down when he returned?

1207. Who was Gideon's oldest son that was afraid to kill the two kings?

1208. When Gideon refused a delegation to be Israel's leader, what did he ask from them instead?

1209. What did Gideon make out of the gold he received?

1210. Who was the son born of Gideon's concubine?

1211. The people of what town rallied behind Abimelech?

1212. How many of Gideon's sons were killed with a single stone?

1213. Who was the only brother to escape Abimelech's massacre?

1214. Jotham told a parable about something looking for a king. What was it?

1215. The people of what town began a revolt against Abimelech?

1216. Who was the leader from Ebed that opposed Abimelech?

1217. What town did Abimelech attack, burning down its strong tower and killing a thousand people?

1218. What did the woman drop from a tower onto Abimelech, cracking his skull?

1219. Instead of dying by the hand of a woman, what did Abimelech asked to be killed with?

1220. Whom did Abimelech ask to kill him?

1221. From what tribe was the judge Tola?

1222. How many sons (and donkeys) did the judge Jair have?

1223. What was the name of Jephthah's father?

1224. What was the occupation of the judge Jephthah's mother?

1225. The elders of Gilead asked Jephthah to fight what enemy?

1226. What vow did Jephthah make if the Lord gave the Ammonites into his hands?

1227. What was the first thing to come out the door to greet Jephthah when he returned from battle?

1228. For how many months did Jephthah's daughter go away before Jephthah finalized his vow?

1229. What did Jephthah's daughter and her friend mourn?

1230. What tribe was upset with Jephthah because he didn't ask them to go to war with the Ammonites?

1231. What word became a pronunciation test to see if someone was an Ephraimite?

1232. How many daughters did the judge Ibzan give away in marriage to those outside his clan?

1233. How many donkeys did the sons and grandsons of the judge Abdon ride?

1234. In what region did Samson's father live?

1235. What was the name of Samson's father?

1236. What tribe was Samson from?

1237. Taking a vow of a Nazirite, what three things did Samson have to stay away from?

1238. How many times did Samson's parents interact with an angel to confirm the birth of Samson?

1239. When talking to Samson's parents, what did the angel cause to come from the altar, which he ascended into?

1240. In what city did Samson see a woman and demand his parents get her for him as a wife?

1241. What nationality was this woman?

1242. What attacked Samson on his way to Timnah (that he tore apart with his bare hands)?

1243. What did Samson later find living inside the dead carcass of that animal?

1244. What food item did Samson pull from the body of the dead lion?

1245. How many sets of linen garments and how many sets of clothes did Samson promise to whomever solved his riddle?

1246. What was the riddle Samson told at the wedding?

1247. How many days did Samson's wife pout until he explained the riddle to her?

1248. Where did Samson get the clothes that he promised to those that solved the riddle?

1249. What did Samson's father-in-law do to Samson's wife when he thought Samson was angry with her?

1250. How many foxes did Samson capture and tie together?

1251. What did Samson tie between each pair of foxes?

1252. What did the fiery foxes burn up?

1253. What did the Philistines do to Samson's father-in-law and wife in retaliation for the incident with the foxes?

1254. What tribe captured Samson and delivered him to the Philistines?

1255. How many Philistines did Samson kill with a jawbone?

1256. What kind of animal was that jawbone from?

1257. What kind of woman did Samson go to see in Gaza?

1258. What city's gates did Samson tear off and deposit far away?

1259. Where did Samson deposit the city gates?

1260. Where did Delilah live?

1261. How much did each Philistine ruler offer Delilah to spy on Samson?

1262. What was the first "secret" that Samson told Delilah would make him weak?

1263. What was the second "secret" that Samson gave for his weakness?

1264. What was the third "secret" that Samson gave for his weakness?

1265. What incessant tactic did Delilah use to make Samson sick to death of her?

1266. After how many times did Samson finally tell Delilah the truth about his hair?

1267. What was the true secret to his strength?

1268. When the Philistines finally subdued Samson, how did they disfigure him?

1269. What did they bind Samson with on his way to prison?

1270. What job did the Philistines make Samson do in prison?

1271. During what god's celebration did the Philistines want Samson to come out and entertain them?

1272. What structure did Samson destroy as he died?

1273. About how many Philistines were watching Samson perform from the rooftop?

1274. What part of the temple did Samson push against to bring the whole structure down?

1275. In whose tomb was Samson buried?

1276. For how many years was Samson a judge?

1277. In Judges 17, who made an idol from eleven hundred shekels of silver?

1278. Besides the idol, what else did Micah have made to put in his shrine?

1279. From what tribe was the man that Micah hired to be his house priest?

1280. In Judges 18, what tribe was searching for a land because they had no inheritance?

1281. What tribe's land did the Danites spy on in Judges 18?

1282. From whose house did the Danites steal the carved image, the ephod, and other idols?

1283. After attacking and burning down Laish, what did the Danites rename the city?

1284. At the end of Judges 18, where was the house of God the entire time?

1285. In Judges 19, from what tribe was the man that went to retrieve his unfaithful concubine?

1286. What was the other name for the city called Jebus?

1287. After nobody else would help, who took in the traveler and his concubine?

1288. In what city was the traveler surrounded by the wicked men that raped and killed his concubine?

1289. What did the men of Gibeah do to the concubine?

1290. Into how many parts did the man cut up his concubine and send them to all the areas of Israel?

1291. In Judges 20, all the tribes turned against which tribe for the awful murder of the concubine?

1292. What physical trait made seven hundred warriors from Benjamin distinct?

1293. What did Judges 20 say those warriors could sling a stone at and not miss?

1294. After how many days of battles did the Israelites finally defeat the Benjamites?

1295. What did the other tribes refuse to offer the Benjamites to help them replenish?

1296. In Judges 21, what tribe did all the other tribes rise up and help?

1297. From what two regions/cities did the Israelites find wives for the Benjamites?

1298. The book of Judges ends by saying that since there was no king in Israel, everyone did what?

Ruth

1299. During the time of Ruth, who was ruling?

1300. Naomi and her husband were originally from what city?

1301. To what country did Naomi, her husband, and her two sons move?

1302. Why crises caused the family to move to Moab?

1303. Who was Naomi's husband?

1304. Who were Naomi's sons?

1305. Who were Naomi's daughters-in-law?

1306. What nation was Ruth from?

1307. What happened to all the men in Naomi's family in Ruth 1?

1308. What city did Naomi want to move back to?

1309. When Naomi returned to her hometown, what new name did she want to be called?

1310. Who owned the grain field where Ruth harvested?

1311. What was the process called when people were allowed to pick the grain left behind by the workers?

1312. What kind of grain was in Boaz's field?

1313. Who was Ruth and Naomi's kinsman-redeemer?

1314. Who encouraged Ruth to woo Boaz?

1315. What three beauty tips did Naomi give Ruth before Ruth met Boaz?

1316. At what part of Boaz's body did Naomi lie during the middle of the night?

1317. Where at the farm did Ruth warm Boaz's feet?

1318. What kind of grain did Boaz give Ruth as a gift?

1319. How many elders witnessed the land transaction at the town gate?

1320. When property was transferred, one party traditionally took off what article of clothing and passed it over to legalize the transaction?

1321. What was the name of Ruth and Boaz's son?

1322. Who was Ruth and Boaz's grandson?

1323. Who was Ruth and Boaz's great-grandson?

1324. What is the last name mentioned in the book of Ruth?

1 Samuel

1325. What nationality was Elkanah?

1326. What were the names of Elkanah's wives?

1327. Who were the priests during this time?

1328. Whose sons were they?

1329. Why did Elkanah give double portions of food to Hannah?

1330. What condition did Hannah face that caused her to be sad?

1331. What did Hannah promise God would never touch her son's head?

1332. Eli the priest saw Hannah praying and thought she was what?

1333. What two beverages did Hannah deny drinking?

1334. What was the name of Hannah's first son?

1335. What does the name Samuel mean?

1336. In 1 Samuel, in what city was the house of the Lord located?

1337. When Hannah gave Samuel to Eli, what three gifts did she bring?

1338. What did Hannah make for Samuel every year?

1339. How many more children did Hannah have after Samuel?

1340. What sinful act did Eli hear that his sons, the priests, were doing?

1341. What part of the sacrificial meat did Eli's sons eat that displeased God?

1342. According to the man of God in 1 Samuel 2, when were Eli's sons going to die?

1343. The boy Samuel kept hearing voices one night. Who was calling him?

1344. Who did Samuel think was calling him at first?

1345. How many times did Samuel hear his name called?

1346. In 1 Samuel 4, what prized Israeli possession did the Philistines capture?

1347. What two people were killed on the day the ark was captured?

1348. Who died when he heard the news that the Philistines captured the ark?

1349. How old was Eli?

1350. How did Eli die?

1351. What physical condition of Eli's probably caused his fall and death?

1352. Name the son of born to Phineas's wife (Eli's daughter-in-law)?

1353. What does the name Ichabod mean?

1354. To what city did the Philistines take the ark?

1355. In which of their god's temples did the Philistines place the ark of the covenant?

1356. While the ark was in the Philistine temple where did the priests find it two times in the morning?

1357. What parts of the idol were broken off the second time?

1358. After the incidents in Dagon's temple, what didn't people step on when entering the temple?

1359. While the ark was in the possession of the Philistines, what kind of plague broke out?

1360. To where did the Philistine rulers suggest moving the ark (its second move)?

1361. Because of the outbreak in that second city, where did the ark get moved (its third move)?

1362. How long had the ark been in the possession of the Philistines when they decided to get rid of it?

1363. What guilt offering did the Philistines put inside the ark of the covenant?

1364. Into what region did the Philistines send the ark, hitched to a cart and pulled by cows?

1365. The five gold tumors and rats placed by the Philistines into the ark of the covenant represented what?

1366. Why did the men die at Beth Shemesh when the ark showed up?

1367. How many men died at Beth Shemesh that day?

1368. To whose house did the people take the ark of the covenant?

1369. During the time of Samuel, the ark remained in Kiriath Jearim (Abinadab's house) for how many years?

1370. What two gods did the people put away so they could be saved from the Philistines?

1371. What was the name of the stone that Samuel set up to remind them of God subduing the Philistines?

1372. What does "Ebenezer" mean?

1373. In what city did Samuel live?

1374. What were the names of Samuel's first two sons that did not walk in his ways?

1375. Because Samuel was old and his sons corrupt, what did Israel ask for?

1376. Why did Israel want a king to rule over them?

1377. Who was Saul's father?

1378. What tribe was Saul from?

1379. What physical characteristic set Saul apart from other people?

1380. What lost animals caused Saul to meet Samuel?

1381. According to 1 Samuel 9, what other name did the people use for prophets?

1382. What characteristic of the tribe of Benjamin made it hard for Saul to believe that he would be king?

1383. What did Samuel pour over Saul's head in 1 Samuel 10?

1384. Where were Saul's missing donkeys found?

1385. A procession of what met Saul at Gibeah, according to Samuel's prediction?

1386. What activity was Saul doing that surprised those that knew him?

1387. When they went looking for Saul to present him to the people, where was he hiding?

1388. Name the Ammonite king that besieged Jabesh Gilead.

1389. As part of a treaty, what did the Ammonite king offer to do to every citizen of Jabesh Gilead?

1390. So that the people would realize how wicked they were asking for a king, what did Samuel pray for (and it happened)?

1391. How old was Saul when he became king?

1392. How many years did Saul reign over Israel?

1393. Who was Saul's son, himself a mighty warrior?

1394. In 1 Samuel 13, whom was Saul impatiently waiting for before they attacked the Philistines?

1395. What did Saul do that caused Samuel to say that a new king would be anointed over him?

1396. Who said that the Lord had sought out a man after his own heart?

1397. Before attacking the Philistines, whom did Saul's army go to and have their weapons sharpened?

1398. What weapons did the Israelite army have when they attacked the Philistines in 1 Samuel 13?

1399. When attacking the Philistines in 1 Samuel 13, what did the other soldiers lack that Saul and Jonathan had?

1400. Who and his armor-bearer attacked the Philistine outpost on a cliff and took out twenty Philistines?

1401. Who broke Saul's command to his army not to eat before battle?

1402. What food did Jonathan eat that made his eyes brighten?

1403. What practice did they do to realize that Jonathan had sinned?

1404. How many sons did Saul have?

1405. Who was Saul's youngest daughter?

1406. Who was Saul's wife?

1407. Who was the commander of Saul's army?

1408. Who was the king that Saul allowed to live but Samuel said must die?

1409. What sound did Samuel hear that revealed Saul's disobedience in not killing everything in the Amalekite camp?

1410. Who finally killed King Agag?

1411. By the end of 1 Samuel 15, how did God feel about making Saul king?

1412. In what town did Samuel find Jesse and his sons?

1413. How many of Jesse's sons passed by Samuel before he found David?

1414. What was David doing when Samuel arrived to anoint him the first time?

1415. What did Samuel anoint David with?

1416. What tormented Saul so much that he needed music to calm him?

1417. What instrument did David play that calmed King Saul?

1418. Besides being Saul's musician, what other job did the king give David when he first met him?

1419. In what valley did the Israelites face off with the Philistines and Goliath?

1420. What town was Goliath from?

1421. In feet, about how tall was Goliath?

1422. How much did Goliath's armor weigh (in pounds)?

1423. What was Goliath's spear compared to?

1424. How much did Goliath's spear weigh (in pounds)?

1425. Who was Jesse's oldest son?

1426. For how many days did the standoff last between the Israelites and Goliath?

1427. What did David transport back and forth from home to his brothers on the front lines?

1428. What did Saul offer any man that killed Goliath?

1429. What two animals did David say he killed, as a shepherd, when they attacked his flock?

1430. What three pieces of armor did David try to wear but later took off?

1431. How many stones did David take with him to battle?

1432. Where did David get those stones?

1433. Besides the stones, what three other things did David take with him to battle?

1434. What animal did Goliath compare himself to when he saw David come at him with a stick?

1435. What three weapons did David say Goliath had?

1436. Where on Goliath's body did David hit him with a stone?

1437. What did David do with Goliath's sword after killing him?

1438. Whose sword did David use to cut off Goliath's head?

1439. Where did David take Goliath's head?

1440. Where did David put Goliath's sword?

1441. Who was the commander of Saul's army when David killed Goliath?

1442. What five items did Jonathan give David after the death of Goliath?

1443. The people sang that Saul had slain his thousands, but David slew how many?

1444. What came upon Saul to make him attack David?

1445. What did Saul throw at David?

1446. Which daughter did Saul offer David before changing his mind and giving her to another man?

1447. Who was the other man that Saul gave his oldest daughter to?

1448. Which daughter did Saul eventually give to David?

1449. Saul asked David for a bride-price before he handed his daughter over to him. What was it?

1450. How many Philistine foreskins did David give Saul?

1451. What did Saul ask Jonathan to do to David but Jonathan refused to carry it out?

1452. How many total times did it say Saul threw a spear at David?

1453. Who warned David and helped him escape by lowering him through a window?

1454. What did she put in his bed to make it look like David slept there?

1455. In 1 Samuel 19, every time Saul and his troops tried to capture David at Ramah, what did they start to do?

1456. What did Jonathan ask David to show toward his family forever?

1457. At what festival did Jonathan indicate to David that Saul intended to kill him?

1458. What did Jonathan use as a signal to David to tell him that Saul wanted him dead?

1459. In what city did David meet Ahimelech the priest?

1460. Since Ahimelech had no regular food, what consecrated item did he give David to eat?

1461. Who was Saul's chief shepherd?

1462. Whose sword did Ahimelech the priest give to David?

1463. What kind of clothing was Goliath's sword hidden behind?

1464. What was the name of the king of Gath?

1465. What did David act like to fool the king of Gath?

1466. What two things did David do to appear crazy?

1467. Who saw David with the priest Ahimelech and then then told King Saul?

1468. How many priests did Doeg kill?

1469. What was the name of the town of priests that Doeg wiped out?

1470. Name the son of Ahimelech that escaped the massacre to join David.

1471. What did Abiathar take with him when he fled that David asked for later?

1472. In what desert was the cave where David spared Saul's life?

1473. What was Saul doing in the cave while David hid in the shadows?

1474. David cut off the corner of what article of Saul's clothing but did not kill him?

1475. Who was the wealthy man of Maon that refused to feed David's men?

1476. Who was Nabal's wife?

1477. Who intervened and kept David from killing Nabal for his rudeness?

1478. What does the name Nabal mean?

1479. When Abigail returned to Nabal, what was going on at her house?

1480. When Abigail told Nabal the news, what happened to his heart?

1481. After Nabal died, what did David do to Nabal's wife?

1482. Whom from Jezreel did David also marry besides Abigail?

1483. To whom did Saul give Michal, David's wife?

1484. With whom did David sneak into Saul's camp?

1485. While Saul slept at his camp, what two items did David steal from him?

1486. Whom did David accuse of not watching King Saul effectively?

1487. What town did Achish, king of Gath, give David and his men to live in?

1488. Where was Samuel buried?

1489. Whom had Samuel expelled from the land (and they were not allowed to practice in Israel)?

1490. Before consulting a medium, what three ways did Saul try to consult the Lord, but heard nothing?

1491. In what town did Saul consult the medium?

1492. Whose spirit did Saul want to consult through the medium?

1493. What did the spirit look like when the medium at Endor saw him?

1494. Whom did the spirit of Samuel predict would die the next day?

1495. Who grew uneasy with David being in the Philistine army and asked King Achish to dismiss him?

1496. What enemy attacked David's town of Ziklag, burned it down, and carried off the wives and children?

1497. Name the priest that traveled with David before David became king.

1498. Before David's raid of the Amalekite camp, how many of his men were too exhausted to move on?

1499. Whom did David and his men encounter that led them to the Amalekites?

1500. What enemy killed Saul's sons?

1501. Who were Saul's three sons?

1502. Whom was Saul wounded by?

1503. Who refused to kill Saul after Saul pleaded with him to do so?

1504. How did Saul kill himself?

1505. The Philistines put the armor of Saul in which god's temple?

1506. The Philistines hung Saul's body from the wall of what city?

1507. The people of what region traveled to Beth Shan to remove and burn the bodies of Saul and his sons?

1508. Under what kind of tree did they bury the bones of Saul and his sons?

2 Samuel

1509. What nationality was the man that broke the news of Saul's death to David?

1510. According to the man who delivered the news, who killed Saul?

1511. What did the man take from Saul and give to David?

1512. How did David repay this man that claimed he killed Saul?

1513. In what town was David anointed king over the tribe of Judah?

1514. David thanked the people that buried King Saul. What region did they come from?

1515. Who was the commander of Saul's army?

1516. Which son of Saul did Abner make king?

1517. What was Ish-Bosheth king over?

1518. How long did Ish-Bosheth reign?

1519. How many years and months did David reign as king in Hebron over Judah?

1520. Where was the pool located where the armies of Saul and David squared off?

1521. How many men from both sides squared off against each other?

1522. Who were the three sons of Zeruiah?

1523. Which one of those sons was described as fleet-footed as a gazelle?

1524. Whom did Asahel chase without turning to the left or right?

1525. With what did Abner kill Asahel?

1526. In 2 Samuel 2, how many from David's army died in the battle?

1527. How many died from Abner's army in that battle?

1528. Who was David's firstborn son?

1529. Which of David's wives gave birth to his first son?

1530. Who was David's second-born son?

1531. Who gave birth to David's second son?

1532. Who was David's third son?

1533. Name the six women that gave birth to David's sons listed in 2 Samuel 3:2-5.

1534. Who was the fourth wife of David mentioned for the first time in 2 Samuel 3:5?

1535. Which wife did David ask to be returned to him after she was given to another man?

1536. Who was this wife's husband that wept when she was returned to David?

1537. What soldier in Ish-Bosheth's army, after being insulted, went over to help David?

1538. Who accused Abner of being a spy and killed him, avenging his brother's death?

1539. Who dropped Jonathan's son, causing him to be lame in both feet?

1540. What news did the nurse hear that caused her to hastily run?

1541. What was the name of that son?

1542. Who murdered Ish-Bosheth?

1543. Where was Ish-Bosheth when he was killed?

1544. What did Ish-Bosheth's killers bring to David?

1545. How did David reward Recab and Baanah for killing Ish-Bosheth?

1546. How old was David when he became king?

1547. How many total years did David reign over Israel?

1548. How many years did David reign over Judah in Hebron?

1549. How many years did David reign over Israel and Judah?

1550. What enemy did David defeat to take over Jerusalem?

1551. What new name did David give Jerusalem when he defeated it?

1552. The king of what nation delivered cedar logs, carpenters, and stonemasons to help build a palace for David?

1553. What was the name of that king?

1554. What kind of a cart does 2 Samuel 6 say brought the ark toward Jerusalem?

1555. According to 2 Samuel 6, in whose house was the ark located before David brought it to Jerusalem?

1556. Who died after touching the ark (and his death made David mad)?

1557. What stumbled and caused the ark to slip?

1558. Who housed the ark of the Lord for three months and his house was blessed?

1559. What was David wearing while dancing before the ark as it entered Jerusalem?

1560. Who despised David because he danced before the ark?

1561. When the ark arrived in Jerusalem, what three food items did the crowd receive?

1562. Because of Michal's reaction to David, what does 2 Samuel 6 say happened to her?

1563. Which prophet encouraged David to make plans to build the temple?

1564. While David lived in a house of cedar, where did the ark of God sit?

1565. What three things did God tell David would be established forever in 2 Samuel 7?

1566. When David defeated the Moabites, they were laid on the ground. Which ones were put to death?

1567. According to 2 Samuel 8, what was Joab's position in David's kingdom?

1568. According to 2 Samuel 8, what positions did Zadok and Ahimelech hold in David's kingdom?

1569. Who was the servant that David asked about showing kindness to those in the family of Jonathan?

1570. To what member of Jonathan's family did David show kindness?

1571. What was Mephibosheth's relationship to Jonathan?

1572. What two ways did David show kindness to Mephibosheth?

1573. What derogatory term did Mephibosheth call himself?

1574. Who was Mephibosheth's son?

1575. What was Mephibosheth's physical affliction?

1576. Name the king of the Ammonites that humiliated David's peaceful delegation.

1577. How did the king of Ammonites humiliate David's men?

1578. Where did David have the envoys stay until their beards grew back?

1579. Whom did the Ammonites hire to help fight against the Israelites, but as a result of the defeat, they were reluctant to ever help the Ammonites again?

1580. During what season did kings normally head off to war but David stayed behind?

1581. What nation were the Israelites fighting at the time?

1582. Who was the woman David saw bathing on her roof?

1583. Who was Bathsheba's husband?

1584. What news did she break to David that caused him to call Uriah back from war?

1585. Instead of going into his house while he was home from the battle, where did Uriah sleep instead?

1586. What did David do to Uriah the second time to get to go home and sleep with his wife?

1587. Who was the army commander that gave the order to withdraw, causing Uriah to die?

1588. After a period of mourning, what did David and Bathsheba do?

1589. Who was the prophet that expressed God's displeasure with David over having Uriah murdered?

1590. David heard a story about what stolen animal that caused him to understand his own sin?

1591. According to Nathan, what would never depart David's house?

1592. What happened to the son born of David's illicit affair with Bathsheba?

1593. Name the son born to David and Bathsheba after the death of their first son.

1594. What alternate name did God send, through Nathan, for Solomon?

1595. Who was Absalom's sister?

1596. Who fell in love with her?

1597. What did Amnon pretend to be to lure Tamar to his room?

1598. Who had Amnon killed?

1599. Who did David originally think was dead?

1600. Who had a wise woman sent to David to deliver a word to him about his relationship with Absalom?

1601. Where was she from?

1602. Approximately how much did Absalom's hair weigh when it was cut (in pounds)?

1603. What did Absalom name his daughter?

1604. Whose fields did Absalom have set on fire in order to get him to respond to his calls?

1605. Where did Absalom stand in the city and intercept people that needed to speak to the king?

1606. Which of David's sons declared himself king in 2 Samuel 15:10?

1607. What city did David's son tell everyone that he was king of?

1608. When David fled Jerusalem in fear of Absalom, what did Zadok take with them but David hoped it would return to Jerusalem some day?

1609. Who met David and misled him about Mephibosheth, saying that Jonathan's son thought he should be king?

1610. Who cursed David and threw stones at him but David did not retaliate?

1611. Whom did Shimei think was taking over the kingdom?

1612. Who wanted to kill this man for defaming the king?

1613. Whom did Absalom sleep with to defy his father in front of all Israel?

1614. According to David and Absalom, whose advice was like that of one that inquired of God?

1615. In 2 Samuel 17, whose better advice did Absalom follow over Ahithophel's advice?

1616. In 2 Samuel 17, where did two messengers heading to David have to hide when Abasalom's men came looking for them?

1617. What did Ahithophel do when he heard his advice was not followed?

1618. Whom did Absalom appoint as head of his army?

1619. When David marched against Absalom, who were the three generals that led his troops?

1620. Whose hair got stuck in a tree and left him vulnerable?

1621. What kind of tree was it?

1622. What was he riding when he got stuck?

1623. Who took three javelins and plunged them into Absalom's heart?

1624. Which two people ran to deliver the news about Absalom's death to David?

1625. Who got mad at David for mourning Absalom?

1626. After cursing the king, who returned to express his allegiance to David?

1627. Who betrayed Mephibosheth by slandering him to the king?

1628. Who was the Gileadite that showed great kindness to David and his troops before they crossed the Jordan?

1629. Name the troublemaker that blew a trumpet and rebelled against David in 2 Samuel 20.

1630. Whom did Joab stab and leave him in the middle of the road?

1631. Who pursued Sheba to Abel Beth Maakah?

1632. Who negotiated to protect Abel Beth Maakah and hand over Sheba?

1633. What did the people of Abel Beth Maakah throw over the wall to prove Sheba was dead?

1634. God told David the reason for a three-year famine was because Saul mistreated what group of people?

1635. What did the Gibeonites ask for as payback for what Saul had done to them?

1636. Whom did David NOT hand over to the Gibeonites?

1637. Whose bones did David receive from Jabesh Gilead and have buried in a tomb in Zela?

1638. Who killed the brother of Goliath the Gittite in 2 Samuel?

1639. How many digits (toes and fingers) did the man killed by Jonathan, son of Shimeah (David's brother), have?

1640. According to 2 Samuel 21, whom were all four of these giant warriors descendants of?

1641. In 2 Samuel 22, David sang that the Lord dealt with him according to his what?

1642. Whose last words were recorded in 2 Samuel 23?

1643. How many did Josheb-Basshebeth, one of David's mighty men, kill in one encounter?

1644. Which of David's mighty men fought so many Philistines that his hand grew tired and froze on the sword?

1645. What did the three mighty men break through Philistine lines to get for David from Bethlehem?

1646. Who was the commander of David's three mighty men and considered the most famous?

1647. Which of David's mighty men killed a lion and a giant Egyptian?

1648. Who was the last listed mighty warrior that David had killed?

1649. How many total mighty warriors made the lists in 2 Samuel 23:39?

1650. In 2 Samuel 24, what did David do that made God angry?

1651. In 2 Samuel 24, which prophet came to David to present three options in response to David's sin?

1652. What three options did God give David?

1653. Which of the three punishments did God choose when David refused to pick one?

1654. How many people died from Dan to Beersheba because of the plague?

1655. What did David see at the threshing floor of Araunah the Jebusite?

1656. What did David buy from Araunah?

1657. What did David build on that threshing floor?

1 Kings

1658. What was the name of the Shunammite girl that kept elderly King David warm?

1659. Which of David's sons, whose mother was Haggith, declared himself king in 1 Kings 1?

1660. What two associates of David gave Adonijah their support?

1661. Who was the prophet that did not follow Adonijah and helped put Solomon into power?

1662. Whom did Nathan advise to talk to David about Solomon becoming king?

1663. Who was the priest that anointed Solomon king?

1664. Who, in fear, clung to the horns of the altar in 1 Kings 1?

1665. Whom did David tell Solomon to deal with according to his wisdom?

1666. What two commanders did that person kill?

1667. Where was David buried?

1668. For how many years was David king in Jerusalem?

1669. For how many total years was David king?

1670. When Adonijah went to Bathsheba, whom did he ask to be his wife?

1671. Whom did Solomon have a throne brought in for and placed at his right hand?

1672. What did Solomon give Adonijah instead of his request for marriage?

1673. What priest did Solomon not have put to death since he had carried the ark for his father?

1674. Who acted as Solomon's assassin, cleaning up any loose ends left by David?

1675. What three people did Benaiah kill to begin Solomon's reign?

1676. Who, in fear for his life, clung to the horns of the altar in 1 Kings 2?

1677. Whom did Solomon put in charge of his army because of his faithful duty?

1678. Whom did Solomon replace Abiathar with as priest?

1679. Whom did Solomon allow to live, as long as he did not cross into Jerusalem, but once he did, Solomon had him killed?

1680. In 1 Kings 3, at the beginning of his reign, Solomon made an alliance with and married whose daughter?

1681. In what city was Solomon when the Lord appeared to him in a dream?

1682. What did Solomon ask for when God offered him anything he wanted?

1683. What three things did God recognize that Solomon did not ask for?

1684. What were the occupations of the two women with the dispute over the one child?

1685. To resolve the dispute, what weapon did Solomon ask for?

1686. What was Solomon's solution to the two women that both claimed a child was hers?

1687. What was the real mother's reaction to Solomon's verdict?

1688. How many stalls did Solomon have for his horses?

1689. What did Solomon possess that was measureless like the sands of the seashore?

1690. It was said that Solomon's wisdom was greater than wisdom found in what two other areas?

1691. According to 1 Kings, how many proverbs did Solomon write?

1692. According to 1 Kings, how many songs did Solomon write?

1693. Solomon's wisdom about plant life extended from the cedars of Lebanon to what other plant?

1694. In addition to plant life, Solomon was wise regarding what four other areas?

1695. Who was the king of Tyre that sent envoys to Solomon in 1 Kings 5?

1696. What did Solomon ask the king of Tyre to supply for the building of the temple?

1697. The king of Tyre promised to haul the trees down from Lebanon and float them across what sea?

1698. In addition to cedars, what other tree was brought in to build the temple?

1699. How many laborers did King Solomon conscript to work on building the temple?

1700. One out of every how many months did a worker spend in Lebanon cutting logs?

1701. How many carriers did Solomon employ?

1702. How many stonecutters did Solomon employ?

1703. How many foremen did Solomon employ?

1704. From where were the craftsmen that Solomon and Hiram hired to cut and prepare the timber and stone?

1705. How many years after the Israelites came out of Egypt did Solomon begin to build the temple?

1706. For how many years was Solomon in office when he began to build the temple?

1707. Where were the rocks dressed before arriving at the temple?

1708. According to 1 Kings 6, what sound was not heard at the location where the temple was built?

1709. From what tree were the paneling and beams of the temple made?

1710. With what metal was the inside of the temple lined?

1711. From what kind of wood were the pair of cherubims in the inner sanctuary of the temple made?

1712. How many years did it take to build Solomon's temple?

1713. How many years did it take to build Solomon's palace?

1714. What was the name of the throne room where Solomon judged?

1715. Solomon made a palace for himself and which wife?

1716. Who was the craftsman that Solomon brought in from Tyre to craft the bronze in the temple?

1717. What two parts of the temple were named Jakin and Boaz?

1718. By the time the ark got to Solomon's temple, what were the only things inside the ark?

1719. During the dedication of temple, 120,000 of what kind of animal were sacrificed?

1720. For how many days did the temple dedication celebration last?

1721. In 1 Kings 9, God told Solomon that if his descendants turn to other gods, what would be reduced to rubble?

1722. In 1 Kings 9, what did Solomon give the king of Tyre for all he supplied to the temple?

1723. Solomon built ships that sailed to Ophir to bring back what?

1724. What queen came to test Solomon with hard questions?

1725. What did the queen bring Solomon that exceeded any amount ever brought before?

1726. What kind of wood was shipped in and used to make support beams in the temple, and harps and lyres for the musicians?

1727. What was Solomon's salary in talents per year?

1728. Out of what did Solomon make five hundred shields, both large and small?

1729. From what two materials was Solomon's throne made?

1730. What animal figure appeared fourteen times in carvings around the throne?

1731. What precious metal was considered of little value in Solomon's time because everything was made of pure gold?

1732. What two animals did Solomon's trading ships return with every three years?

1733. During Solomon's reign, what metal was as common as stones in Jerusalem?

1734. What animal was imported from Egypt for Solomon, of which he had twelve thousand?

1735. How many wives did Solomon have?

1736. How many concubines did Solomon have?

1737. Name the three gods that Solomon's wives drew him to?

1738. Who was the detestable god of the Sidonians?

1739. Who was the detestable god of the Moabites?

1740. Who was the detestable god of the Ammonites?

1741. Who was the Edomite the Lord raised up against Solomon?

1742. Who was the leader in Aram that God raised up against Solomon?

1743. Who was the foreman in charge of the labor force that rebelled against Solomon?

1744. Who was the prophet from Shiloh that met Jeroboam outside of Jerusalem?

1745. What did Ahijah the prophet tear into twelve pieces and give ten of those pieces to Jeroboam?

1746. What did the ten pieces of the cloak stand for?

1747. Where did Jeroboam go to hide from Solomon?

1748. Who was the king of Egypt at that time?

1749. For how many years did Solomon reign?

1750. Who was Solomon's son that succeeded him on the throne?

1751. Whom did Rehoboam listen to instead of his father's elders?

1752. Rehoboam replied to the people by saying, "My father scourged you with whips; I will scourge you with ________."

1753. Which two tribes sided with Rehoboam?

1754. Who was the man of God that stopped Rehoboam from going to war with Jeroboam?

1755. What kind of idols did Jeroboam make for the ten tribes to worship?

1756. In what cities did Jeroboam place two golden calves?

1757. In 1 Kings 13, who did the man of God say would one day sacrifice the priests of the high places?

1758. What happened to King Jeroboam's hand when he reached out to seize the man of God?

1759. When the altar split open as a sign, what poured out of it?

1760. What killed the man of God after he returned to the house of the old prophet?

1761. What two animals stood over the body of the prophet on the road?

1762. When Abijah, son of Jeroboam, got sick, who did Jeroboam tell to disguise herself and visit Ahijah the prophet?

1763. What physical affliction did Ahijah the prophet suffer from in his old age?

1764. What happened to Jeroboam's son the moment his mother arrived home, crossing the threshold?

1765. Who was Jeroboam's son that succeeded him as king?

1766. Who was Rehoboam's mother?

1767. In 1 Kings 14, what kingdom attacked Jerusalem and carried off the treasures of the temple and royal palace?

1768. Who was the leader of that kingdom?

1769. What prized golden items of Solomon's were taken (and Rehoboam replaced them with bronze ones)?

1770. Who succeeded Rehoboam to the throne?

1771. First Kings 15 says David kept all of the Lord's commands except in how he dealt with one man. Who was that man?

1772. Who was the first good king of Judah since Solomon?

1773. Whom did Asa remove from her position as queen mother for making a detestable idol?

1774. Even though Asa cleaned up a lot of the idol worship in Judah, what was the one thing Asa failed to do?

1775. Which king of Israel did Asa fight?

1776. Whom did Asa give all the temple treasuries to as a treaty between their nations to deter Israel from fighting Judah?

1777. In his old age, what part of King Asa's body became diseased?

1778. Which king killed all of Jeroboam's family in accordance with the prophecy of Ahijah?

1779. Which prophet received word about the house of Baasha?

1780. Who was Baasha's son that succeeded him?

1781. Who murdered Elah, king of Israel?

1782. Which king of Israel only lasted seven days?

1783. What did Zimri do to the palace when he saw it surrounded by Omri's army?

1784. Who was the commander of the army that replaced Zimri as king of Israel?

1785. What was the name of the city on the hill that Omri bought and built on?

1786. Who was Omri's son that succeeded him?

1787. How many years did Ahab reign?

1788. Whom did King Ahab marry?

1789. What city was Jezebel from, meaning she was of what nationality?

1790. What famous city was rebuilt during the time of Ahab?

1791. While rebuilding Jericho, the builder, Hiel of Bethel, lost his son in accordance to whose prophecy?

1792. Which prophet was a Tishbite?

1793. What weather disaster did Elijah proclaim at the beginning of his job as prophet?

1794. What fed Elijah during the drought?

1795. What two food items did the ravens bring Elijah?

1796. In what city did Elijah live with a widow?

1797. What was the widow collecting for a meal when she met Elijah?

1798. What two food items did Elijah tell the widow would always be provided for her?

1799. Whom did Elijah raise from the dead?

1800. How many times did Elijah stretch himself out on the boy before he came to life?

1801. Who was the prophet that met up with Elijah (his name is also a book of the Bible)?

1802. How many prophets did Obadiah hide from Jezebel when she started killing them?

1803. In how many caves did Obadiah hide the prophets?

1804. What was the name of the mountain where Elijah told the people of Israel and the prophets of Baal to meet him?

1805. How many total prophets did Elijah tell Ahab should meet them on the mountain?

1806. Four hundred and fifty of those prophets served what god?

1807. Four hundred of those prophets served what other god?

1808. What animal sacrifice did Elijah challenge the prophets of Baal to divinely set on fire?

1809. Elijah sarcastically suggested that the prophets should cry louder, suggesting that their god was doing one of four things. What were they?

1810. What did the prophets of Baal slash themselves with to awaken their god?

1811. How many stones did Elijah place on the altar he built on Mount Carmel?

1812. How many times did Elijah have water poured over the altar before God set it on fire?

1813. In what valley were the prophets of Baal slaughtered?

1814. How many times did Elijah tell the servant to look for rain clouds?

1815. Elijah outran Ahab in a chariot all the way to what city?

1816. Who threatened Elijah and caused him to fear for his life?

1817. Under what kind of tree did Elijah sit and pray to die?

1818. When the angel woke Elijah, what food was waiting for him to eat?

1819. Elijah traveled forty days and nights to what mountain?

1820. Three "acts of God" occurred on Mount Horeb, but God told Elijah he was not in any of them. What were they?

1821. God told Elijah to anoint three people. Who were they?

1822. How many people did God reserve, keeping them from bowing to Baal?

1823. How many yoke of oxen was Elisha plowing with when Elijah found him?

1824. When Elijah met Elisha, what did Elijah throw over Elisha's shoulders?

1825. After being commissioned to follow Elijah, what did Elisha do to his oxen and farming equipment?

1826. With what kind of officers did a prophet tell King Ahab to lead the attack against the Arameans?

1827. In 1 Kings 20, what king of Aram did King Ahab defeat?

1828. A prophet in 1 Kings 20 told his companion to strike him. When the companion refused, what killed him?

1829. Who owned the vineyard that King Ahab wanted?

1830. What did Ahab want the vineyard to be used for?

1831. Whom had Naboth killed for his vineyard?

1832. What was Naboth accused of blaspheming?

1833. Elijah prophesied that what would lick up Ahab's blood?

1834. Elijah prophesied that what would devour Jezebel by the wall of Jezreel?

1835. After Ahab heard the deadly prophecy from Elijah, what did he do that caused God to ease off him?

1836. What city did Jehoshaphat, king of Judah, and Ahab, king of Israel, want to free from the Arameans?

1837. How many prophets said attacking Aram was a good thing?

1838. What prophet did the king of Israel tell Jehoshaphat, king of Judah, that he didn't like because he never prophesied anything good?

1839. What kind of spirit did Micaiah say enticed the four hundred prophets?

1840. Who slapped Micaiah in the mouth for his prophecy?

1841. What killed King Ahab in battle?

1842. Ahab's blood was washed into a pool where who bathed?

1843. What licked up Ahab's blood according to Elijah's prophecy?

1844. What did King Jehoshaphat build to go to Ophir for gold?

1845. Who was King Jehosphat's son that succeeded him?

1846. Who was Ahab's son that replace him on the throne?

2 Kings

1847. Which king of Israel fell through the lattice of his upper room in Samaria and injured himself?

1848. What god did Ahaziah want to consult to see if he would recover from his injury?

1849. What Old Testament prophet was described wearing a garment of hair and a leather belt around his waist?

1850. In total, King Ahaziah sent how many companies of fifty men to Elijah to retrieve him?

1851. What fell and killed two companies of fifty men that were trying to detain Elijah?

1852. Because Ahaziah had no son, who succeeded him on the throne?

1853. In 2 Kings 2, what three places did Elijah travel to and Elisha followed him?

1854. In 2 Kings 2, who went out and met Elisha at every place they visited?

1855. In 2 Kings 2, what river did Elijah strike?

1856. What did Elijah strike the water with?

1857. What happened to the water when Elijah struck it?

1858. How much more of a portion of Elijah's spirit did Elisha ask for?

1859. What suddenly arrived to take Elijah away to heaven?

1860. What pulled the chariot that took Elijah away?

1861. What did Elisha do to his garment when Elijah was swept away?

1862. When Elisha struck the Jordan with his cloak, what happened to it?

1863. How many prophets from Jericho met Elisha and offered to look for Elijah?

1864. What did Elisha add to the bad water to heal it?

1865. What name did the boys mock Elisha with?

1866. What animals came out of the woods and mauled the boys?

1867. How many animals mauled the boys that jeered at Elisha?

1868. How many boys were killed for jeering at Elisha?

1869. The kings of what three regions got together to fight against the king of Moab in 2 Kings 3?

1870. After seven days of marching, what did the three armies run out of?

1871. Whom was Elisha the son of?

1872. Before he prophesied to Jehoshaphat, Elisha asked for what musical instrument to be played?

1873. Elisha prophesied that the valley would fill with water, but in the morning it looked like pools of what to the enemy?

1874. What did Elisha miraculously help a widow fill her jars with so she could pay her debts?

1875. What was the widow's husband's previous occupation?

1876. What four pieces of furniture did the Shunammite woman set up in the guest room for Elisha?

1877. What was the name of Elisha's servant?

1878. What did Elisha predict the Shunammite woman would have next year since she didn't have one currently?

1879. What part of the body did the Shunammite woman's son complain was hurting?

1880. What did Elisha first try to lay on the Shunammite woman's son to heal him?

1881. How did Elisha eventually heal the Shunammite woman's son?

1882. How many times did the boy sneeze, indicating he was alive?

1883. What was wrong with the pot of stew served to Elisha and the prophets?

1884. What did Elisha put into the poisoned pot of stew to purify it?

1885. Who in the Old Testament miraculously fed a hundred men bread from only twenty loaves?

1886. What kind of bread was it?

1887. Who was the valiant soldier that Elisha healed of his sickness?

1888. What disease did the soldier have?

1889. What nation was this army commander from?

1890. How many times did Elisha tell Naaman to dip himself in the river to be healed of leprosy?

1891. In what river did Elisha tell Naaman to dip himself to be healed of leprosy?

1892. What did Elisha take as compensation for healing Naaman?

1893. What was the name of Elisha's servant that lied to Naaman about compensation?

1894. What was Gehazi afflicted with because he lied to Elisha?

1895. What item did Elisha cause to float in the Jordan?

1896. What did Elisha throw into the Jordan to make the ax head float?

1897. When surrounded by the Arameans, what did Elisha's servant see around them after his eyes were opened?

1898. With what did Elisha strike the Arameans that were about to attack Israel?

1899. To what city did Elisha lead the blind Arameans?

1900. Instead of killing them, what did Elisha have the king of Israel do instead?

1901. What cost eighty shekels during the Arameans' siege around Samaria?

1902. Four men stricken with what disease wandered into the Aramean camp and found it empty?

1903. What sound did the Arameans hear that caused them to run away during a siege of Samaria?

1904. How many years did Elisha predict the famine would occur?

1905. Whom did Ben-Hadad, king of Aram, send to Elisha to ask about his illness?

1906. Who did Elisha prophesy would kill Ben-Hadad?

1907. How did Hazael kill Ben-Hadad?

1908. Which king of Judah's mother was named Athaliah?

1909. Whom did Elisha send a young prophet to and anoint as king of Israel?

1910. What did Elisha tell the young prophet to do after he anointed Jehu?

1911. Whose lineage was Jehu told to destroy?

1912. What two kings did Jehu meet on chariots and then kill?

1913. What did Jezebel put on before her death?

1914. What group tossed Jezebel off the tower to her death?

1915. When they went to bury Jezebel, what was left of her body?

1916. What had devoured her?

1917. How many sons of Ahab were in Samaria when Jehu went after them?

1918. What king had everyone in the house of Ahab killed?

1919. What did the people do with the heads of the seventy princes that were murdered?

1920. Jehu pretended to be a worshiper so all the ministers would come to a meeting and eventually be killed. What god did he worship?

1921. After Jehu burned the sacred stone of Baal, what did people use the stone for?

1922. Who was the mother of Ahaziah that proceeded to destroy the entire royal family?

1923. Which heir to the throne was hidden from Athaliah and survived the slaughter?

1924. Which priest had Athaliah killed?

1925. Who was the youngest king to begin his reign over Judah?

1926. What was the age of the youngest king to reign over Judah?

1927. Who was Joash's mother?

1928. What was the one important thing Joash failed to do as king?

1929. Name three reasons money was donated to the temple.

1930. What did Joash want the temple money used for?

1931. When Joash became king, what had the priests not done to the temple in years?

1932. Name the four trades of workers that were hired to repair the temple.

1933. Who was the king of Aram that threatened to invade during the reign of Joash?

1934. What did Joash give to the king of Aram to withdraw his attack on Jerusalem?

1935. Who assassinated Joash?

1936. Where was Joash assassinated?

1937. Who was which country King Joash's son and successor?

1938. Which country's king destroyed Jehoahaz's army, leaving it down to fifty horsemen and ten chariots?

1939. What did Elisha die from?

1940. Elisha had King Jehoash shoot what out the window to declare his upcoming victory?

1941. Following Elisha's instructions, how many times did Jehoash strike the ground with an arrow?

1942. What happened to the dead raider whose body touched Elisha's bones in the tomb?

1943. Which king of Israel captured Amaziah, king of Judah, and took the articles from the temple and hostages?

1944. Which king succeeded Amaziah at the age of sixteen?

1945. Which king had leprosy until the day he died and had to live in a separate house?

1946. Who was the king that assassinated Zechariah, king of Israel, then reigned for only one month until he, too, was assassinated?

1947. Which king of Israel took money from all the wealthy people to give Assyria a thousand talents of silver to not invade their country?

1948. Who was the king of Assyria that threatened Israel but backed off when they got the thousand talents of silver?

1949. During which king of Israel's reign did Assyria first deport people to their country?

1950. Who was the king of Assyria that started deporting Israelites to his country?

1951. Who assassinated Pekah and became king of Israel?

1952. Whom did King Ahaz of Judah sacrifice in the fire?

1953. King Ahaz turned to the king of what country when he was besieged by Aram and Israel?

1954. What country was Tiglath-Pileser king of?

1955. What did Ahaz pay that king for his help?

1956. What did King Ahaz sketch in Damascus and ask Uriah the priest to build a replica of?

1957. Who was the last king of Israel before the Assyrians invaded?

1958. Which king of Assyria invaded Israel and laid siege for three years?

1959. Assyria invaded Israel because they learned Hoshea sent envoys to what country?

1960. What country was So the king of?

1961. What did the king of Assyria do with the Israelites when he invaded the country?

1962. What did God send to the settlers of Israel after Assyria invaded it?

1963. What do the names Sukkoth Benoth, Nergal, Ashima, Nibhaz, Tartak, Adrammelek, Anammelek, and Sepharvaim describe?

1964. What article from the time of Moses did Hezekiah have broken into pieces?

1965. What was the article that the people were worshiping called?

1966. Who was ruling Judah when Shalmaneser, king of Assyria, invaded Israel?

1967. Who was the king of Assyria that first attacked the fortified cities of Judah during Hezekiah's fourteenth year of reign?

1968. In order to pay the king of Assyria, what did Hezekiah have stripped for gold?

1969. Which prophet that also has a book in the Bible advised Hezekiah?

1970. What did Hezekiah do after he received a threatening letter from Assyria?

1971. During the reign of Hezekiah, how many in the Assyrian camp were put to death by the angel of the Lord?

1972. After this devastating defeat, to what city did the king of Assyria retreat (and stay there)?

1973. Which Assyrian king was killed by his sons while worshiping his idol?

1974. What was the name of the god he was praying to at the time?

1975. What were the names of his sons?

1976. Who succeeded Sennacherib as king of Assyria?

1977. Who told Hezekiah he was going to die from illness, then went back and told him he would live after his prayer?

1978. What was Hezekiah facing when he prayed for more life?

1979. How many more years did God add to his life?

1980. From what nation's king did God promise he would deliver Hezekiah?

1981. What did Isaiah have a poultice of prepared and applied to Hezekiah's boil?

1982. What sign did God give Hezekiah that he would be healed?

1983. How many steps would the shadow move?

1984. Hezekiah showed the envoys of the king of what country his entire temple treasury?

1985. Who was the Babylonian king at the time?

1986. Who was the Babylonian king's son that visited Jerusalem?

1987. What six items did Hezekiah show the envoys from the other country?

1988. Which prophet warned Hezekiah that everything would be carried off to Babylon?

1989. What did Hezekiah make that brought water into the city?

1990. Who was Hezekiah's son that took over his throne?

1991. How old was Manasseh when he became king?

1992. What three false idols did Manasseh rebuild altars to in the temple?

1993. To what god did Manasseh put a carved pole right in the temple?

1994. Who was Manasseh's son that succeeded him as king?

1995. Who assassinated King Amon of Judah?

1996. Who was the second-youngest king to rule Judah?

1997. How old was Josiah when he started his reign?

1998. Who was the high priest that found the Book of the Law during Josiah's reign?

1999. Name the secretary that read the Book of the Law to King Josiah after it was found in the temple.

2000. When Josiah heard the word of the Book of the Law, what did he tear?

2001. On the Hill of Corruption, Josiah desecrated the high places. Which predecessor had built them?

2002. Who was the vile goddess of the Sidonians?

2003. Who was the vile god of Moab?

2004. Who was the detestable god of Ammon?

2005. With what did Josiah cover the idol sites to desecrate them?

2006. What celebration did Josiah insist the kingdom must observe?

2007. In 2 Kings 23, which king was like no other and turned to the Lord with all his heart, soul, and strength?

2008. Whose army killed King Josiah?

2009. Where was Josiah killed?

2010. Name Josiah's son that followed him to the throne.

2011. Which king did Pharaoh Necho put in chains to keep him from reigning?

2012. Whom did Pharaoh Necho put into power after capturing him?

2013. During Jehoiakim's reign, what king of Babylon invaded the land?

2014. Name the first king to rebel against Nebuchadnezzar.

2015. Which king surrendered Jerusalem to Nebuchadnezzar?

2016. What did Nebuchadnezzar remove from the temple?

2017. What group of people did Nebuchadnezzar leave behind in Jerusalem?

2018. How many fighting men did Nebuchadnezzar exile to Babylon?

2019. Whom did Nebuchadnezzar make king after his invasion?

2020. What was Mattaniah's relationship to his predecessor, Jehoiachin?

2021. After Zedekiah's rebellion, what did Nebuchadnezzar do to Jerusalem that caused a severe famine in the city?

2022. Whom from Zedekiah's family did Nebuchadnezzar kill before his eyes?

2023. What harm did Nebuchadnezzar do to Zedekiah after that?

2024. Name the commander of the Babylonians that set fire to the temple of the Lord and tore down the walls of Jerusalem.

2025. Whom did Nebuchadnezzar make governor after the temple was burned down?

2026. After Gedaliah was assassinated, where did everyone in Israel flee in fear of the Babylonians?

2027. Who led Babylon after Nebuchadnezzar?

2028. Whom did Awel-Marduk release from prison and allow to sit in a seat of honor?

1 Chronicles

2029. What name begins the genealogy in Chronicles 1?

2030. Who is the only son of Adam listed?

2031. What enemy of Israel did the Kasluhites spawn according to 1 Chronicles 1?

2032. In 1 Chronicles 2, who was the firstborn son of Judah that was considered wicked and thus put to death by the Lord?

2033. How many sons of Jesse does 1 Chronicles list?

2034. How many of David's sisters were listed?

2035. Who was the firstborn son of David?

2036. Which of David's wives bore him his first son?

2037. Who was David's second son?

2038. Which of David's wives bore him his second son?

2039. Who was David's third son?

2040. How many of David's sons were born in Hebron?

2041. Who was the only daughter of David mentioned?

2042. How many sons of Solomon are listed in 1 Chronicles?

2043. Who (mentioned only in 1 Chronicles) asked God to be blessed, to have his territory enlarged, and for God's hand to remain on him?

2044. Which of Jacob's sons lost his birth status by defiling his father's marriage bed?

2045. Which of Jacob's sons retained the rights of the firstborn?

2046. Whom did God stir up to take the Reubenites, the Gadites, and the half tribe of Manesseh into exile?

2047. Name the three sons of Levi that had jobs keeping the tabernacle running.

2048. From which of Levi's sons was Moses descended?

2049. What kind of cities were Hebron and Shechem called in 1 Chronicles 6?

2050. What descendant of Manasseh had only daughters?

2051. From what tribe of Jacob was Joshua, son of Nun, born?

2052. From what line of Jacob was King Saul born?

2053. Who was King Saul's father?

2054. What other name did Jonathan's son Merib-Baal go by?

2055. From whose line did the gatekeepers of the temple come?

2056. What three sons of Saul died on the same day that he did?

2057. Which enemy killed Saul's sons?

2058. Who was too afraid to kill a wounded King Saul and ran away?

2059. How did King Saul and his armor-bearer both die?

2060. In what god's temple did the Philistines hang the head of King Saul?

2061. First Chronicles 10:13 lists three reasons why Saul died: he was unfaithful to the Lord, he didn't keep the word of the Lord, and he consulted someone else instead of the Lord. To whom did he go for guidance?

2062. First Chronicles 11 says the Jebusites lived in what city (also named Jebus)?

2063. Which commander took David's offer to lead the attack on the Jebusites?

2064. Once David took up residence in the fortress of Jebus, what was the city then called?

2065. One of David's mighty men, Jashobeam, killed how many men in one encounter?

2066. What did David desire, so the three mighty men went into Philistine territory to get it?

2067. What brother of Joab raised his spear and killed three hundred men, making him famous?

2068. What did Benaiah, one of David's mighty warriors, kill in a pit on a snowy day?

2069. Where was the seven-and-a-half-foot-tall warrior that Benaiah killed with a club from?

2070. From which tribe came the warriors that were able to shoot arrows and sling stones with their left or right hand?

2071. What tribe's defectors to David's armies were described as having faces of lions and being swift as gazelles?

2072. Who reached out his hand to steady the ark, but God struck him down?

2073. What caused the ark to stumble when it was being transported to Jerusalem?

2074. Because God's wrath struck against Uzzah, what was the place called?

2075. Instead of taking the ark to the City of David, in whose house did David put the ark?

2076. What happened to his house for three months while the ark stayed there?

2077. Name the king of Tyre that sent cedar logs and workmen to build a palace for David.

2078. Because of David's "break out" defeat of the Philistines and because they abandoned their gods, what did David call the place where he had defeated the Philistines?

2079. What did David realize they did wrong when carrying the ark the first time?

2080. How did the Levites carry the ark into Jerusalem?

2081. Which of David's wives despised David when she saw him dancing as the ark arrived in Jerusalem?

2082. When the ark first arrived in Jerusalem, where was it housed?

2083. When the ark arrived in Jerusalem, what three food items did David give every Israelite man and woman?

2084. Which chief priest was left in charge of the ark when it arrived in Jerusalem?

2085. What was David living in a house made of, while the ark sat in a tent?

2086. What did God promise never to take away from David's son, as he had from David's predecessors?

2087. Which prophet reported to David that his throne would be established forever?

2088. What fighting weapons did David take from Hadadezer, king of Zobah, numbering a thousand?

2089. What enemy tribe embarrassed a delegation of David's men sent to express sympathy for the death of their king?

2090. Where did the humiliated men stay until their beards grew back?

2091. What nation realized they had become an obnoxious stench in David's nostrils?

2092. What nation did the Ammonites hire to fight against David?

2093. After David defeated the Arameans, what did they refuse to do for the Ammonites anymore?

2094. According to 1 Chronicles 20, what should kings be doing in the spring?

2095. Who killed the brother of Goliath?

2096. What was the name of Goliath's brother?

2097. How many total digits (fingers and toes) did the huge man in Gath killed by Jonathan, son of Shimea, have?

2098. Whom were these large men descendants of?

2099. According to 1 Chronicles 21, who incited David to take a census of Israel?

2100. What seer brought the bad news to David about his sin regarding the census?

2101. What three painful consequences did David need to choose from, in response to his sin of the census?

2102. How many died as a result of God's judgment on Israel because of David's sin of the census?

2103. Who owned the threshing floor where David saw the angel?

2104. How much did David pay for the threshing floor?

2105. What did David build on that threshing floor?

2106. What did David want to build on the threshing floor?

2107. Whom did David call and charge with building the temple?

2108. According to God, why couldn't David build the temple?

2109. How old did the Levites need to be in order to be counted?

2110. How old did the Levites need to be to work in the temple?

2111. Who was the priest that helped David separate the Levites into divisions for ministering?

2112. The sons of what man are listed as musicians in 1 Chronicles 25 and also credited with psalms in the book of Psalms?

2113. According to 1 Chronicles 26, what was some of the plunder taken from war dedicated to repair?

2114. According to 1 Chronicles 27, how many men were in each division of the army?

2115. How many times a year did each army division serve?

2116. In the list of King David's overseers, what was Joab in charge of?

2117. Who did David say gave him the plans for the temple, courts, and treasuries?

2118. In 1 Chronicles 29, David said our days on earth like a ___________ (without hope).

2119. When Solomon was anointed to be ruler, which priest was also appointed?

2120. How many total years did David rule Israel?

2121. David ruled how many years in Hebron and how many years in Jerusalem?

2122. The records of three prophets/seers are mentioned at end of 1 Chronicles. Who are they?

2 Chronicles

2123. In what city was God's tent of meeting when Solomon visited it to inquire of the Lord?

2124. How many sacrifices did Solomon offer when he reached the tent of meeting?

2125. When God spoke to Solomon and told him to ask for whatever he wanted, what did Solomon ask for?

2126. What other three things did God give to Solomon besides what he asked for?

2127. Second Chronicles says God made gold and silver as common as what in Jerusalem?

2128. Whom did Solomon appeal to in order to find a skilled craftsman to build the temple?

2129. Who was the master craftsman that Hiram sent to Solomon to build the temple?

2130. How did the logs from the temple get from Lebanon to Joppa?

2131. How many people did Solomon assign to work on the temple?

2132. Solomon built the temple on what mount?

2133. The spot where the temple was built was previously used as what?

2134. What did Solomon name the northern and southern pillars of the temple?

2135. In regards to the basins, lampstands, and tables, how many of each were built for the original temple?

2136. What extended so far out from the ark that it could be seen from in front of the inner sanctuary?

2137. What were the only things in the ark when Solomon placed it in the temple?

2138. During the dedication of the temple, what prevented the priests from performing their service?

2139. Solomon prayed that when God's people needed help, they could turn toward what and pray?

2140. What came down from heaven when Solomon finished praying for the temple?

2141. According to 2 Chronicles 7:14, what four things did God's people need to do for him to heal the land?

2142. Whom did Solomon specifically not conscript to work in his slave-labor force?

2143. The queen of Sheba's caravan carried what three gifts to Solomon?

2144. What precious metal from Ophir did Solomon use to make the steps of the temple?

2145. What was the weight of gold that Solomon received yearly?

2146. What animal's image was carved into Solomon's throne (over a dozen of them)?

2147. Every three years, Solomon's ships returned with gold, silver, ivory, and what exotic animals?

2148. Solomon made what precious metal as plentiful as stones in Jerusalem?

2149. Where were Solomon's horses imported from?

2150. For how many years did Solomon reign?

2151. To what country did Jeroboam flee from King Solomon?

2152. Instead of listening to his father's trusted advisers, whom did Rehoboam listen to instead?

2153. Rehoboam's advisers told him to whip the people so brutally that it would be like whipping them with what?

2154. Who was Solomon's son that succeeded him and caused rebellion in the country?

2155. What two tribes did Rehoboam prepare to battle Israel?

2156. Who was the man of God that stopped Rehoboam from attacking Israel?

2157. Who sold their pasturelands and property and moved to Judah because Jeroboam had rejected them?

2158. Which wife did Rehoboam love more than any other?

2159. Who was the king of Egypt that attacked Rehoboam?

2160. Who was Rehoboam's mother, and what was her country of origin?

2161. Who succeeded Rehoboam to the throne?

2162. Who was Abijah's mother, the wife of Rehoboam?

2163. Who won the first battle of Abijah versus Jeroboam (Judah versus Israel)?

2164. Who succeeded Abijah to the throne?

2165. Whom was Zerah the leader of (that marched against Asa)?

2166. Who was the prophet that King Asa listened to and helped to make significant reforms for God?

2167. The remnant of what three other nations settled among Judah and Benjamin during the time of Asa?

2168. Whom did King Asa depose as queen mother because she made an Asherah pole?

2169. King Asa removed her Asherah images and burned them in what valley?

2170. Which king of Israel sieged Ramah during the reign of Asa?

2171. Whom did Asa convince to break his treaty with Israel and fight against Israel?

2172. A seer named Hanani told Asa that he trusted in what army before trusting God?

2173. King Asa suffered from a disease that affected what part of his body?

2174. Who was Asa's son that succeeded him on the throne?

2175. In 2 Chronicles 17, why did Jehoshaphat send officials to all the towns of Judah?

2176. King Jehoshaphat of Judah married into the family of what king of Israel?

2177. What king wanted to align with Jehoshaphat to defeat Ramoth Gilead?

2178. What prophet did Ahab suggest to Jehoshaphat, but he never told Jehoshaphat anything good?

2179. What did Micaiah say the Lord had put in the mouths of Ahab's prophets?

2180. What did King Ahab wear when he went into battle against the Aramean army?

2181. Who was the one person the Aramean army was looking for when they battled Israel and Judah?

2182. Where was King Ahab shot?

2183. Who fired the arrow that killed Ahab?

2184. In 2 Chronicles 19, whom did Jehoshaphat appoint in the towns of Judah?

2185. In 2 Chronicles 20, what two armies came up against Jehoshaphat, but God caused them to destroy each other?

2186. What did King Jehoshaphat ally with King Ahaziah to build together?

2187. When Jehoram established himself as king, whom did he kill?

2188. From whose family was the wife of Jehoram?

2189. Which prophet sent a condemning letter to King Jehoram?

2190. Jehoram died of an incurable disease that affected what part of his body?

2191. Who killed Ahaziah, king of Judah?

2192. What future king survived the murders on the royal family of Judah by Athaliah, mother of Ahaziah?

2193. Who was the woman that hid Joash while his family was murdered?

2194. To whom was Jehosheba married?

2195. Where did they hide Joash?

2196. How long did Joash remain hidden while Athaliah ruled the land?

2197. Who was the only queen of Judah?

2198. Who was the priest that led the charge to make Joash king?

2199. When Joash became king, who was put to death by the priests?

2200. How old was Joash when he became king?

2201. What did Joash place in the temple to collect contributions for the repair of the temple?

2202. Who was the good prophet (and son of Jehoiada) that Joash had stoned to death?

2203. What army easily invaded Jerusalem, killed the leaders, took plunder, and wounded King Joash?

2204. Where was Joash eventually murdered by his officials?

2205. Which king brought home the gods of Seir after slaughtering the Edomites?

2206. Where did Amaziah, king of Judah, and Jehoash, king of Israel, battle?

2207. In 2 Chronicles 25, who won the battle between Israel and Judah?

2208. How old was Uzziah when he became king?

2209. According to 2 Chronicles 26, from what prophet did King Uzziah seek advice?

2210. King Uzziah made machines designed to shoot what two objects from towers?

2211. Who was the priest, with eighty other courageous priests, that followed King Uzziah to the altar of incense and warned him not to burn incense to the Lord?

2212. What disease broke out on King Uzziah's forehead because of his pride?

2213. Who was King Uzziah's son that succeeded him to the throne and walked steadfastly with the Lord?

2214. Who did King Ahaz sacrifice in the fire?

2215. According to 2 Chronicles 28, because King Ahaz did detestable practices of idol worship, God gave him trouble with what five nations?

2216. In 2 Chronicles 28, name the warrior that was attributed with killing 120,000 soldiers?

2217. Who was the prophet that told the army of Israel to return what they had taken after defeating King Ahaz?

2218. What did a prophet tell the army of Israel to return to Judah, or face God's anger?

2219. What nation did King Ahaz appeal to for help against the Edomites and Philistines but that nation gave them more trouble than help?

2220. Who was the leader of that nation at the time?

2221. What did King Ahaz shut the doors to?

2222. Where did King Ahaz set up altars in Jerusalem?

2223. Who was King Ahaz's son that succeeded him and undid all the atrocities Ahaz had done?

2224. What was the first recorded thing Hezekiah did during the first month of the first year of his reign?

2225. During the opening of the temple, Hezekiah commanded that the people sing the words of which two writers of Psalms?

2226. What celebration did Hezekiah reestablish, since priests had not consecrated themselves and there hadn't been an assembly of people?

2227. What did Hezekiah send out to all of Judah to call people to come to Jerusalem for Passover?

2228. What did Hezekiah do when he heard the people had not properly purified themselves before Passover?

2229. When Hezekiah reinstituted the Passover, how many more days did the people extend the celebration?

2230. During the reign of Hezekiah, what did the people bring from all over and pile in heaps in Jerusalem?

2231. What king of Assyria threatened Jerusalem and Hezekiah?

2232. Sennacherib wrote letters to Hezekiah ridiculing whom?

2233. What prophet cried out in prayer with King Hezekiah for the defeat of the Assyrians?

2234. Where was Sennacherib murdered?

2235. Who murdered Sennacherib?

2236. What king's pride was tested by envoys from Babylon?

2237. In what prophet's book does 2 Chronicles 32 say other events of Hezekiah's reign are written?

2238. Who was Hezekiah's son that took his throne?

2239. How old was Manesseh when he became king?

2240. What nation took Manesseh captive, putting a hook in his nose and taking him to Babylon?

2241. God allowed Manesseh to return to Jerusalem after he did what?

2242. Who was Manesseh's son that took his throne?

2243. According to 2 Chronicles 33, what did Amon never do, unlike his father?

2244. Who killed Amon?

2245. How old was Josiah when he became king?

2246. What did King Josiah have burned on the altars of the idols?

2247. Who was the high priest during the time of Josiah?

2248. What did Hilkiah find in the temple during the reign of Josiah?

2249. Who was the prophetess that told Josiah that God would allow him to see peace if he kept the commands of the Book of the Covenant?

2250. During Josiah's first Passover celebration, whom were the musicians the descendants of, as they were in the time of David?

2251. According to 2 Chronicles, Josiah's Passover had not been observed like that since the days of what prophet?

2252. Who was the king of Egypt that Josiah went out to fight in the battle at Carchemish?

2253. On what plain did that battle occur?

2254. How did Josiah die in battle?

2255. What prophet composed laments for King Josiah?

2256. Which king succeeded Josiah but was dethroned by the king of Egypt?

2257. Whom did the king of Egypt appoint as king in Jehoahaz's place?

2258. What name did the king of Egypt give to Eliakim?

2259. What did the king of Egypt do to Jehoahaz?

2260. What king bound Jehoiakim, king of Judah, in bronze shackles and took him to Babylon?

2261. What did Nebuchadnezzar take from the temple in Jerusalem and bring to his temple in Babylon?

2262. How many months did Jehoiachin reign?

2263. Who was the second king that Nebuchadnezzar brought to Babylon?

2264. Whom did Nebuchadnezzar appoint as king in Jehoiachin's place?

2265. What was Zedekiah's relationship to Jehoiachin?

2266. Who was the prophet that Zedekiah did not humble himself before?

2267. According to 2 Chronicles 36, what two places in Jerusalem did Nebuchadnezzar burn down?

2268. In 2 Chronicles 36, what kind of a rest did the land experience after the desolation?

2269. For how many years did the rest occur?

2270. Who prophesied that this desolation would happen?

2271. What king of Persia rose into power and took over Babylon?

2272. Who prophesied that this would happen?

2273. What did the king of Persia say God had appointed him to build?

Ezra

2274. Which two Bible books list the exiles that returned to Jerusalem from Babylon?

2275. What three prophets with Bible books named after them are mentioned in Ezra?

2276. Which Persian king made the proclamation to rebuild Jerusalem in the time of Ezra?

2277. Which prophet prophesied that King Cyrus would rebuild Jerusalem?

2278. Members of what three tribes of Israel returned to Jerusalem?

2279. King Cyrus returned the articles belonging in the temple that were stolen by what Babylonian king?

2280. How many total articles from the temple were returned to Jerusalem?

2281. If no records were found confirming someone in the priesthood, what were they considered?

2282. When the exiles returned to Jerusalem, what was the first thing they built according to Ezra 3?

2283. The rebuilding of what part of the temple caused the people that had seen the previous temple to weep and cry out?

2284. What two emotions were so loud that no one could distinguish one from the other?

2285. The enemies that offered to help build the temple said they were seeking to sacrifice to God since what king of Assyria?

2286. The opposition against the temple construction lasted during the reign of which four kings of Persia?

2287. In what language did the enemies of the exiles write the accusation letter to King Artaxerxes?

2288. What did the opposition's letter speculate that the Jews would no longer pay?

2289. What kind of city did the opposition call Jerusalem, as seen throughout history?

2290. Work on the temple came to a standstill until the second year of what king's reign?

2291. After the reconstruction was stopped, what two prophets prophesied to the exiles to continue working?

2292. According to the book of Ezra, what two men were instrumental in the construction of the temple?

2293. Who was the governor of the Trans-Euphrates that sent a letter to King Darius to alert him that the rebuilding of Jerusalem was continuing?

2294. Whom did King Cyrus appoint as governor while the temple was rebuilt?

2295. Which Persian king sent a letter and restarted the stalled construction of the temple in the book of Ezra?

2296. According to the book of Ezra, the foundation of the temple was how many feet high and wide?

2297. According to the book of Ezra, who paid for the rebuilding of the temple of God?

2298. According to the decree, anyone that interfered with the construction of the temple would have a beam torn from their house and what would happen to that person?

2299. And what would happen to his house?

2300. From what tribe was Ezra?

2301. Which king sent a letter with Ezra, granting him certain powers?

2302. According to the king's letter, no taxes would be imposed on whom?

2303. Because he had told the king that God would protect them, what didn't Ezra ask for when he traveled to Jerusalem?

2304. What sin caused Ezra to tear his tunic and pull hair from his head and beard?

2305. The book of Ezra ends with a list of priests that had committed what sin?

Nehemiah

2306. In what place was the citadel where Nehemiah first heard the news about the exiles?

2307. Who was Nehemiah's brother that told him the news?

2308. Nehemiah was concerned about what city?

2309. Nehemiah wept when he heard what two parts of Jerusalem were still not fixed?

2310. What was Nehemiah's job for the king?

2311. Which king allowed Nehemiah to go to Jerusalem and rebuild the walls?

2312. What beverage did Nehemiah bring the king on a regular basis?

2313. What had Nehemiah never before looked like in the presence of the king?

2314. Nehemiah wanted letters of passage written to the governor of what region?

2315. Who was the keeper of the king's forest?

2316. In chapter 2, what four gates did Nehemiah inspect?

2317. Name the three men that mocked and ridiculed Nehemiah's efforts.

2318. Which one of Nehemiah's naysayers was a Horonite?

2319. Which one of Nehemiah's naysayers was an Ammonite?

2320. Which one of Nehemiah's naysayers was an Arab?

2321. In Nehemiah, what do these names all describe: Fountain, Valley, Dung, Sheep, Fish, Jeshanah, Horse, and Water?

2322. In Nehemiah, Tobiah criticized the wall, saying what animal's weight could topple it?

2323. During the wall construction, workers carried materials in one hand and what in the other?

2324. What did Nehemiah ask people to stop charging on those that were helping to pay for the building of the wall?

2325. To what political office was Nehemiah eventually appointed?

2326. What did Nehemiah not take even though it was allotted for a governor?

2327. What did Sanballat accuse the Jews of planning?

2328. What was the name of the female prophet that was intimidating Nehemiah?

2329. How many days did it take to the build the wall around Jerusalem according to Nehemiah?

2330. In chapter 7, whom did Nehemiah put in charge of Jerusalem?

2331. Nehemiah 7 is a repeat of what other chapter in the Bible?

2332. In Nehemiah 8, who was told to bring out the Book of the Law and read it?

2333. How long did it take him to read it?

2334. In order to celebrate the festival of temporary shelters, what did the people need to collect to build the shelters?

2335. In Nehemiah 9, as the people fasted and wore sackcloth, what did they throw into their hair?

2336. When the people sealed the agreement to follow God in Nehemiah 10, who signed it first?

2337. To whom did the people of Nehemiah's time promise not to give their daughters?

2338. On what day did the people of Nehemiah's time promise not to buy and sell?

2339. Out of every ten people, how many moved into Jerusalem by the casting of lots?

2340. What were the two large groups that Nehemiah assigned to walk along the top of the wall during the dedication ceremony?

2341. During the wall dedication ceremony, what sound could be heard far away?

2342. After reading the Book of Moses, what two nationalities of people did the Israelites exclude from Israel?

2343. Where did Eliashib allow Tobiah to live, which caused Nehemiah to kick Tobiah out?

2344. When Nehemiah returned to Jerusalem, what did he find the people doing on the Sabbath?

2345. What language did Nehemiah find the children of Judah speaking, which was not their native tongue?

2346. What did Nehemiah physically do to those men that married foreign women?

2347. Nehemiah remind the people did that what king did the same thing by marrying foreign women?

Esther

2348. What was the name of the king in the book of Esther?

2349. Over how many provinces did the king rule in Esther?

2350. Those provinces stretched from what nation to what nation?

2351. In Esther, what was the name of the citadel from which the king reigned?

2352. For how many days did he display his vast wealth?

2353. How long did King Xerxes' party last in Esther 1?

2354. What was the name of the first queen before Esther?

2355. Whom did she give a banquet for at the same time as the king's party?

2356. How did Vashti respond to the king's request to show off her beauty to the people?

2357. Who were the wise men afraid would emulate Vashti's behavior?

2358. In the book of Esther, what was the name of the eunuch in charge of the virgins?

2359. What Jewish tribe was Mordecai from?

2360. What other name did Esther go by?

2361. What was Mordecai's relationship to Esther?

2362. What did Esther keep secret during the queen contest?

2363. Who told Esther to keep her secret?

2364. How many months of beauty treatments did Esther receive?

2365. What was the name of Esther's father?

2366. What were the names of king's officers that conspired against King Xerxes?

2367. Whom did Mordecai tell of the plot to assassinate King Xerxes?

2368. What was the name of the man that Mordecai refused to bow down to?

2369. In Esther, what did they cast to decide on what day they would kill the Jews?

2370. With what did the king seal the decree to wipe out the Jews?

2371. According to the edict, who could be killed in a single day?

2372. What was the date on which the Jews could be annihilated?

2373. According to Esther 4, someone could not enter the city if they were wearing what?

2374. What did Esther send Mordecai but he refused because he was mourning?

2375. In Esther, what happened to someone if they approached the king without being summoned?

2376. What could a king extend to someone and save their life?

2377. What did King Xerxes offer Esther up to half of when he saw her?

2378. What was Esther's request?

2379. Who were the only people invited to Esther's banquet?

2380. After the first banquet, what did Esther invite Xerxes and Haman to again?

2381. What did Esther promise to do at the second banquet?

2382. What was the name of Haman's wife?

2383. How high (in feet) was the pole that Haman built for Mordecai?

2384. Who suggested that Haman have the gallows built?

2385. Why did King Xerxes have the book of Chronicles read to him?

2386. What royal article of clothing did Haman suggest to Xerxes should be put on the person that was to be honored?

2387. Where did Haman suggest that the royal crest should be worn?

2388. What did Mordecai ride through the streets, with Haman in the lead?

2389. What did King Xerxes think Haman was doing to his wife Esther after she announced Haman's conspiracy?

2390. Who was first impaled on the pole Haman built?

2391. Who was appointed over Haman's estate?

2392. What did the new edict allow the Jews to do?

2393. What color were the king's royal garments that Mordecai wore?

2394. Since so many nationalities feared the Jews, what did they become because of the events in Esther?

2395. On the first day, how many men did the Jews kill at the citadel in Susa in defense of themselves?

2396. How many sons of Haman were also hung?

2397. While the Jews defended themselves and killed their enemies, what did they not touch?

2398. How many people were killed in all the provinces when the Jews defended themselves?

2399. Who recorded all the events in Esther?

2400. In what month does it say that the people celebrated the victory?

2401. What do people do to celebrate Purim?

2402. What does *pur* mean?

2403. What is the name of the Jewish holiday that celebrates their victory over their enemies in the book of Esther?

2404. For how many days did the celebration continue?

2405. In what place did Mordecai rank after King Xerxes?

2406. In what book of the Bible is God never mentioned by name?

Job

2407. What Old Testament person was described as blameless and upright, one who feared God and shunned evil?

2408. In what land did Job live?

2409. How many children did Job first have?

2410. What Old Testament person had 7,000 sheep, 3,000 camels, 500 yoke of oxen, and 500 donkeys?

2411. What occasion did Job's children like to celebrate?

2412. What did Job do to his children after a party in case they had sinned?

2413. In Job, when God asked Satan where he had come from, what was Satan's answer?

2414. What did Satan accuse God of putting around Job?

2415. What did God first mark as off-limits with Job that Satan couldn't touch?

2416. What tribe carried off Job's oxen and donkeys and killed his servants?

2417. What burned up Job's sheep and servants?

2418. What tribe of people carried off Job's camels?

2419. What destroyed Job's house and killed his children?

2420. Who said, "Naked I came from my mother's womb and naked I will depart"?

2421. When asked a second time where he came from, where did Satan tell God he had been roaming?

2422. What did Satan ask to strike of Job's that would certainly cause him to curse God?

2423. What did Satan inflict Job's body with?

2424. How far did the sores on Job spread throughout his body?

2425. What did Job use to scrape his skin?

2426. Who told Job to "curse God and die"?

2427. Job felt they should accept the good from God and what else?

2428. Name Job's three friends that sat with him.

2429. What three nationalities were these friends?

2430. When the friends saw Job, what did they tear?

2431. What did Job's friends sprinkle on their heads?

2432. How long did Job's friends sit with him?

2433. In Job 3, what day did Job curse?

2434. In Job 4, which of Job's friends was first to respond to Job?

2435. What did Eliphaz say visited him, causing his hair to stand on end?

2436. In Job 5, according to Eliphaz, what does not just spring up from the soil or sprout from the ground?

2437. In Job 6, what did Job wish his anguish and misery could be placed on?

2438. In Job 7, what two things did Job say his body was clothed with?

2439. According to Job, those that go down to the grave do not ever what?

2440. In Job 8, who was the second friend to speak up?

2441. Job 8 says that the trust of the godless is as fragile as what?

2442. In Job 9, what constellations created by God did Job mention by name?

2443. What two things did Job say he could wash with?

2444. In chapter 10, Job felt that God stalked him like a what?

2445. Job wished he had been carried from the womb to where?

2446. In Job 11, it says the witless cannot become wise, like a wild donkey's colt cannot be born like a what?

2447. According to chapter 12, what did Job believe he had become to his friends?

2448. What four things did Job say could teach his friends about the Lord?

2449. Whom did Job wish to argue his case before?

2450. Who said, "Though he slay me, yet will I hope in him"?

2451. According to Job 13, a man wastes away like a garment eaten by what?

2452. In chapter 14, what vegetation did Job say had more hope than he did?

2453. What did Job hope God would not keep track of, but seal up and cover over?

2454. In Job 15, Eliphaz asked Job if he was the first person ever to be what?

2455. In chapter 16, how did Job describe his comforters' speeches?

2456. In chapter 17, what was the only home Job could hope for?

2457. In Job 18, to what stupid animal did Bildad believe Job was comparing his friends?

2458. In chapter 19, what did Job say was offensive to his wife?

2459. What familiar phrase in Job 19:20 did Job use to communicate how closely he had escaped death?

2460. In Job 20, Bildad said a godless person would perish like his own what?

2461. Bildad said a wicked person would be struck by an arrow that pierced what important organ?

2462. According to Job 21, what animal of the wicked person's flock never fails to breed?

2463. According to Job 22, whom did the wicked want to leave them alone?

2464. In chapter 23, what four places did Job say he could go and not find or see God?

2465. In Job 24, what time of the day was morning for thieves?

2466. Which friend's response to Job was the shortest of any chapter in Job, only six verses long?

2467. In Job 26, what does God wrap up in the clouds yet the clouds don't burst under the weight?

2468. In chapter 27, despite his friends' words, what did Job refuse to deny?

2469. Job compared a wicked person's house to a moth's what?

2470. In Job 28, people knew where to dig for precious metals, but what did they have a hard time finding?

2471. In chapter 29, what did Job say he put on as his clothing?

2472. In chapter 30, since everyone has abandoned him, Job said he had become a brother of jackals and a companion of what bird?

2473. In chapter 31, Job said if he had mistreated the fatherless, then he asked that what part of his body would just fall off?

2474. According to chapter 32, why did Job's three friends stop talking to him?

2475. What was the name of the fourth person that talked to Job?

2476. From what tribe was Elihu?

2477. Why was Elihu angry with Job's three friends?

2478. Why did Elihu wait to speak last?

2479. In Job 33, according to Elihu, what does God do to people in dreams or directly into their ears?

2480. In Job 34, according to Elihu, what did Job drink like water?

2481. According to Elihu, if God withdrew his spirit and breath, what would man return to?

2482. In Job 35, whom did Elihu accuse of opening his mouth with empty talk?

2483. In Job 37, what three weather patterns did Elihu say no one could understand how God did them?

2484. Of all the weather conditions mentioned in Job 37, which one did it say God produced with his breath?

2485. God spoke to Job out of what weather pattern?

2486. In Job 38, God asked Job where he was when He laid the earth's what?

2487. What sang together as the earth's cornerstones were laid?

2488. What on earth did God say he shut up behind doors?

2489. What daily occurrence did God say He gave orders to?

2490. What two "gates" did God ask Job if he had seen?

2491. What were in the two "storehouses" God asked Job if he'd encountered?

2492. What two weather occurrences did God say he "fathered"?

2493. Whose "belt" did God ask if anyone had loosened?

2494. What three constellations did God mention in Job 38?

2495. What two birds did God ask Job if he had given them wisdom and understanding?

2496. What two animals did God ask Job if he knew about their birth patterns?

2497. What flightless bird did God describe as joyful yet without wisdom?

2498. In Job 39, according to God, what bird laughed at the horse and rider when it ran?

2499. What animal did God describe to Job as a leaping locust?

2500. What animal of God's creation did he say laughed at fear and was not afraid of the sword?

2501. How many times did Job say he spoke to God, but he would speak no more?

2502. What attribute of God's was described like thunder?

2503. What name did God give the animal that fed on grass like an ox and had bones like bronze?

2504. What did the Behemoth feed on?

2505. What did the Behemoth's tail sway like?

2506. What kind of plant did the Behemoth lie under?

2507. What name did God give the animal that could not be pulled down with a fishhook and its tongue tied down with a rope?

2508. In Job 41, what did God describe as pouring from the mouth and nostrils of this beast?

2509. What eight weapons could not bring down the beast?

2510. Which of Job's three friends did God speak directly to?

2511. What did God tell Job's friends to do in repentance for their words?

2512. In Job 42, how many times more did God bless Job?

2513. What two precious materials did each of Job's friends give Job after God spoke?

2514. After God restored Job, how many sons and daughters did he have?

2515. What were the names of Job's three daughters?

2516. For how many years did Job live?

2517. Job lived to see his children through how many generations?

Psalms

2518. In terms of chapters, what is the longest book of the Old Testament?

2519. According to Psalm 1, a man is blessed if he does not walk in the counsel of whom?

2520. According to Psalm 1, a man is blessed if he does not stand in the way of whom?

2521. According to Psalm 1, a man is blessed if he does not sit in the company of whom?

2522. According to Psalm 1, what should a man meditate on day and night?

2523. According to Psalm 1, a wicked man blows away like what?

2524. According to Psalm 2, with what kind of scepter does God promise to rule with?

2525. According to Psalm 3, what part of his enemies' body does the writer want God to break?

2526. According to Psalm 4, what should people not do while lying in their beds?

2527. According to Psalm 5, what does the writer lay before God in the morning?

2528. According to Psalm 5, what part of an enemies' body was described as an open grave?

2529. According to Psalm 6, what parts of the writer's body were in agony?

2530. According to Psalm 7, the writer felt his enemies would tear him apart like what animal?

2531. According to Psalm 7, God is a righteous judge but he displays what every day?

2532. According to Psalm 8, who was made a little lower than the heavenly beings?

2533. According to Psalm 9, what do the nations fall into?

2534. According to Psalm 10, who does a wicked person think will never notice his actions?

2535. According to Psalm 10, what two groups of needy people does God defend?

2536. According to Psalm 11, where is the Lord and what is he sitting on?

2537. According to Psalm 12, to whom does everyone lie?

2538. In Psalm 13, the writer wondered how long God would hide what from him?

2539. In Psalm 14, a fool says in his heart that there is no what?

2540. In Psalm 15, a blameless person lends money to the poor without charging what?

2541. According to Psalm 16, the psalmist knew God would not abandon him where?

2542. In Psalm 17, the writer asked to hide in the shadow of God's what?

2543. In Psalm 17, the writer compared his hungry and crouching enemies to what animal?

2544. Psalm 18 says that the Lord is "my rock, my fortress and my ________"?

2545. In Psalm 18, the writer said God made his feet like that of what animal standing on high places?

2546. In Psalm 19, what two things proclaim the glory and work of God?

2547. What two things in Psalm 20 do people trust in, but the psalmist trusted in the name of the Lord?

2548. In Psalm 21, with what weapon did the writer describe God using to aim at the backs of the enemies?

2549. Which psalm was sung to the tune of "The Doe of the Morning"?

2550. Which psalm did Jesus quote the first line of while on the cross?

2551. In Psalm 22, the writer said he was not a man but what tiny creature?

2552. In Psalm 22, what did the people hurl at the one being mocked?

2553. In Psalm 22, what three animals surrounded the writer?

2554. In Psalm 22, the writer said he was poured out like what?

2555. In Psalm 22, what did the writer say was out of joint?

2556. According to the writer of Psalm 22, what two parts of the body have been pierced?

2557. According to Psalm 22:17, what could the psalmist count every one of?

2558. In Psalm 22, what did they divide up among themselves and cast lots for?

2559. In Psalm 23, what does the shepherd make the writer lie down in?

2560. In Psalm 23, what did the writer walk through but feared no evil?

2561. In Psalm 23, what two weapons did the shepherd carry with him?

2562. In Psalm 23, what does God prepare in the presence of the enemies?

2563. In Psalm 23, what did God anoint the psalmist with?

2564. According to Psalm 23, what overflowed?

2565. According to Psalm 23, where did the writer say he would dwell forever?

2566. In Psalm 24, what two parts of the city walls did the writer tell to lift up so God could come in?

2567. From what time period in the psalmist's life did he not want God to remember his sins?

2568. What two things did the writer of Psalm 26 ask the Lord to test, try, and examine?

2569. In Psalm 27, where did the writer ask to dwell forever?

2570. In Psalm 27, what did the writer want to gaze on all the days of his life?

2571. In Psalm 28, what part of the writer's body leapt for joy while praising God?

2572. In Psalm 29, what aspect of God did the writer call thundering, powerful, and earth shattering?

2573. In Psalm 29, God made Lebanon skip like what animal?

2574. In Psalm 30, what did the writer say God brought him up from?

2575. In Psalm 30, the writer said God turned his wailing into what?

2576. In Psalm 31, what did the writer say that he committed into the hands of God?

2577. When did Jesus quote Psalm 31:5?

2578. In Psalm 32, a man was blessed if the Lord did not count what against him?

2579. According to Psalm 32, what two animals must be controlled by a bit and bridle or they will not come to you?

2580. In Psalm 33, God gathers the waters of sea into what?

2581. In Psalm 34, what did the writer encourage readers to taste and see?

2582. According to Psalm 34:20, what part of the body of a righteous man was protected and not broken?

2583. In Psalm 35, to what animal did the psalmist compare the slanderers and mockers?

2584. Psalm 36 says that people take refuge in the shadow of God's what?

2585. Psalm 37 says that if we delight in the Lord, he will give us what?

2586. Psalm 37 says that the meek will inherit what?

2587. In Psalm 38, why did the writer believe his bones had lost their soundness?

2588. In Psalm 38, while standing before the Lord, what two physical abilities did he feel like he lost?

2589. Psalm 39 says each man's life is but a what?

2590. In Psalm 40, what kind of song did God put in the psalmist's mouth?

2591. In Psalm 40, what numbered more than the hairs of the psalmist's head?

2592. In Psalm 41, what did the writer share with the close friend that lifted up his heel against him?

2593. In Psalm 42, what animal panted for streams of water?

2594. In Psalm 42, what had been the psalmist's food day and night?

2595. In Psalm 43, what did the writer address, asking why it was so downcast?

2596. In Psalm 44, what two weapons did the psalmist not trust in?

2597. In Psalm 45, what of God's did the psalmist describe as smelling of myrrh and aloes?

2598. In Psalm 46, the writer said he would not fear even if what land masses fell into the sea?

2599. In Psalm 46, the psalmist said that we must be still and know what?

2600. In Psalm 47, whom did the writer tell to clap their hands?

2601. In Psalm 48, where did the psalmist meditate on God's unfailing love?

2602. In Psalm 49, what animal, like humans, was described as destined for the grave?

2603. According to Psalm 50, God owns the cattle on how many hills?

2604. In Psalm 51, what plant did the writer ask to be cleansed with?

2605. In Psalm 51, the writer asked God to create a pure what in him?

2606. In Psalm 51, what did the psalmist not want taken away from him?

2607. According to Psalm 51, what kind of heart was considered a true sacrifice?

2608. In Psalm 52, what kind of tree did the writer compare himself to, flourishing in the house of God?

2609. According to Psalm 53, how many have done good?

2610. In Psalm 53, where did the writer want salvation for Israel to come from?

2611. In Psalm 54, the psalmist faced arrogant, ruthless people with no regard for whom?

2612. In Psalm 55, during what three parts of the day did the writer call out to God in distress?

2613. In Psalm 55, what two slippery substances did the writer use to describe his companion's words?

2614. In Psalm 55, what did the writer say we should cast on the Lord?

2615. In Psalm 56, what did the psalmist want listed on God's scroll?

2616. The writer of Psalm 57 described the teeth and tongue of his enemies by comparing them to what three weapons?

2617. In Psalm 57, what two traps did the writer say were set for him?

2618. According to Psalm 57, God's love reaches to the heavens, but what reaches to the skies?

2619. What did the writer of Psalm 58 compare his enemies to (that melts away as it moves along)?

2620. What snarling animals did the writer of Psalm 59 compare his enemies to?

2621. In Psalm 60, which nation did God call his scepter?

2622. According to Psalm 60, at what nation did Goes toss his sandal?

2623. In Psalm 61, what did the writer ask to be led to that was higher than him?

2624. In Psalm 61, the psalmist wanted to take refuge in the shadow of God's what?

2625. In Psalm 62, the writer said he would not be shaken because God was his what?

2626. In Psalm 63:3, the writer said God's love is better than what?

2627. In Psalm 64, what were the evildoers' cruel words like?

2628. In Psalm 65, what did the writer say God did to the roaring seas and waves?

2629. In Psalm 66, whom did the psalmist ask to shout with joy to God?

2630. In Psalm 67, what did the psalmist want to shine on the people?

2631. In Psalm 68, the psalmist called God a father to the fatherless and a defender of whom?

2632. In Psalm 68, what weapon of God's did the psalmist say numbered tens of thousands?

2633. In Psalm 69, the writer said zeal for what consumed him?

2634. In Psalm 69, what did the psalmist say that they put in his food?

2635. In Psalm 69, what did the writer want his enemies blotted out of?

2636. In Psalm 70, what did the writer's enemies want to take away from him?

2637. In Psalm 71, with what two musical instruments did the writer want to praise God?

2638. In Psalm 71, with what two parts of his body did the writer want to praise God?

2639. In Psalm 72, the psalmist wanted God to endure longer than what two celestial bodies?

2640. In Psalm 72, where did the psalmist want the gold given to God to come from?

2641. In Psalm 73, the writer said the arrogant wear their pride like what piece of jewelry?

2642. In Psalm 74, what creature mentioned in Job did the writer reference?

2643. In Psalm 75, what did God hold in his hand and pour out on the earth?

2644. In Psalm 76, where was God's tent?

2645. What famous miracle does Psalm 77 remember?

2646. In Psalm 78, the writer said he used what form of speaking when he opened his mouth?

2647. In Psalm 78, which tribe of Jacob did the writer say that God chose over all the others?

2648. In Psalm 79, what did the writer ask God to pour out on the nations?

2649. In Psalm 80, what was the bread that God fed the people made from?

2650. In Psalm 81, during what festival did the writer ask for the ram's horn to be sounded?

2651. In Psalm 81, what tasty treat did God promise to satisfy Israel with if they listened to him?

2652. In Psalm 82, who knew nothing, understood nothing, and walked around in darkness?

2653. In Psalm 83, which nation was hated by enemies who wanted to destroy it, so that its name would not be remembered anymore ?

2654. According to Psalm 84, better is one day in God's courts than how many days elsewhere?

2655. In Psalm 85, what do righteousness and peace do to each other?

2656. In Psalm 86, what kind of heart did the psalmist want God to give him?

2657. In Psalm 87, what name did the psalmist use for the city on the holy mountain?

2658. In Psalm 88, who did the writer say was his closest friend?

2659. In Psalm 89, what did the psalmist say would endure like the sun rather than be cast to the ground?

2660. In Psalm 90, the writer said a thousand years was like what period of time in God's sight?

2661. How many years at best does Psalm 90 say an average man will live?

2662. According to Psalm 91, God will cover us with his what?

2663. In Psalm 91, what two animals did the writer say that someone could trample on and God would rescue them?

2664. In Psalm 92, the writer said it was good to proclaim God's love in the morning and what at night?

2665. In Psalm 93, what part of the earth lifted its voice to God?

2666. In Psalm 94, what three groups of people were crushed, slayed, and murdered by the evildoers?

2667. In Psalm 95, what two places during the Israelites' wanderings in the desert were remembered as locations where their hearts were hardened?

2668. According to Psalm 95, how many years was God angry with that generation in the wilderness?

2669. In Psalm 96, what kind of a song did the writer encourage people to sing?

2670. In Psalm 97, what did the mountains melt like before the Lord?

2671. According to Psalm 97, what did the heavens proclaim?

2672. In Psalm 98, what geographical locations clap their hands to God?

2673. In Psalm 98, what geographical locations sing together for God?

2674. In Psalm 99, who were the three Old Testament priests that called on God's name?

2675. According to Psalm 100, how long does God's faithfulness continue?

2676. In Psalm 101, no one that practices what can dwell in God's house?

2677. According to Psalm 102, the psalmist's days vanish like what?

2678. In Psalm 102, the distraught psalmist eats what with his food?

2679. According to Psalm 103, God is slow to anger and abounding in what?

2680. According to Psalm 103, God removes our transgressions as far as what is from what?

2681. According to Psalm 103, God knows how we are formed and that we are nothing but what?

2682. According to Psalm 103, what plant are man's days like?

2683. According to Psalm 104, what does God wrap himself in like a garment?

2684. According to Psalm 104, what has God set on its foundation?

2685. In Psalm 105, every plague in Egypt is recounted except which two?

2686. In Psalm 106, the writer remembered the people's rebellion against what two leaders?

2687. According to Psalm 106, Phineas' act to stop the plague gave him a credit of what?

2688. According to Psalm 106, to whom did the Israelites in the wilderness sacrifice their sons and daughters?

2689. According to Psalm 107, the people reeled and staggered around like what during a storm?

2690. What maritime miracle of Jesus was alluded to in Psalm 107?

2691. What is unique about Psalm 60 and Psalm 108?

2692. In Psalm 109, the psalmist asked God to make the wife of his enemy into a what?

2693. According to Psalm 110, what will God turn "your enemies" into?

2694. According to Psalm 110, "you are a priest forever" in the order of who?

2695. According to Psalm 111, what is the beginning of wisdom?

2696. According to Psalm 112:7, what will the righteous never fear?

2697. According to Psalm 113, what two groups of people does God raise from the dust and ash heap?

2698. In Psalm 114, what geographical formations skipped like rams and lambs?

2699. In Psalm 115, what has ears but cannot hear, noses but cannot smell?

2700. In Psalm 116, the death of whom is precious in the sight of the Lord?

2701. What is the shortest chapter in the entire Bible?

2702. How many total verses does the shortest chapter in the Bible have?

2703. Psalm 118 says it is better to take refuge in the Lord than to trust whom?

2704. Psalm 118 says the stone the builders rejected has become what?

2705. Psalm 118 says blessed is the man "who comes in the ________ of the Lord."

2706. What is the longest chapter in the entire Bible?

2707. According to Psalm 119, what had the writer hidden in his heart so he wouldn't sin against God?

2708. What did the writer say fainted with longing for God's salvation?

2709. In Psalm 119, whom did the psalmist feel he had more wisdom than because he obeyed God's precepts?

2710. According to Psalm 119, what acts as a lamp to the writer's feet?

2711. In Psalm 119, what did the psalmist love less than God's commands?

2712. In Psalm 119, how many times a day did the writer praise God for his laws?

2713. In Psalm 119, the psalmist felt like he had strayed like a lost what?

2714. How many total verses are in Psalm 119, the longest chapter in the Bible?

2715. In Psalm 120, what two lying and deceitful parts of the human head did the writer want God to save him from?

2716. In Psalm 121, where did the writer lift his eyes to in order to find help?

2717. In Psalm 122, the writer asked people to pray for peace for what city?

2718. In Psalm 123, the eyes of the slave looked to whose hand?

2719. In Psalm 124, like what creature escaping from a snare did the psalmist compare his escape from trouble?

2720. According to Psalm 125, those that trust in the Lord were like what mount?

2721. According to Psalm 126, those that sow in tears will reap with songs of what?

2722. According to Psalm 127, the builders build the house in vain unless who builds it?

2723. According to Psalm 127, unless the Lord watches over a city, who stands guard in vain?

2724. According to Psalm 127, who are a heritage and a reward from the Lord?

2725. According to Psalm 127, children are like what in the hands of a warrior?

2726. According to Psalm 127, a man is blessed if his what is full of sons?

2727. In Psalm 128, who will be a fruitful vine in the house?

2728. In Psalm 128, who will be olive shoots around the table?

2729. In Psalm 129, the psalmist wanted his enemies to be like grass that grew in what place?

2730. In Psalm 130, what of the Lord's did the writer put his hope in?

2731. In Psalm 131, the writer said he was as content as a what?

2732. In Psalm 132, if David's sons kept God's commands, they would have a seat where?

2733. In Psalm 132, where has the Lord desired to live forever and ever?

2734. In Psalm 132, what would the Lord allow to grow for David?

2735. In Psalm 133, how good and pleasant it is when who live together in unity?

2736. In Psalm 134, the psalmist praised those that minister at night in what place?

2737. In Psalm 135, with what four weather conditions did the psalmist credit God?

2738. In Psalms 135 and 136, two kings that God defeated were mentioned by name. Who were they?

2739. Psalm 136 repeats what phrase twenty-six times?

2740. The writer of Psalm 137 said he sat by the rivers of what country and wept, thinking about Zion?

2741. The writer of Psalm 138 said he would bow down in the direction of what and praise God?

2742. In Psalm 139, where did the psalmist say God knit him together?

2743. In Psalm 139:14, how did the writer describe the way he was made?

2744. In Psalm 139, what was ordained and written in God's book before any of them came to be?

2745. In Psalm 139, the writer asked God to search him and know his what?

2746. According to Psalm 140, evil men's tongues are as sharp as what?

2747. In Psalm 140, what burning object did the writer want to fall on the heads of his enemies?

2748. In Psalm 141, what did the writer ask to be set before God like incense?

2749. In Psalm 141, what did the writer want God to set a guard over?

2750. In Psalm 142, what did the writer want to be set free from?

2751. In Psalm 143, the writer thirsted for God like what kind of land?

2752. According to Psalm 144, what did God prepare the psalmist's fingers for?

2753. In Psalm 144, how many strings were on the lyre the psalmist wanted to play?

2754. According to Psalm 145, as everyone's eyes look to God, what does he give them at the proper time?

2755. In Psalm 146, whom did the writer say we should not to put our trust in?

2756. In Psalm 147, what does God bind up the wounds of?

2757. In Psalm 147, what does God call each by name?

2758. In Psalm 148, what did the writer tell the sun, moon, stars, sea creatures, mountains, hills, fruit trees, and all animals and birds to do?

2759. In Psalm 149, the writer asked for praise to be in the people's mouth while what was in their hands?

2760. Name the seven instruments the psalmist asked people to praise God with in Psalm 150.

2761. What are the last three words of the book of Psalms?

Proverbs

2762. At the beginning of Proverbs, which king was credited for the proverbs?

2763. According to Proverbs 1, what is the beginning of knowledge?

2764. According to Proverbs 1, what two people should a son listen to?

2765. In Proverbs 1, it's useless to spread a net in front of what kind of animals?

2766. In Proverbs 1, who calls aloud in the streets?

2767. According to Proverbs 2, a son should look for wisdom as if looking for what precious metal?

2768. According to Proverbs 2, what will save you from wicked men?

2769. According to Proverbs 2, what kind of a woman will wisdom save you from?

2770. According to Proverbs 2, whose house leads to death?

2771. According to Proverbs 3, if the son follows wise teachings, what will it prolong?

2772. According to Proverbs 3, what two things should we bind around our neck?

2773. Proverbs 3 says we should trust in the Lord and not lean on what?

2774. According to Proverbs 3, if we are not wise in our own eyes, what will it bring nourishment to?

2775. According to Proverbs 3, if we honor the Lord with our wealth, what will be filled to overflowing?

2776. According to Proverbs 3:12, whom does the Lord discipline?

2777. According to Proverbs 3, what three precious items is wisdom better than?

2778. According to Proverbs 3, long life is found in Wisdom's right hand. What is in her left hand?

2779. According to Proverbs 3, what did the Lord use to lay the earth's foundation?

2780. What should we not withhold from someone that deserves it?

2781. According to Proverbs 3, whom should we not tell to come back tomorrow if we have what they need today?

2782. According to Proverbs 3, whose house does the Lord curse?

2783. What does Proverbs 4 say we must love, and she will watch over us?

2784. According to Proverbs 4, what will wisdom set on your head?

2785. According to Proverbs 4, what do the wicked eat the bread of?

2786. What does Proverbs 4 say we should guard because everything flows from it?

2787. What do the lips of an adulterous women drip with?

2788. What is an adulterous woman as bitter as?

2789. Where do an adulterous woman's steps lead straight to?

2790. What part of the adulteress's house should a man stay away from?

2791. If you are caught up with an adulterous woman, who could feast on your wealth?

2792. According to Proverbs 5, what should we drink from our own cistern?

2793. To what animal does the writer compare a wife from his youth?

2794. According to Proverbs 6, what insect should a lazy person go to and consider?

2795. What is an ant lacking, yet it stores up provisions and food?

2796. What will come upon a sluggard like a thief?

2797. How many things does Proverbs 6:16–19 say are detestable to the Lord?

2798. According to Proverbs 6, whom can you have for a loaf of bread?

2799. According to Proverbs 7, where should we bind the commands and teachings?

2800. In Proverbs 7, what three scents does the prostitute use to perfume her bed?

2801. According to Proverbs 7, if you follow a prostitute, it's like what animal going to slaughter?

2802. Proverbs 8 says to choose wisdom over what two precious metals?

2803. According to Proverbs 8:23, how long has wisdom been around?

2804. According to Proverbs 9, how many pillars does wisdom's house have?

2805. According to Proverbs 9, you invite insult by correcting whom?

2806. But whom can you rebuke and they will love you?

2807. What is described as a loud, undisciplined woman that sits at the door of her house and calls out to those that pass by?

2808. How does stolen water taste?

2809. According to Proverbs 10, if a wise son brings joy to his father, what does a foolish son bring to his mother?

2810. Proverbs 10 says hatred stirs up dissension, but what covers all wrongs?

2811. While wisdom is found on the lips of the discerning, what is best for the back of a senseless person?

2812. Proverbs 10 compares a sluggard to what liquid on teeth?

2813. According to Proverbs 11, a lack of what causes a nation to fall?

2814. According to Proverbs 11, a woman without discretion is like what in a pig's snout?

2815. According to Proverbs 11, a person that brings trouble on his family will inherit what?

2816. According to Proverbs 12, whoever loves discipline, loves what?

2817. According to Proverbs 12, a wife of noble character is her husband's what?

2818. But a disgraceful wife brings decay to his what?

2819. Proverbs 12:10 says a righteous man cares for the needs of his what?

2820. According to Proverbs 12, what weighs a heart down?

2821. What cheers the heart up?

2822. According to Proverbs 13, whose appetite is never filled?

2823. While one man pretends to be rich and has nothing, the one that pretends to be poor has what?

2824. Hope deferred makes what sick?

2825. He that spares what hates his son?

2826. According to Proverbs 14, the strength of what animal causes an abundant harvest?

2827. According to Proverbs 14, there is a way that seems right to a man, but in the end it leads to what?

2828. The fear of the Lord is a fountain of what?

2829. According to Proverbs 14, what rots the bones?

2830. According to Proverbs 14, if you oppress the poor, whom are you really showing contempt for?

2831. According to Proverbs 15, what does a gentle answer turn away?

2832. According to Proverbs 15, what brings healing like a tree of life?

2833. What small serving of food served with love is better than a fattened calf served with hatred?

2834. According to Proverbs 15, plans succeed with many what?

2835. According to Proverbs 15, the Lord tears down a proud man's what?

2836. According to Proverbs 16, it is better to get wisdom than what?

2837. According to Proverbs 16, what goes before destruction?

2838. There is a way that seems right to man, but in the end it leads to what?

2839. According to Proverbs, what color hair is a crown a splendor?

2840. It's better to have a dry crust with peace and quiet, than eat a feast in a house full of what?

2841. Crucibles and furnaces are for silver and gold, but what does the Lord test?

2842. According to Proverbs 17, it's better to meet a bear robbed of what than a fool bent on folly?

2843. Starting a quarrel is like breaching a what?

2844. A friend loves at all times, and who is born for adversity?

2845. According to Proverbs 17, a cheerful heart is like what?

2846. According to Proverbs 18, a fool's lips bring him strife and his mouth invites what?

2847. According to Proverbs 18, the name of the Lord is like a strong what?

2848. According to Proverbs 18, what part of the body has the power of life and death?

2849. According to Proverbs 18, he that finds what, finds what is good and receives favor from the Lord?

2850. According to Proverbs 18, who sticks closer than a brother?

2851. According to Proverbs 19, what attracts many friends?

2852. According to Proverbs 19, whose rage is like the roar of a lion?

2853. According to Proverbs 19, while we inherit houses and wealth from parents, what comes from the Lord?

2854. According to Proverbs 19, you should discipline your children so you are not a willing party in their what?

2855. In Proverbs 19, it says a person has many plans. What ultimately prevails?

2856. What does a sluggard bury his hand in, too lazy to bring it to his mouth?

2857. According to Proverbs 20, wine is a mocker and beer is a what?

2858. In Proverbs 20, a king's wrath is like the roar of what animal?

2859. According to Proverbs 20, what two senses has God made both of?

2860. According to Proverbs 20, there are plenty of gold and rubies, but lips that speak what are a rare jewel?

2861. According to Proverbs 20, how does food gained by fraud taste?

2862. But in the end, the mouth of that person is full of what?

2863. In Proverbs 20, the glory of young men is their strength, but what is the splendor of the old?

2864. A man's ways seem right to him, but what does the Lord weigh?

2865. What two places mentioned in Proverbs 21 are better to live than with a quarrelsome wife?

2866. In Proverbs 21, what given in secret soothes anger?

2867. In Proverbs 21, the love for what two liquids will make one poor?

2868. What animal is made ready for battle, but victory rests with the Lord?

2869. Who, once started off correctly, will not depart from the way he should go when he gets old?

2870. Who is a slave to the lender?

2871. In Proverbs 22, what animal does a sluggard say is running around outside?

2872. What kind of trap is the mouth of an adulteress compared to?

2873. What should someone not move, once set up by the forefathers?

2874. If you are given to gluttony, what should you put to your throat?

2875. According to Proverbs 23, what drink bites like a snake and poisons like a viper?

2876. Being drunk is like sleeping on what vessel?

2877. According to Proverbs 24, what does wisdom build and fill its rooms with treasures?

2878. According to Proverbs 24, victory is won with many what?

2879. In Proverbs 24, honey is sweet to the taste as what is sweet to the soul?

2880. Proverbs 24 says not to gloat when who falls?

2881. According to Proverbs 24, an honest answer is like what?

2882. According to Proverbs 24, after you get your fields outside ready, what should you build next?

2883. According to Proverbs 24, a little rest, a little folding of hands, and poverty comes upon you like a what?

2884. According to Proverbs 25, a word aptly spoken is like what fruit of gold?

2885. According to Proverbs 25, what will you vomit if you gorge too much of?

2886. In whose house should you seldom set your foot or he'll hate you?

2887. According to Proverbs 25, if you give food or water to your enemy, it's like piling what on his head?

2888. What, from a distant land, is like cold water to a weary soul?

2889. Like a city without walls, so is a man that lacks what?

2890. If a whip is for a horse and a bridle for a donkey, what is for the backs of fools?

2891. The useless legs of the lame are like what from the mouth of a fool?

2892. According to Proverbs 26, a fool repeats his folly like a dog returns to his what?

2893. What animal is the sluggard afraid might be in the street, so he can't go outside?

2894. As a door turns on its hinges, so does a fool turn where?

2895. Like a fire goes out without wood, the lack of what causes a quarrel to die down?

2896. According to Proverbs 26, if you dig a pit, what will ultimately happen to you?

2897. According to Proverbs 27, anger and fury are bad, but what's worse?

2898. Wounds from a friend can be trusted, but what does an enemy multiply?

2899. According to Proverbs 28, what metal is likened to two people sharpening each other?

2900. As water reflects a face, what reflects a man's life?

2901. A ruler that oppresses the poor is a driving rain destroying what?

2902. What kind of a wicked person deals with a helpless person like a roaring lion or a charging bear?

2903. According to Proverbs 28, a man will do wrong for a piece of what?

2904. According to Proverbs 28, when the wicked perish, who thrives?

2905. According to Proverbs 29, those that flatter their neighbors spread what at their feet?

2906. According to Proverbs 29, who stirs up a city?

2907. According to Proverbs 29, if we discipline our children, what will they give us?

2908. According to Proverbs 29, the people cast off restraint if there is no what?

2909. To whom are the sayings in Proverbs 30 credited?

2910. The writer of Proverbs 30 describes what parts of a disgraceful person's body as swords and knives?

2911. According to Proverbs 30, what do the leech's two daughters cry out?

2912. According to Proverbs 30:16, what are the four things that never are never satisfied?

2913. In Proverbs 30, what did the writer say will peck out the eye of the one that mocks a father?

2914. In Proverbs 30, what does an ant do that makes him so wise?

2915. In Proverbs 30, the small hyrax/coney wisely makes his home in what?

2916. In Proverbs 30, the locust is small yet wise because it advances in ranks without a what?

2917. In Proverbs 30, the lizard is wise because it's easily captured and yet it finds its way into what place?

2918. Proverbs 31 includes the sayings of what king?

2919. According to Proverbs 31, what two beverages should rulers and kings not drink?

2920. To whom should those two beverages be given instead?

2921. What is a wife of noble character worth far more than?

2922. Who has full confidence in the wife of noble character?

2923. With what two clothing materials do the hands of a Proverbs 31 woman work eagerly?

2924. A Proverbs 31 woman is like what vessel that brings food from afar?

2925. What does not go out at night for a Proverbs 31 woman?

2926. What items does a Proverbs 31 woman seem to have in her hands at all times?

2927. To whom does the Proverbs 31 woman reach out her hands?

2928. The household of a Proverbs 31 woman is dressed in what color out in the snow?

2929. What color clothes does a Proverbs 31 woman wear?

2930. Where is the Proverbs 31 woman's husband respected?

2931. What does a Proverbs 31 woman supply the merchants with?

2932. How does a Proverbs 31 woman react to the days to come?

2933. What does a Proverbs 31 woman not eat the bread of?

2934. Who rises up and calls a Proverbs 31 woman blessed?

2935. What two characteristics of a woman are deceptive and fleeting?

2936. What characteristic of a Proverbs 31 woman is to be praised?

Ecclesiastes

2937. Whose son claimed that Ecclesiastes were his words?

2938. What does Ecclesiastes repeatedly claim everything is?

2939. According to Ecclesiastes 1, what goes south, north, round and round, and then returns to its course?

2940. According to Ecclesiastes 1, there is nothing new under what?

2941. What political position did the Teacher (or Preacher) of Ecclesiastes hold?

2942. Ecclesiastes states that with more knowledge comes more what?

2943. What building projects did the writer of Ecclesiastes undertake?

2944. According to a famous phrase in Ecclesiastes, it's meaningless to chase after what?

2945. According to Ecclesiastes 2, what is better than folly?

2946. According to Ecclesiastes 3, there's a time to be born and a time to what?

2947. According to Ecclesiastes 3, there's a time to kill and a time to what?

2948. According to Ecclesiastes 3, there's a time to weep and a time to what?

2949. According to Ecclesiastes 3, there's a time to mourn and a time to what?

2950. According to Ecclesiastes 3, there's a time to search and a time to what?

2951. According to Ecclesiastes 3, there's a time to tear and a time to what?

2952. According to Ecclesiastes 3, there's a time to be silent and a time to what?

2953. According to Ecclesiastes 3, there's a time to love and a time to what?

2954. According to Ecclesiastes 3, there's a time for war and a time for what?

2955. According to Ecclesiastes, what has God set in the hearts of people?

2956. According to Ecclesiastes 3, the fate of human beings is like that of what?

2957. According to Ecclesiastes 3, to what place does every living thing go?

2958. Ecclesiastes 4:2 says who is happier than the living?

2959. According to Ecclesiastes 4, who is better off than the living or the dead?

2960. According to Ecclesiastes 4, if one falls down, who will pick him up?

2961. According to Ecclesiastes 4, what type of cord is not easily broken?

2962. According to Ecclesiastes 4, a poor, wise youth is better than an old, foolish what?

2963. According to Ecclesiastes 5, since God is in heaven and we're on earth, what should we use few of?

2964. According to Ecclesiastes 5, what do people love and never have enough of?

2965. In Ecclesiastes 5, the abundance of wealth keeps the rich from what?

2966. In what condition does everyone come from their mother's womb (the same way they will depart)?

2967. Who is better off than a man that never enjoyed his prosperity and didn't receive a proper burial?

2968. Ecclesiastes 6 says everyone's efforts are for their what, yet it is never satisfied?

2969. According to Ecclesiastes 7, what is better than fine perfume?

2970. According to Ecclesiastes 7, it is better to go to a house of mourning than to a house of what?

2971. According to Ecclesiastes 7, extortion turns a wise person into a what?

2972. Wisdom makes a wise person more powerful than how many rulers of a city?

2973. According to Ecclesiastes 8, what brightens a person's face and changes his appearance?

2974. According to Ecclesiastes 8, it's meaningless when a wicked person gets the same thing as whom?

2975. According to Ecclesiastes 9, a live dog is better than a dead what?

2976. What color clothes does Ecclesiastes 9 suggest you always wear?

2977. In Ecclesiastes 9, what did the poor wise man save but nobody remembered him?

2978. In Ecclesiastes 9, what does the writer say is better than weapons of war?

2979. According to Ecclesiastes 10, what do dead flies give a bad smell to?

2980. The writer of Ecclesiastes saw whom on horseback while princes walked on foot?

2981. According to Ecclesiastes 10, what may happen to someone that digs a pit?

2982. According to Ecclesiastes 10, if an ax is dull, then what more is required?

2983. According to Ecclesiastes 10, if a man is lazy, what begins to sag?

2984. According to Ecclesiastes 11, what does the writer say to ship across the waters, then days later get a return?

2985. What two things, if watched too closely, will cause someone not to plant or reap?

2986. In Ecclesiastes 11:5, what two examples did the writer use to show that we cannot understand the work of God?

2987. According to Ecclesiastes 12, what we should remember in our youth?

2988. The writer of Ecclesiastes said the collected sayings of the wise are like firmly embedded what?

2989. What does Ecclesiastes 12 say there is no end to the making of, and too much study only wearies the body?

2990. Now that everything has been heard, what does the writer of Ecclesiastes say is the conclusion to the whole matter?

Song of Songs

2991. In Song of Songs 1, the woman said the man's love was more delightful than what beverage?

2992. In Song of Songs 1, the man's name was like what fragrance poured out?

2993. In Song of Songs 1, the woman called herself dark like the tents of what place?

2994. In Song of Songs 1, the beloved asked not be stared at because she was what?

2995. In Song of Songs 1, the man likened his darling to which of Pharaoh's animals?

2996. In Song of Songs 1, what kind of jewelry did the man promise to make the woman?

2997. In Song of Songs 1, her beloved was like a sachet of what fragrance resting between her breasts?

2998. In Song of Songs 1, to what bird did the beloved compare his bride's eyes?

2999. In Song of Songs 2, the woman described herself as what flower from Sharon?

3000. In Song of Songs 2, she compared him to what fruit tree whose fruit was sweet to her taste?

3001. In Song of Songs 2, what should we not arouse or awaken before it so desires?

3002. In Song of Songs 2, the beloved described her lover as what young animal?

3003. In Song of Songs 2, the lover asked to catch what animal that ruins the vineyards?

3004. In Song of Songs 2, what kind of flowers did he browse among?

3005. As the beloved searched for her lover, who found her as they made their rounds in the city?

3006. In Song of Songs 3, when she found her man, to whose house did she take him?

3007. In Song of Songs 3, whose carriage arrived escorted by sixty warriors?

3008. In Song of Songs 3, who crowned Solomon on his wedding day?

3009. In Song of Songs 4, the lover described the beloved's hair as a flock of what?

3010. In Song of Songs 4, the lover described what part of the beloved's body as a flock of sheep just shorn?

3011. In Song of Songs 4, the lover described what part of the beloved's body as halves of a pomegranate?

3012. In Song of Songs 4, the lover described what part of the beloved's body as a tower of David?

3013. In Song of Songs 4, what parts of her body were like two fawns?

3014. In Song of Songs 4, what two foods were under her tongue?

3015. In Song of Songs 5, the beloved's hands drip with what fragrance?

3016. In Song of Songs 5, who found the beloved wandering around the city, then beat her?

3017. In Song of Songs 5, the beloved described her lover's hair as black as what bird?

3018. In Song of Songs 5, the beloved described her lover's eyes like what bird washed in milk?

3019. In Song of Songs 5, the beloved described her lover's lips like what flowers?

3020. In Song of Songs 5, the beloved described her lover's arms like rods of what?

3021. In Song of Songs 5, the beloved described her lover's legs like pillars of what?

3022. In Song of Songs 6, the man described his beloved's hair like a flock of what animal?

3023. In Song of Songs 6, the beloved more unique than how many queens?

3024. In Song of Songs 6, what national origin does the lover say his beloved was?

3025. In Song of Songs 7, the man described the woman's legs as what?

3026. In Song of Songs 7, what did the beloved describe as a rounded goblet that never lacks blended wine?

3027. In Song of Songs 7, the man compared the pools of Heshbon to what part of the women's body?

3028. In Song of Songs 7, the lover described what part of the beloved's body as the tower of Lebanon?

3029. In Song of Songs 7, the lover described the lover's breath as the fragrance of what?

3030. In Song of Songs 8, under what kind of tree did the woman say she roused the man?

3031. In Song of Songs 8, whom did the friends inquire about, wondering what they should do for her on the day she was spoken for?

Isaiah

3032. What two nations did Isaiah say his visions concerned?

3033. Isaiah was the son of whom?

3034. During the reigns of what four kings of Judah did Isaiah see his vision?

3035. What two animals knew their master yet Israel did not know God?

3036. According to Isaiah 1, what two cities could Israel have become like if it hadn't been for God's mercy?

3037. What three animals did God say he had no pleasure in their sacrificial blood since the people sinned so much?

3038. In Isaiah 1, what feast did the Lord hate with all his being?

3039. According to Isaiah 1, sins are like what color?

3040. In Isaiah 1, God promised to make those sins as white as what two things?

3041. What two names would Zion be called after God restored the city?

3042. According to Isaiah 2, who would all stream to the mountain of the Lord in the last days?

3043. What would the people beat their swords into?

3044. What would the people beat their spears into?

3045. In that day of the Lord, people would throw their idols toward what two animals?

3046. In Isaiah 3, whom did God threaten to put in charge as their officials?

3047. What did God promise to do to the heads of the haughty women of Zion?

3048. In that day described in Isaiah 4, how many women would desperately grab one man and plead for his help?

3049. In that day described in Isaiah 4, those that were left in Zion would be called what?

3050. In Isaiah 5, what kind of garden did the Lord describe the nation of Israel as?

3051. God spoke a woe to those that called evil what?

3052. God spoke a woe to those that were heroes and champions at doing what?

3053. Which king died in Isaiah 6, the year the prophet had his vision?

3054. In Isaiah 6's vision of God, the train of what filled the temple?

3055. In Isaiah 6's vision of God, how many wings did each seraphim have?

3056. What three things were the wings doing?

3057. When the seraphim spoke, what two parts of the temple shook?

3058. In Isaiah 6, Isaiah cried out that what part of him was unclean?

3059. In Isaiah 6's vision of God, what did the seraphim use to retrieve the hot coal?

3060. In Isaiah 6's vision of God, with what did the seraphim touch Isaiah's lips?

3061. As a result of his lips being touched, what two things happened?

3062. When Isaiah heard the voice of Lord asking, "Whom shall I send," what was Isaiah's response?

3063. In Isaiah 7, what two kings marched up against King Ahaz in Judah?

3064. From what nations were those two kings?

3065. What famous chapter and verse in Isaiah says that the virgin will be with child?

3066. According to Isaiah 7, the virgin will call her son by what name?

3067. In Isaiah 7, what two insects could God whistle for and they would arrive?

3068. In Isaiah 8, what was the long name of the son born to the prophetess?

3069. Before Isaiah's son could say "my father," the wealth of Damascus would be carried off by what army?

3070. In Isaiah 8, what thing caused men to stumble?

3071. In Isaiah 8, what did Isaiah tell people not to consult?

3072. According to Isaiah 9, what will be on the child's shoulders?

3073. In Isaiah 9:6, what four titles would the child be called?

3074. There would be an increase and no end to what two things as this child reigned on David's throne?

3075. In Isaiah 10, what nation was described as God's rod of anger and club of wrath?

3076. According to Isaiah 11, a shoot will come up from the stump of whom?

3077. According to Isaiah 11, what will figuratively be the belt and the sash of this branch?

3078. According to Isaiah 11, five groups of animals will live in peace. What will the lion live with?

3079. What will the leopard lie down with?

3080. According to Isaiah 11, who will lead all these groups of animals?

3081. What will the lion and ox eat together?

3082. In Isaiah 11, what dangerous animal could a little child play with?

3083. In Isaiah 11, what will the Root of Jesse raise for all people and nations?

3084. In Isaiah 12, the people would praise the Lord even though the Lord felt which way about them?

3085. According to Isaiah 13, when the day of Lord comes, what four celestial things will be darkened?

3086. According to Isaiah 13, who would rise up against Babylon?

3087. According to Isaiah 13, when Babylon was overthrown, what animal would live in the Babylonians' houses and palaces?

3088. In Isaiah 14, what fell from heaven?

3089. Isaiah 15 mentions the cities of Ar, Kir, and Dibon, all found in what country?

3090. According to Isaiah 15, the waters of Dimon would be filled with what?

3091. In Isaiah 16, how many years did Moab have left before it lost its splendor?

3092. According to Isaiah 17, what great city would become a heap of ruins?

3093. In Isaiah 19, what feared nation was described as a tall, smooth-skinned people, aggressive and with a strange language?

3094. Isaiah prophesied that the plants of what river would dry up in Egypt?

3095. In Isaiah 19, the prophet said there would be a highway from Egypt to what country where they would worship together?

3096. In Isaiah 20, who was the king of Assyria that attacked and captured Ashdod?

3097. In Isaiah 20, how many years did Isaiah go around stripped and barefoot as a sign against Egypt and Cush?

3098. In Isaiah 21, the Lord told Isaiahto have the lookout watch for riders on what three animals?

3099. According to Isaiah 22, those in mourning will put on sackcloth and tear out what part of their body?

3100. In Isaiah 22, to whom did God promise to give authority (and this someone would become like a father to those that lived in Jerusalem)?

3101. Isaiah 23 tells the ships of what city to wail?

3102. According to the prophecy in Isaiah 23, how many years would Tyre be forgotten, which is the span of a king's lifetime?

3103. In Isaiah 24, what will be completely laid to waste, its inhabitants burned up, and its leaders gathered in dungeons?

3104. In Isaiah 25, what will God swallow up forever in addition to wiping away all tears?

3105. In chapter 26, Isaiah said they were like people pregnant with child, but what did they ultimately give birth to?

3106. In Isaiah 27, what monster of the sea did the Lord slay with his sword?

3107. In Isaiah 28, where does the Lord lay a precious cornerstone?

3108. In Isaiah 29, the people come to God with their mouth and lips, but what is far from him?

3109. In Isaiah 29, whom can't the pot talk back to and question?

3110. What nation did God refer to as Rahab?

3111. In Isaiah 21, what country did God say the people should not trust in their horses and chariots for help?

3112. According to Isaiah 31, what did the Egyptians possess that were only flesh and not spirit?

3113. In Isaiah 31, what country will fall by nonhuman/nonmortal sword?

3114. In Isaiah 32, God addressed what complacent group in Jerusalem that would tremble in more than a year?

3115. In Isaiah 33, God told the people that they conceived chaff and gave birth to what?

3116. After God's judgment in Isaiah 34, what will the mountains be soaked in?

3117. According to Isaiah 34, three different kinds of owls would inhabit Edom. What were they?

3118. According to Isaiah 35, when the Lord comes, what four human disabilities will be cured?

3119. In Isaiah 36, who was the king of Assyria that threatened to attack Judah?

3120. Who was the king of Judah during that time?

3121. Which country did Assyria call a splintered reed?

3122. In what language did the representatives of Judah ask the field commander from Assyria to speak?

3123. What language did he speak in anyway?

3124. In Isaiah 37, after King Hezekiah tore his clothes over the report about Assyria, what did he put on?

3125. What was Tirhakah king of?

3126. As a result of Hezekiah's prayer in Isaiah 37, how many Assyrians died in their camp?

3127. What god was Sennacherib praying to when he was killed?

3128. Who killed Sennacherib?

3129. Who succeeded Sennacherib?

3130. What Old Testament king was sick to the point of death, but he prayed and lived?

3131. How many more years of life did Hezekiah receive after praying for more life?

3132. From what enemy did God also promise he would deliver Hezekiah?

3133. What sign did Hezekiah receive that he would recover from his illness?

3134. What did Isaiah command be applied to Hezekiah's boil?

3135. Who sent envoys expressing get-well wishes to Hezekiah?

3136. What country did King Hezekiah allow to tour the nation's treasury?

3137. What was calling in the wilderness to prepare the way of the Lord?

3138. Isaiah said that two pieces of vegetation whither but the word of our God endures forever. What were they?

3139. In Isaiah 40, the nations are like a drop in what, when compared to God?

3140. Isaiah said those that hope in the Lord will soar on the wings of what bird?

3141. In Isaiah 41, what did God promise to turn the desert into?

3142. In chapter 42, Isaiah described a servant that will not break what?

3143. In chapter 42, Isaiah described a servant that will not snuff out what?

3144. The servant, described in Isaiah 42, promised to be a light for what group of people?

3145. In Isaiah 43, what does God promise to blot out and remember no more?

3146. According to Isaiah 44, those that make what are nothing?

3147. Name four kinds of trees mentioned that were made into idols in Isaiah 44.

3148. To what king of Persia did Isaiah send a message?

3149. In Isaiah 45, God said he can break down gates made from what two metals?

3150. What object would never quarrel with the potter?

3151. In Isaiah 45, which group of people were described as tall (or men of stature)?

3152. According to Isaiah 45, whom will God put to shame and disgrace?

3153. Name the two false gods whose idols were born of beasts of burden and were unable to rescue the burden.

3154. In Isaiah 47, God said that the queen city of what country would face disaster?

3155. In Isaiah 47, the predictions of what two groups could not save Babylon from destruction?

3156. In Isaiah 48, God said he made predictions so what would not get any credit for bringing events about?

3157. In Isaiah 48, God said that if Israel had obeyed, their peace would be like what?

3158. In Isaiah 48, God said there was no peace for whom?

3159. In Isaiah 49, a servant will come to be a light to what group of people?

3160. In Isaiah 49, God will make the oppressors of Israel eat their own what?

3161. In Isaiah 50, God said he offered his cheeks to his enemy and what did they do in return?

3162. In Isaiah 50, God said he did not hide his face from his enemy and what did they do in return?

3163. According to Isaiah 51, God promised to restore Zion's desert into what famous garden?

3164. According to Isaiah 51, Jerusalem drank a cup of what?

3165. According to Isaiah 52, beautiful were the feet of those that brought what?

3166. According to Isaiah 53, the servant grew up like a tender what?

3167. What was this servant lacking that didn't attract anyone to him?

3168. In Isaiah 53, who despised and rejected the servant?

3169. What was this servant familiar with?

3170. According to Isaiah 53, the servant was pierced for our what?

3171. His punishment brought us what?

3172. By his wounds we are what?

3173. According to Isaiah 53, we have gone astray like what?

3174. In Isaiah 53, what did God lay on the servant for us?

3175. According to Isaiah 53, this oppressed person was led like a what to slaughter?

3176. Just like a sheep, whom was he silent before?

3177. What was he cut off from?

3178. What two groups of people was he assigned to the grave with?

3179. What was not found in his mouth?

3180. Isaiah 54 begins by telling what kind of woman to sing?

3181. In Isaiah 54, what land masses could be shaken and removed, but God's unfailing love would never crumble?

3182. In Isaiah 54, what forged item will not prevail against God's people?

3183. According to Isaiah 55, what will not return to God empty?

3184. Jesus quoted Isaiah 56, saying God's house will be a house of what?

3185. Isaiah 56 compares Israel's watchmen to what animal with a mighty appetite?

3186. In Isaiah 57, God called out the children of what three types of people?

3187. In Isaiah 57, which false idol received offerings of olive oil and perfume?

3188. In Isaiah 57, what type of people were described as a tossing sea, which can't rest and whose waves stir up mud?

3189. For whom did God say there is no peace?

3190. What religious act did the people do but it always ended in quarreling and fist fights?

3191. According to Isaiah 59, what part of God is not too short to save his people?

3192. In Isaiah 59, what do the people's feet rush into?

3193. In Isaiah 59:17, what two pieces of the Ephesians 6 armor of God are mentioned?

3194. In Isaiah 60, God promised Zion's walls would be rebuilt by whom?

3195. In Isaiah 60, what will be the everlasting light for Zion?

3196. Who quoted Isaiah 61:1–2 and was almost thrown off a cliff?

3197. According to Isaiah 62, on what city's walls did God promise to post watchmen that would never be silent day and night?

3198. In Isaiah 63, what color are the garments of the one coming from Edom?

3199. What splattered on those garments, causing them to turn this color?

3200. In Isaiah 63, who was grieved because of the people's rebellion?

3201. According to Isaiah 64:6, what are all our righteous acts like?

3202. According to Isaiah 64:9, what do we not want God to remember forever?

3203. According to Isaiah 65, what two "new" things will God create?

3204. According to Isaiah 65, what two sounds will not be heard in Jerusalem?

3205. In Isaiah 65, what food will the lion eat with the ox?

3206. On the day of restoration of Jerusalem, what will the serpent eat?

3207. In Isaiah 66, God said heaven is his throne and earth is what piece of furniture?

3208. In Isaiah 66, God said he would extend peace like what kind of body of water?

3209. Mentioned in Isaiah 66, the Lydians were famous because of what battle skill?

3210. In Isaiah 66, what creature will not die as it eats all the dead bodies?

Jeremiah

3211. Who was Jeremiah's father?

3212. When Jeremiah was called to be a prophet, what was his current job?

3213. During the reign of which three kings did Jeremiah prophesy?

3214. What excuse did God tell Jeremiah not to give when asked to prophesy?

3215. When God called Jeremiah, what kind of tree did Jeremiah see during his first vision?

3216. During his second vision, what was the pot doing that Jeremiah saw?

3217. According to Jeremiah 2, what did a nation never change before?

3218. In Jeremiah 2, the people had forsaken springs of living water and dug what for themselves instead?

3219. In Jeremiah 2, God asked why his people would go to Egypt and drink the waters of what two famous rivers?

3220. According to Jeremiah 2, what did the people call a piece of wood?

3221. In Jeremiah 3, what did God call Israel's unfaithful sister?

3222. With what two things did Israel commit adultery against God?

3223. God said to Jeremiah that a faithless Israel is more righteous than an unfaithful what?

3224. In Jeremiah 3, what famous object did the people say they would no longer miss since it never entered their minds?

3225. In Jeremiah 3, what did God promise to cure the people of?

3226. In Jeremiah 4, God's judgment comes down like horses swifter than what bird?

3227. According to Jeremiah 4, what did the people need washed to be saved?

3228. In Jeremiah 5, God promised not to destroy Jerusalem if they could find how many honest people?

3229. In Jeremiah 5, God said they made their faces harder than what and refused to repent?

3230. In Jeremiah 5:6, what three fierce animals did God say would attack them?

3231. In Jeremiah 5, God compared his people to lusty stallions neighing after what?

3232. In Jeremiah 5, what deadly weapon of the enemy did God compare to an open grave?

3233. In Jeremiah 5, God compared their deceitful houses to cages full of what?

3234. According to Jeremiah 6, from what direction was the enemy coming to attack Jerusalem?

3235. In Jeremiah 7, God said the people had turned his house into a den of what?

3236. In Jeremiah 7, God told the people to go and see what he had done because of the people's wickedness in what city?

3237. Who was the queen that God accused them of worshiping?

3238. What did God tell Jeremiah that the people were burning in the Valley of Ben Hinnom?

3239. In Jeremiah 7, what new name would Topheth or the Valley of Ben Hinnom take on after God judged them for practices going on there?

3240. In Jeremiah 8, the prophet asked if there was any balm in what city?

3241. In Jeremiah 9, the people used their tongues like bows to shoot what?

3242. In Jeremiah 9, God said he would make Jerusalem a heap of ruins and it would become a haunt for what pack of animals?

3243. According to Jeremiah 9, what climbed in through their windows and entered their fortresses?

3244. In Jeremiah 10, what was compared to a scarecrow in a cucumber field?

3245. In Jeremiah 11, God said Judah had as many gods as they had what?

3246. In Jeremiah 11, God said Jerusalem had as many altars to Baal as they had what?

3247. The people of what region were trying to kill Jeremiah?

3248. In Jeremiah 12, God said his enemies would sow wheat but reap what?

3249. What material was the belt that Jeremiah bought made from?

3250. What could this belt never touch?

3251. Where did God tell Jeremiah to hide the belt?

3252. In questioning Judah's ability to change, God asked if an Ethiopian could change the color of his what?

3253. In questioning Judah's ability to change, God asked if what animal could change his spots?

3254. In Jeremiah 14, what disaster did God call on Judah that caused jars to be unfilled and the ground to crack?

3255. In Jeremiah 15, God said that even if which two Old Testament prophets stood before him, he would not change his heart?

3256. In Jeremiah 15, what four kinds of destroyers did God promise to send to his people?

3257. In Jeremiah 15, God promised to make Judah abhorrent to all the kingdoms because of the evil deeds of what king?

3258. In Jeremiah 16, because things were going to get so bad in Judah, what did God tell Jeremiah not to do in his personal life?

3259. In Jeremiah 16, what did God tell Jeremiah not to do during a funeral?

3260. In Jeremiah 16, what did God tell Jeremiah not to do during a party?

3261. In Jeremiah 17, what book of the Bible did Jeremiah seem to quote about a person being like a tree planted by the water, yielding fruit all the time?

3262. In Jeremiah 17, what act did God mention four times that he didn't want his people doing on the Sabbath?

3263. In Jeremiah 18, whose house did Jeremiah visit to watch him work?

3264. What did Jeremiah buy and then break in front of the elders?

3265. What did God want the broken, unrepairable object to represent?

3266. What was the name of the priest that had Jeremiah beaten and put into stocks?

3267. In chapter 20, Jeremiah prophesied that all of Judah would be handed to what nation?

3268. Which king asked Jeremiah to intervene with God because the Babylonians were attacking?

3269. In Jeremiah 21, God told the people of Jerusalem to either die by sword, famine, or plague, or to live by doing what?

3270. In Jeremiah 22, God asked if having a palace built with what kind of wood made a person a king?

3271. Which king's burial did Jeremiah say would be like a donkey's funeral?

3272. In Jeremiah 22, God said that even if King Jehoiachin were what piece of jewelry on God's right hand, God would still throw him away?

3273. In Jeremiah 23, whom did God declare a woe to because they were scattering the sheep of God's pasture?

3274. What kind of a branch did God promise to raise up that would save Judah?

3275. God showed Jeremiah two baskets filled with what kind of good and bad fruit?

3276. Whom did the basket of good fruit represent?

3277. Whom did the basket of bad fruit represent?

3278. In chapter 25, Jeremiah proclaimed that he had been prophesying for how many years?

3279. How many years did Jeremiah prophesy that Judah would be exiled?

3280. After those seventy years, whom did God promise to punish?

3281. God asked Jeremiah to take a cup filled with the wine of God's what?

3282. In Jeremiah 26, who was the prophet during the time of Hezekiah that prophesied about Jerusalem's destruction?

3283. In Jeremiah 26, who was the other prophet that prophesied the same things Jeremiah did at the same time, yet fled to Egypt in fear of his life?

3284. In Jeremiah 27, what did God ask Jeremiah to strap to his neck?

3285. What king did Jeremiah tell Zedekiah to bow down to and serve?

3286. Jeremiah said that articles from what place would be carried off by Nebuchadnezzar to Babylon?

3287. Who was the false prophet that took the yoke off Jeremiah's neck and broke it?

3288. Jeremiah said the yoke of wood would be replaced by a yoke made of what?

3289. In Jeremiah 28, God promised that Nebuchadnezzar would not only rule over the people but what else?

3290. In Jeremiah 29:11, what kind of plans did God have for the people of Judah?

3291. Name the rebellious letter writer in chapter 29 that Jeremiah prophesied would be punished.

3292. In Jeremiah 30, who was the king that God promised the exiles he would raise up?

3293. In Jeremiah 30, God promised he would restore the fortunes of whose tents?

3294. In Jeremiah 31, who was mourning and weeping for her children?

3295. From where was this voice of mourning heard?

3296. According to Jeremiah 31, the fathers had eaten sour grapes and whose teeth were set on edge?

3297. According to the new covenant God would make with Israel, where would he write his law?

3298. In chapter 32, which king had Jeremiah put in prison for his prophesying?

3299. What did God tell Jeremiah that Hanamel would come and ask him to buy?

3300. In Jeremiah 23, what kind of a branch did God promise, which would sprout from David's line?

3301. Whom did God tell Jeremiah that Zedekiah would see face-to-face?

3302. What kind of death did Jeremiah promise Zedekiah he would have?

3303. In Jeremiah 34, whom did God ask the people in Jerusalem to set free?

3304. Which king did Jeremiah prophesy would be handed over to the enemy?

3305. What family line did Jeremiah visit that showed incredible obedience among the people of Judah?

3306. What did Jeremiah set before the Rekabites but they refused to take it because of a vow their ancestors had made?

3307. In chapter 36, who copied the words of Jeremiah on a scroll and then read it to the people?

3308. Where did Jeremiah tell him to read the words?

3309. What did King Jehoiakim do to the scroll sent to him by Jeremiah?

3310. Who was made king by Nebuchadnezzar, replacing Jehoiachin?

3311. What country's army caused the Babylonians to withdraw their siege on Jerusalem?

3312. What happened to Jeremiah when he reached the Benjamin Gate?

3313. Jeremiah was imprisoned in the house of what secretary?

3314. Because of his prophecies against Judah, Jeremiah was lowered into what as punishment?

3315. What official of the royal palace helped pull Jeremiah from the cistern?

3316. What did Jeremiah tell Zedekiah to do in order to spare his life and his family, and to keep Jerusalem from being burned down?

3317. About how long did Nebuchadnezzar lay siege on Jerusalem until breaking through?

3318. Nebuchadnezzar captured Zedekiah on the plains of what city?

3319. Whom did Nebuchadnezzar slaughter right in front of King Zedekiah?

3320. What part of Zedekiah's body did Nebuchadnezzar have removed?

3321. What was the name of the commander of Babylon's imperial guard?

3322. After invading Jerusalem and exiling the people, whom did the Babylonians leave behind?

3323. In Jeremiah 39, what royal official did the Lord rescue from disaster because he trusted in God?

3324. Who freed Jeremiah from chains and gave him the choice to go into exile or stay behind in Jerusalem?

3325. What did Jeremiah choose to do?

3326. After King Zedekiah was overthrown, whom did the Babylonians appoint as governor?

3327. Who came with ten men to eat with King Gedaliah, then assassinated him?

3328. Where did Ishmael throw the bodies of the seventy men he had slaughtered?

3329. In Jeremiah 42, God told the remnant in Judah not to go to what country for protection?

3330. To what city in Egypt did the remnant flee?

3331. In Jeremiah 43, what country did Jeremiah prophesy that Nebuchadnezzar would destroy and burn its temples?

3332. In Jeremiah 44, the remnant of Jews living in Egypt burned incense and poured out drink offerings to the queen of what?

3333. In addition to pouring out drink offerings to her, what did they make with the Queen of Heaven's picture on it?

3334. In Jeremiah 44, what was the name of the pharaoh at the time?

3335. In Jeremiah 45, whom did Jeremiah comfort by saying he would escape and not be harmed?

3336. In Jeremiah 46, who was the pharaoh that Nebuchadnezzar defeated?

3337. Where did Nebuchadnezzar defeat the Egyptians?

3338. In Jeremiah 46, what weapon did God say would devour until it was satisfied and had quenched its thirst for blood?

3339. In Jeremiah 46, what was the name of the god of Thebes that the Lord promised to punish?

3340. In Jeremiah 47, what group of people did God promise to destroy whose cities included Gaza and Ashkelon?

3341. In Jeremiah 48, what nation did God say to put salt on, whose horn would be cut off and her arm broken?

3342. In Jeremiah 49, what god had taken over Gad?

3343. In Jeremiah 49, unlike grape pickers and thieves, what did God promise to do to Edom?

3344. In Jeremiah 49, God promised pain and anguish on Damascus like a woman in the midst of what?

3345. According to Jeremiah 50, what two gods of Babylon did God want to put to shame?

3346. In Jeremiah 51, what country did God describe as a gold cup in his hand that made other nations drunk?

3347. According to Jeremiah 51, God had stirred up the kings of what country to destroy Babylon?

3348. According to Jeremiah 51, God would have vengeance on Babylon because they destroyed what?

3349. In Jeremiah 51, whom did the prophet give a message to and have read it aloud when he arrived in Babylon?

3350. When these words were read to Babylon, Jeremiah had the scroll tied to a stone and thrown into what river?

3351. Who was the Babylonian commander that set fire to the temple, the royal palace, and the important buildings in Jerusalem?

3352. Why did he leave the poorest people behind in Jerusalem?

3353. According to Jeremiah 52, how many total people were carried into exile by Nebuchadnezzar?

3354. Which king of Judah was released from prison and treated kindly, and ate regularly at the king's table?

3355. Who was the Babylonian king that released Jehoiachin?

Lamentations

3356. What city did the writer of Lamentations mourn?

3357. In Lamentations 1, the writer said all his sins were bound and formed what around his neck?

3358. What did the elders of Zion sprinkle on their head while they wore sackcloth?

3359. In Lamentations 2, who fainted in the streets of the fallen city?

3360. According to Lamentations 2, whose visions were false and worthless?

3361. According to Lamentations 3, because God's compassions are new every morning, great is the Lord's what?

3362. In Lamentations 3, what did God cover himself with so no prayer could get through?

3363. In Lamentations 4, the heartless people were compared to what bird in the desert?

3364. What city was better off than this one because it was overthrown in a moment?

3365. In Lamentations 4, those that died by the sword were better off than those that died how?

3366. Because of the destruction of Jerusalem, compassionate women would cook what?

3367. In Lamentations 5, what two enemies did the city need to turn to for bread?

3368. In Lamentations 5, what had dancing turned into?

Ezekiel

3369. Next to what river did Ezekiel receive his first vision?

3370. Ezekiel received his vision while living in what nation?

3371. What occupation did Ezekiel hold when he received his vision?

3372. How many living creatures did Ezekiel see in the center of the fire?

3373. How many faces and wings did these living creatures have?

3374. What did the faces of the four creatures in Ezekiel's vision look like?

3375. What circular object did Ezekiel see in his vision?

3376. What were the wheels in Ezekiel's vision filled with all around?

3377. The sound of the angels' wings reminded Ezekiel of the roar of what?

3378. The man Ezekiel saw in chapter 1 glowed like what?

3379. What did the man from Ezekiel's first vision address Ezekiel as?

3380. To what obstinate and stubborn people was Ezekiel sent?

3381. In chapter 3, what did the man offer Ezekiel to eat?

3382. What did it taste like?

3383. The man in Ezekiel's vision promised to make Ezekiel's forehead as hard as what?

3384. How many days did Ezekiel need to recover after the first vision?

3385. On what did Ezekiel draw the city of Jerusalem?

3386. What did Ezekiel build around the clay tablet?

3387. How many days did Ezekiel lay on his left side, putting the sin of Israel on himself?

3388. How many days did Ezekiel lay on his right side, looking at the drawing of Jerusalem?

3389. What did God tell Ezekiel he would tie him up with for forty days?

3390. What six ingredients were in Ezekiel's bread?

3391. In chapter 4, how many shekels' weight of food did Ezekiel eat every day?

3392. What was the only thing Ezekiel could drink during this time?

3393. What kind of fuel did God first tell Ezekiel to cook his bread over?

3394. After hearing Ezekiel's protest, what did God allow Ezekiel to bake his bread over?

3395. What did God ask Ezekiel to use as a razor?

3396. What of Ezekiel's did God ask him to burn, strike with a sword, and then throw into the wind?

3397. In Ezekiel 5, in what five ways did God say he would punish the people?

3398. In Ezekiel 6, God promised to slay the people as they stood in front of what?

3399. According to Ezekiel 7, because of the people's fear of God, what would their legs be wet with?

3400. According to Ezekiel 7, things would get so bad in Israel that people would throw what into the streets?

3401. In chapter 8, when the spirit took Ezekiel away, by what part of his body was he lifted up?

3402. To what city did the Spirit take Ezekiel?

3403. In Ezekiel 8, when the man showed Ezekiel around the city, what was he pointing out?

3404. What god was the woman mourning over in Ezekiel's chapter 8 vision?

3405. During Ezekiel's vision in chapter 9, what kind of kit did the man in linen have in his hands?

3406. In Ezekiel's vision, where did God tell the man in linen to put a mark on the people that were grieving?

3407. In Ezekiel 10, what did the man in linen remove from the cherubim and scatter all over the city?

3408. What completely covered the bodies, backs, hands, and wings of the cherubim (just like the wheels) in Ezekiel's vision?

3409. In chapter 10, each of the cherubims in Ezekiel's vision had four faces that looked like what?

3410. Where had Ezekiel seen these living creatures before?

3411. In Ezekiel 10, what departed from the temple?

3412. In Ezekiel 10, what did the things under the wings of each cherubim look like?

3413. In Ezekiel 11, God told Ezekiel that the city was a pot and the bodies were what?

3414. In chapter 11, while Ezekiel prophesied, what happened to the man named Pelatiah?

3415. In chapter 11, the Spirit picked up Ezekiel and took him to the exiles in what country?

3416. In chapter 12, the Lord told Ezekiel to pack up his things in front of the people and dig through what structure?

3417. In Ezekiel 13, God accused the false prophets of covering the walls with what material?

3418. In Ezekiel 13, what were the women sewing on their wrists that displeased the Lord?

3419. In chapter 14, what three righteous Old Testament heroes did Ezekiel mention twice?

3420. What four dreadful judgments did God say he would send to Jerusalem?

3421. In Ezekiel 15, God compared the people living in Jerusalem to a vine consumed by what?

3422. In Ezekiel 16, God talked about raising Jerusalem to be a queen, but she became a what?

3423. God said Jerusalem really was not like a prostitute because she denied what?

3424. In Ezekiel 16, what two cities did God say Jerusalem was worse than?

3425. In Ezekiel 17, the prophet had a vision where he saw two of what kind of bird planting vegetation?

3426. What nation was named as the allegorical bird?

3427. In Ezekiel 17, God later compared Jerusalem to a sprig off what kind of tree that he would plant and grow?

3428. In Ezekiel 18, God said the Jews would no longer quote the proverb about teeth and what fruit?

3429. According to Ezekiel 18, a child would not die because of whose sins?

3430. In Ezekiel 19, God compared the princes of Israel to what animal caught in a cage and sent to Babylon?

3431. In Ezekiel 20, God promised to rule over Israel "with a mighty ________ and an overstretched ________ and with outpoured wrath."

3432. In Ezekiel 21, what sharp and polished weapon did God reference in his judgment against Israel?

3433. In Ezekiel 21, what instrument of royalty did this weapon despise?

3434. In chapter 21, God told Ezekiel that the king of Babylon would determine his future after examining what organ (of an animal)?

3435. According to Ezekiel 22, what part of melted metal had the people become to God?

3436. In Ezekiel 22, God promised to melt the people of Israel like which five metals?

3437. What two cities did Ezekiel call adulterous sisters?

3438. What were the names of the two prostitutes?

3439. In Ezekiel 23, what two nations did Jerusalem prostitute themselves with (and then were ultimately destroyed by)?

3440. According to Ezekiel 23, where did Israel's propensity to prostitute themselves begin?

3441. In chapter 24, God asked Ezekiel to put what cooking instrument on the fire to represent the burning away of impurities in Jerusalem?

3442. Who was the "delight of your eyes" that God told Ezekiel would die?

3443. After her death, what did God tell Ezekiel not to do?

3444. In Ezekiel 25, God promised to turn the territories of the Ammonites into pasturelands for what two animals?

3445. For three chapters, Ezekiel 26–28, what Phoenician seaport in modern-day Lebanon did Ezekiel prophesy against?

3446. In Ezekiel 26, who was the king that would decimate Tyre?

3447. Ezekiel 27 lists all the countries that engaged in what kind of business with Tyre?

3448. In Ezekiel 28, God asked if the king of Tyre was wiser than what Old Testament prophet?

3449. Which king did Ezekiel lament over, saying he thought he was a model of perfection?

3450. According to Ezekiel 28, what made Tyre proud?

3451. In Ezekiel 29, what river did God say he owned?

3452. In Ezekiel 29, what nation did God promise to scatter and desolate, and then regather its people after forty years?

3453. What city did Nebuchadnezzar campaign hard against but got no reward?

3454. Thebes, Pelusium, Memphis, Heliopolis, Bubastis, and Tahpanhes were all places in what country?

3455. In Ezekiel 30, whose arms did God promise to break?

3456. In Ezekiel 30, whose arms did God promise to strengthen?

3457. In Ezekiel 31, to what kind of tree did God compare Assyria?

3458. In Ezekiel 32, to what realm did God say Egypt would descend?

3459. In Ezekiel 33, whom did God appoint to the position of watchman?

3460. In Ezekiel 34, God compared Israel to what farm animal?

3461. In Ezekiel 34, to what job on the farm did God compare Israel's leaders?

3462. In Ezekiel 34, what was the name of the servant that would truly shepherd his flock?

3463. In Ezekiel 35, Mount Seir was located in what nation?

3464. In Ezekiel 36, God promised to replace Israel's heart made of stone with a heart made of what?

3465. In Ezekiel 37, the prophet saw a vision of a valley filled with what?

3466. When the bones became flesh and stood on their feet, what did they become?

3467. What nation did the dry bones of Ezekiel's prophecy represent?

3468. What two items did Ezekiel write on and then bring together, representing two nations?

3469. What two nations did those items represent?

3470. According to Ezekiel 38, what nation was Gog the leader of?

3471. According to Ezekiel 39, after Gog was destroyed, Israel would not need to gather wood for fire because they would use what instead?

3472. In chapter 40, what six-cubit-long object was in the hand of a man that Ezekiel saw?

3473. What did the man in Ezekiel 40–43 measure?

3474. According to the vision in Ezekiel 41, how many cubits long was the temple?

3475. According to the vision in Ezekiel 41, the faces of what two things were carved on the cherubs found throughout the temple?

3476. When the man measured the wall outside the temple in Ezekiel's vision, each side measured how many cubits long?

3477. When Ezekiel stood at the gate in his vision, he saw the glory of the Lord coming from what direction?

3478. In Ezekiel 44, God said only priests descended from what other priest could minister in the sanctuary?

3479. In Ezekiel 44, God directed the priests not to wear wool clothing but what fabric instead?

3480. According to Ezekiel 44, why did God tell the priests not to wear wool clothing?

3481. In Ezekiel 44, God told the priests that they could not marry what kind of women?

3482. In Ezekiel 44, God told the priests that they could only marry virgins or a widow previously married to whom?

3483. According to Ezekiel 45, the measurement of a bath and an ephah equaled what fraction of a homer?

3484. In Ezekiel 45, a shekel equaled how many gerahs?

3485. What did sixty shekels equal?

3486. During the appointed feasts, when someone entered through a gate for a sacrifice, which gate did they need to exit through?

3487. In Ezekiel's vision in chapter 47, what flowed out from under the threshold of the temple?

3488. Where did this water eventually flow?

3489. When the waters emptied there, what did it turn the salt water into?

3490. What kind of trees would then grow on the banks of the river?

3491. What would the leaves of these trees be used for?

3492. In Ezekiel 47, what sea was described as the western boundary for Israel?

3493. What was the name of the line of consecrated priests that faithfully served God and did not go astray like the Levites?

3494. In Ezekiel 48, God told Ezekiel to name the gates of the city after whom?

3495. In the last line of Ezekiel, what was the name of this city from that time on?

Daniel

3496. Which king of Babylon captured Jerusalem?

3497. Who was the king of Judah at the time?

3498. What did Nebuchadnezzar take from the temple in Jerusalem and put in the temple of his god?

3499. Who was the chief of the king's courts assigned to bring well-educated, handsome young men from Judah into the king's service?

3500. What two things about Babylon were all the young men taught?

3501. What two things were they assigned daily from the king's table?

3502. How many years were the young Israelite men trained in Babylonian culture?

3503. What were the Jewish names of Daniel's three friends?

3504. What were the Babylonian names of Daniel's three friends?

3505. What was Daniel's Babylonian name?

3506. For how many days did Daniel and his friends ask to stay on their diet?

3507. What food item did Daniel ask to eat instead of the king's food?

3508. What two kinds of knowledge did God give Daniel and his three friends?

3509. What special ability did God give specifically to Daniel?

3510. How many times better than everyone else did the king find Daniel and his three friends?

3511. Daniel remained in service until the first year of what king?

3512. Name the four groups of people that could not interpret the king's dream.

3513. What two things did King Nebuchadnezzar threaten to do to his astrologers and magicians if they could not interpret his dream?

3514. Who was the king's commander that was going to put to death all the wise men of Babylon?

3515. What four metals were Nebuchadnezzar's dream statue made of?

3516. What item struck Nebuchadnezzar's dream statue and smashed its feet to pieces?

3517. What part of Nebuchadnezzar's dream statue represented Babylon?

3518. What did all the parts of Nebuchadnezzar's dream statue represent?

3519. As a result of Daniel successfully interpreting the dream, to what position was he appointed?

3520. To what position were Daniel's friends appointed?

3521. How many feet tall was the image Nebuchadnezzar made in the book of Daniel?

3522. What was the image made of?

3523. What did Nebuchadnezzar decree should happen every time people heard the music play?

3524. Which three men refused to worship the image of gold?

3525. What were they thrown into because they refused to worship Nebuchadnezzar's statue?

3526. How much hotter did Nebuchadnezzar turn up the fire to burn Daniel's friends?

3527. In Daniel 3, who was killed in the fiery furnace?

3528. How many men did Nebuchadnezzar see walking around inside the fire?

3529. What did Nebuchadnezzar say the fourth man in the fire looked like?

3530. When Shadrach, Meshach, and Abednego stepped out of the furnace, what did they not smell like?

3531. According to chapter 4, Daniel's name was changed to Belteshazzar, which was the name of what?

3532. In Daniel 4, what object did Nebuchadnezzar dream about?

3533. When Daniel interpreted the tree dream, whom did the tree represent?

3534. Where was Nebuchadnezzar walking when the voice from heaven spoke to him?

3535. What animal did Nebuchadnezzar eat like after his dream was fulfilled?

3536. When Nebuchadnezzar was driven away from the people, what was his body drenched in?

3537. What food did he consume?

3538. After Nebuchadnezzar praised God, what happened to him?

3539. In Daniel 5, which Babylonian king threw the great banquet?

3540. What items from the temple did the king ask to be brought out during the great banquet?

3541. In Daniel 5, what did the king see written on the wall?

3542. What three rewards did the king offer to anyone that could read the writing on the wall?

3543. Who reminded the king that Daniel had the ability to interpret dreams and explain riddles?

3544. Who was Belshazzar's father?

3545. In Daniel 5, what three words did the mysterious hand write on the wall?

3546. What two nations did Daniel say would take over Belshazzar's kingdom?

3547. After Daniel interpreted the writing on the wall, what happened to King Belshazzar that night?

3548. In Daniel 5, who replaced Belshazzar as king?

3549. According to the edict in Daniel 6, who was the only person someone could pray to?

3550. In Daniel 6, how many days did the decree last?

3551. What was the punishment for breaking this decree?

3552. How many times a day did it say Daniel prayed?

3553. Which king put Daniel into the lions' den?

3554. In Daniel 6, with what did the king seal the rock that covered the lions' den?

3555. According to Daniel, whom did God send to shut the mouths of the lions in the den?

3556. Whom did the king throw into the lions' den after Daniel was rescued?

3557. Daniel prospered during the reigns of what two Persian kings?

3558. In chapter 7, Daniel had his vision during the reign of what Babylonian king?

3559. In Daniel's chapter 7 vision, what four things came out of the sea?

3560. The lion in Daniel's chapter 7 dream had wings that looked like what bird?

3561. What did the bear in Daniel's chapter 7 dream have in its mouth?

3562. In Daniel's chapter 7 dream, how many wings and heads did the leopard have?

3563. In Daniel's chapter 7 dream, what kind of teeth did the fourth beast have?

3564. In Daniel's chapter 7 dream, how many horns did the fourth beast start out with?

3565. According to Daniel 7, how did the little horn speak?

3566. In Daniel 7, what did the son of man arrive on?

3567. In Daniel's chapter 7 dream, what did the four great beasts represent?

3568. In Daniel 7, what did the ten horns represent?

3569. During what king's third year of reign did Daniel have his chapter 8 dream?

3570. In Daniel's chapter 8 dream, what two animals did he watch fight?

3571. Which animal won the fight?

3572. After the goat's large horn was broken off, how many other horns grew in its place?

3573. Name the angel that was told to interpret the dream for Daniel in chapter 8?

3574. In Daniel's chapter 8 dream, what did the two-horned ram represent?

3575. In Daniel's chapter 8 dream, what did the shaggy goat represent?

3576. What did the four horns on the shaggy goat represent?

3577. Daniel 9 took place during the first year of what Persian king's reign?

3578. In chapter 9, Daniel said he understood what prophet's vision of seventy years of desolation?

3579. In chapter 9, what angel arrived to give Daniel the answer to his prayer?

3580. How many total "sevens" were decreed for Daniel's people?

3581. Gabriel told Daniel that a ruler would set up an abomination in the temple that caused what?

3582. In chapter 10, Daniel received this revelation when what king of Persia was in power?

3583. How long did Daniel mourn as a result of the frightening vision?

3584. When Daniel received the vision in chapter 10, on what river's banks was he standing?

3585. In chapter 10, the man that Daniel saw was dressed in what material?

3586. What was his belt made of?

3587. For how many days did the prince of the Persian kingdom resist the angel?

3588. In Daniel 10, who came to rescue the man from the prince of Persia?

3589. The angel warned that after the Persians, the prince of what nation would come?

3590. In Daniel 11, how many kings did the man say would rise in Persia?

3591. Which country would the Persian king stir up everyone against?

3592. After the mighty king rose, his empire would be divided among how many leaders that were not his descendants?

3593. In Daniel's chapter 11 vision, by what titles did the man call the two opposing kings?

3594. In Daniel 12, who was the great prince that would arise and protect the people?

3595. In Daniel 12, the man in linen told Daniel it would take how long for these visions to occur?

3596. In Daniel 12, how many days would pass from the time the daily sacrifice was abolished to the abomination that caused desolation?

Hosea

3597. Who was Hosea's father?

3598. Hosea prophesied during the reigns of what four kings of Judah?

3599. What was the name of the prophet Hosea's promiscuous wife?

3600. How many children did Gomer have with Hosea?

3601. What was the name of Hosea's firstborn son, named after the place where the house of Jehu led a massacre?

3602. What was the meaning of the name of Hosea's daughter Lo-Ruhamah?

3603. What was the meaning of the name of Hosea's son Lo-Ammi?

3604. In Hosea 2, on that day when God restored Israel, he said the people would not call him "my master" but what instead?

3605. In Hosea 2, what god's name did God promise to remove from their lips?

3606. With what two items did Hosea buy Gomer back?

3607. The people of Israel behaved like Gomer because they were led away by a spirit of what?

3608. In Hosea 4, God wanted to pasture Israel like a lamb, but they acted like what stubborn animal?

3609. In Hosea 5, what specific tribe did God say would be laid to waste because they pursued idols and turned to Assyria for help?

3610. In Hosea 6, what from Ephraim was described as a morning mist, an early dew that disappears?

3611. In Hosea 6, God said he desired mercy and not what?

3612. In Hosea 7, the hearts of Israel are described as like what kitchen appliances?

3613. In Hosea 8, what bird flew over the house of the Lord because the people had broken God's covenant?

3614. What was the likeness of the idol in Samaria that God said would be broken into pieces?

3615. In Hosea 9, Ephraim's sins were so many that inspired people were considered to be what?

3616. In Hosea 9, God said that when he found Israel, it was like finding what fruit in the desert?

3617. In Hosea 10, what in Samaria would eventually be carried away to Assyria?

3618. In Hosea 11, whom did God call out of Egypt?

3619. In Hosea 11, when God roared, his children would tremble like sparrows and flutter like what other birds?

3620. In Hosea 12, God said he had been the God of Israel ever since they came from where?

3621. In Hosea 13, what three wild animals did God threaten to become when dealing with Ephraim?

3622. In Hosea 13, what did God give the nation in anger and then take away in wrath?

3623. What New Testament writer quoted Hosea 13:14 by saying, "Where, O death, are your plagues? Where, O grave, is your destruction?"

3624. In Hosea 14, to what three trees did God compare a newly restored Israel?

Joel

3625. Who was Joel's father?

3626. What insects buzzed all throughout the book of Joel?

3627. In chapter 1, whom did Joel tell to wake up?

3628. In Joel 1, what two people were described as wearing sackcloth?

3629. What doomsday phrase appears five times beginning with Joel 1:15?

3630. In Joel 2, when the army strikes, what three things go dark and no longer shine?

3631. According to Joel 2:21, what land was Joel telling not to be afraid?

3632. In Joel 2, God promised to repay for the years that were eaten by what?

3633. In Joel 2:28, what will the old men do?

3634. In Joel 2:28, what will the young men do?

3635. According to Joel 2:31, what will the sun turn to?

3636. According to Joel, what will the moon turn to?

3637. What will happen to everyone that calls on the name of the Lord?

3638. In Joel 3, God said he was judging Tyre and Sidon for selling the people of Judah to what group of people?

3639. What did God ask the plowshares be beaten into?

3640. According to the prophecy in Joel 3, once Jerusalem was restored, what three liquids would drip and flow from the hills and mountains?

Amos

3641. What was the occupation of the prophet Amos?

3642. Where was Amos from?

3643. What event shook up Israel two years before Amos received his vision?

3644. When Amos received his vision, who was the king of Judah?

3645. Who was the king of neighboring Israel when Amos received his vision?

3646. In Amos 1, for every nation God spoke against, he said he would not turn his back from how many sins?

3647. What did God say he would break down in Damascus?

3648. Name the eight cities/regions/nations that God prophesied against in Amos 1–2.

3649. In Amos 2, God promised to punish Israel for trampling on whose heads?

3650. In Amos 2, God accused Israel for making the Nazirites drink what?

3651. In Amos 2, what three types of warriors did God say could not escape or survive?

3652. In Amos 3, God said he did nothing until he revealed his plans to whom?

3653. In Amos 3, in what city were the altars that God promised to destroy?

3654. In Amos 4, how did God promise to take away the women that oppressed the poor?

3655. In Amos 4, what did God allow in one town or field but not in another town or field?

3656. Name the two constellations mentioned in the book of Amos.

3657. According to Amos, the day of the Lord would be like a man fleeing a lion only to meet up with what?

3658. In Amos 6, what two pieces of furniture did the complacent lounge on?

3659. Amos mentioned a swarm of what insect that struck the land?

3660. Amos saw the Lord standing by a wall holding what in his hand?

3661. In Amos 7, who was the priest that thought Amos was raising a conspiracy against the king?

3662. Who was the king that this priest sent a message to, complaining about Amos?

3663. What profession did Amos say his father was not?

3664. What kind of trees did Amos take care of?

3665. What did God show Amos a basket of, saying that the time was ripe for Israel?

3666. In Amos 8, God promised a famine not of food or water but of what?

3667. In Amos 9, on what famous mountain did God promise to find his people if they hid there?

3668. In Amos 9, with what weapon did God promise to kill all sinners?

3669. According to Amos 9, during a time of restoration of Israel, what would drip off the mountains and hills?

Obadiah

3670. What is the shortest book of the Old Testament?

3671. According to verse 1, what enemy country did the prophet Obadiah speak against?

3672. Who was the father of the Edomites mentioned in Obadiah 6?

3673. Who was the "brother" that Edom did not take care of and as a result God judged them?

3674. Obadiah said that Jacob would be fire and Joseph a flame, while Esau would be turned into what?

Jonah

3675. Who was Jonah's father?

3676. Where did God ask Jonah to go preach?

3677. Why did God ask Jonah to go there?

3678. Where did Jonah head toward instead?

3679. In what city did Jonah catch the ship to get there?

3680. What did the ship encounter on the sea that threatened to sink them?

3681. Whom did the sailors cry out to when the storm hit the ship?

3682. In Jonah 1, what did the sailors first throw into the sea to lighten the ship?

3683. What was Jonah doing when the storm hit the ship?

3684. How did the sailors determine that the storm was Jonah's fault?

3685. What did Jonah suggest the sailors should do to calm the storm?

3686. Instead of throwing Jonah into the sea, what did the sailors first try to do?

3687. How long was Jonah in the belly of the huge fish?

3688. What did Jonah say was wrapped around his head inside the great fish?

3689. What did the fish do to get Jonah on dry land?

3690. In the book of Jonah, the city of Nineveh was so big that it took how many days to visit it?

3691. How many days did Jonah give Nineveh before it would be overthrown?

3692. After hearing Jonah's message, what material did people cover themselves with?

3693. After hearing Jonah's message, what did the king declare for every man and beast?

3694. In what direction did Jonah sit to see what would happen to Nineveh?

3695. What did Jonah build as he waited for God to do something to the city?

3696. While Jonah pouted in the sun, what did God provide him to ease his discomfort from the sun?

3697. What insect did God send to destroy Jonah's vine?

3698. In the book of Jonah, how many Ninevites lived in the city according to God?

Micah

3699. During the reign of what three kings did Micah prophesy?

3700. All of these kings were from what kingdom?

3701. What two cities did Micah have a vision about?

3702. In Micah 1, because of Israel's sin, what animal would Micah howl like and what bird would he moan like?

3703. God told the people to shave their heads so they would be as bald as what bird?

3704. In Micah 2, he warned the people against any prophet that promised to prophesy for what two drinks?

3705. In Micah 3, because of Israel's sin, what two places would be plowed like a field and turned into a heap of rubble?

3706. According to Micah 4, to which mountain would many people stream to in the last days?

3707. In Micah 4, what would the people beat their swords into?

3708. In Micah 4, what country did Judah need to go to before they were rescued?

3709. According to Micah 5:2, what city was smallest among the cities of Judah?

3710. What would come out of that city?

3711. The ruler in Micah 5:2 would come from what origin?

3712. What king of Moab and son of Beor did Micah mention?

3713. Micah asked if the Lord would be pleased with thousands of what and ten thousand rivers of what?

3714. In Micah 6, God accused Israel for following the practices of what king's house?

3715. In Micah 7, on the day God would visit them in judgment, who would be a man's enemies?

3716. According to Micah 7, where does God hurl all our iniquities?

Nahum

3717. What was Nahum's heritage?

3718. According to Nahum 1, what is the Lord slow to do?

3719. According to Nahum 1, what can the Lord rebuke and it will dry up?

3720. What city did the prophet Nahum prophesy against?

3721. In Nahum 1, what did God promise to break from Judah's neck?

3722. In Nahum 2, who would moan like doves when Nineveh's attackers came?

3723. In Nahum 2, what military weapon did the Lord promise to burn up in Nineveh?

3724. What did God symbolically say he would lift up over Nineveh's face and reveal her nakedness?

3725. To what insect did the prophet Nahum compare the enemies' guards and officials?

Habakkuk

3726. What nation did God tell Habakkuk he was raising up?

3727. God told Habakkuk that the enemies' horses were swifter than what animal?

3728. Habakkuk said that the people were like fish in the sea and that the enemy pulled them up with what two fishing tools?

3729. What did God warn a city not to build on?

3730. Like the waters of the sea, the knowledge of what would fill the earth?

3731. What musical terms did Habakkuk 3 use?

3732. What animal did Habakkuk say God made his feet to be like as it ascended high places?

Zephaniah

3733. Zephaniah prophesied during the reign of what king?

3734. In Zephaniah 1, what two gods did God mention by name?

3735. Zephaniah 1 promised such distress on the people that they would grope around like whom?

3736. Zephaniah 1 declared such anguish on the people that their blood would be poured out like what?

3737. What city in Assyria did Zephaniah say would be left utterly desolate?

3738. In Zephaniah 2, what two types of owls would hoot and roost in the city?

3739. According to Zephaniah 3, what three groups of people were to blame for the destruction of Jerusalem?

Haggai

3740. During the reign of what Persian king did Haggai prophesy?

3741. During what year of Darius' reign did these prophecies in Haggai occur?

3742. How many different times in Haggai did the word of the Lord come to him?

3743. To what two people did Haggai deliver the Lord's message?

3744. What was God encouraging them to build?

3745. God's house had not been built because they were busy building what?

3746. What political position did Zerubabbel hold?

3747. What spiritual title did Joshua hold?

3748. For how many months, from the first prophecy to the last, did the word of the Lord come to Haggai?

3749. Like what piece of royal jewelry did God tell Haggai that he was going to make Zerubbabel?

Zechariah

3750. Who was the king of Persia when the first message came to Zechariah?

3751. In Zechariah 1, what color were the three horses Zechariah saw?

3752. What kind of tree was the man standing among when Zechariah saw him?

3753. The angel told Zechariah that the four horns scattered the people from what three areas?

3754. In Zechariah 2, what was the man going to measure?

3755. In Zechariah 3, whom did the prophet see in filthy rags being accused?

3756. Who was accusing him?

3757. In Zechariah 3, what clean item did the angel put on Joshua's head?

3758. In Zechariah 3, the stone in front of Joshua had how many eyes?

3759. In Zechariah 3, what did God say he would remove from this land in a single day?

3760. In Zechariah 4, what did Zechariah see that was made of gold with seven lights on top?

3761. According to Zechariah 4, who was the person that would lay the foundation of the temple?

3762. What kind of trees from Zechariah's vision represented the two that were anointed to serve the Lord?

3763. In chapter 5, what flying object did Zechariah see?

3764. Who was in the basket Zechariah saw in his vision?

3765. What did the basket in Zechariah's vision represent?

3766. To what country was the basket being taken?

3767. In Zechariah 6, what were the colors of the four horses?

3768. In Zechariah 6, the four horses pulling chariots represented what?

3769. In Zechariah 6, whom was the silver and gold crown given to?

3770. What was the name given to this man?

3771. In Zechariah 7, the people were described as having hearts as hard as what?

3772. In Zechariah 8, what name would Jerusalem be called when the Lord returned to dwell there?

3773. In Zechariah 8, what practices held during the fourth, fifth, seventh, and tenth months would end and turn into joyful occasions?

3774. In Zechariah 8, the Lord promised that how many people would take hold of a Jew and beg to go with him to Jerusalem?

3775. Zechariah 9 speaks of a king riding on two animals. What were they?

3776. In Zechariah 10, God's anger burned against whom?

3777. According to Zechariah 10, from where would the cornerstone come?

3778. Where did the cedars referenced in Zechariah 11 come from?

3779. Where did the oaks referenced in Zechariah 11 come from?

3780. In Zechariah 11, what were the names of the two staffs?

3781. How long did it take to get rid of three shepherds?

3782. In chapter 11, Zechariah was paid how much money?

3783. Whom was the money thrown at?

3784. The breaking of the second staff symbolized the breaking of the bond between what two nations?

3785. A foolish shepherd tears what off the choicest sheep?

3786. Which eye of the worthless shepherd did God ask to be blinded?

3787. What kind of immovable object did God promise to make Jerusalem in Zechariah 12?

3788. Zechariah 12 said that the people would look and mourn at the one that had been what?

3789. According to Zechariah 13, what was a prophet's garment made of?

3790. According to Zechariah 13, what happens when the shepherd is struck?

3791. In Zechariah 14, the Lord would stand on what mountain as it split in two?

3792. According to Zechariah, an earthquake would cause the people to flee, just like the one that struck during the reign of what king of Judah?

3793. On that day in Zechariah 14, what kind of water would flow from Jerusalem, half to the Dead Sea and half to the Mediterranean?

3794. In Zechariah 14, God said he would inflict a plague on the Egyptians if they did not celebrate what Jewish holiday?

3795. In Zechariah 14, what kitchen item in the Lord's house would be like sacred bowls in front of the altar?

Malachi

3796. What is the last book of the Old Testament?

3797. In Malachi 1, God said he loved Jacob but hated whom?

3798. In Malachi 1, what nation might try to rebuild but God would crush them?

3799. In Malachi 1, what kind of sacrifices did the priest offer that displeased God?

3800. In Malachi 2, what did God threaten to spread on the priests' faces?

3801. Which of Jacob's sons, that walked in peace and righteousness, turning many from sins, did God mention in Malachi?

3802. In Malachi 2, on the subject of marriage, what did God make clear that he hated?

3803. In Malachi 3, the Lord compared his coming messenger to what two cleansing agents?

3804. In Malachi 3, whom would this coming messenger cleanse?

3805. According to Malachi 3, how do people rob God?

3806. According to Malachi 3, if we bring the whole tithe to God, he will throw open the floodgates of what?

3807. Which prophet did God promise to send in the final chapter of the Old Testament?

3808. In Malachi 4, God promised that the coming prophet would turn the hearts from whom to whom and vice versa?

PART TWO

THE ANSWERS

Genesis

1. In the beginning (Genesis 1:1)
2. The Spirit of God (Genesis 1:2)
3. "Let there be light" (Genesis 1:3)
4. Light (Genesis 1:3)
5. Darkness (Genesis 1:3)
6. Light/day and night (Genesis 1:5)
7. Sky (Genesis 1:8)
8. The third day (Genesis 1:11)
9. The third day (Genesis 1:11)
10. The fourth day (Genesis 1:16)
11. The fourth day (Genesis 1:16)
12. The fifth day (Genesis 1:20)
13. The sixth day (Genesis 1:24)
14. The sixth day (Genesis 1:26)
15. Man (Genesis 1:26)
16. Multiply/increase in number (Genesis 1:28)
17. Plants and fruit (Genesis 1:29)
18. Every green plant (Genesis 1:30)
19. The sixth day (Genesis 1:31)
20. The seventh day (Genesis 2:2)
21. The seventh day (Genesis 2:3)
22. From the streams in the earth (Genesis 2:6)
23. The dust on the ground (Genesis 2:7)
24. His nostrils (Genesis 2:7)
25. East (Genesis 2:8)
26. Eden (Genesis 2:8)
27. The tree of life and the tree of knowledge of good and evil (Genesis 2:9)
28. Pishon, Gihon, Tigris, and Euphrates (Genesis 2:11–14)
29. Pishon (Genesis 2:11)
30. Gihon (Genesis 2:13)
31. The tree of knowledge of good and evil (Genesis 2:17)
32. The fact that the man was alone (Genesis 2:18)
33. So he could name them (Genesis 2:19)
34. His rib (Genesis 2:21–22)
35. Their father and mother (Genesis 2:24)
36. Flesh (Genesis 2:24)
37. The serpent (Genesis 3:1)
38. The middle (Genesis 3:3)
39. They would die (Genesis 3:3)
40. They were opened (Genesis 3:7)
41. Fig leaves (Genesis 3:7)
42. It was the cool of the day (Genesis 3:8)
43. Because he was naked (Genesis 3:10)
44. The woman (Genesis 3:12)
45. The serpent (Genesis 3:13)
46. Dust (Genesis 3:14)
47. Childbearing (Genesis 3:16)

48. Thorns and thistles (Genesis 3:18)
49. The dust/the ground (Genesis 3:19)
50. Adam (Genesis 3:20)
51. Garments of skin (Genesis 3:21)
52. A cherubim and flaming sword (Genesis 3:24)
53. Cain (Genesis 4:1)
54. Abel (Genesis 4:2)
55. He kept flocks/shepherd (Genesis 4:2)
56. He worked the land/farmer (Genesis 4:2)
57. Fruits of the soil (Genesis 4:3)
58. Fat portions (Genesis 4:4)
59. Abel (Genesis 4:4)
60. Cain (Genesis 4:7)
61. Cain (Genesis 4:8)
62. Cain (Genesis 4:9)
63. Abel (Genesis 4:11)
64. Cain (Genesis 4:12)
65. Seven (Genesis 4:15)
66. A mark (Genesis 4:15)
67. Nod (Genesis 4:16)
68. Eden (Genesis 4:16)
69. Enoch (Genesis 4:17)
70. A city (Genesis 4:17)
71. Enoch (Genesis 4:17)
72. Jabal (Genesis 4:20)
73. Jubal (Genesis 4:21)
74. Tools (Genesis 4:22)
75. Seth (Genesis 4:25)
76. Enosh (Genesis 4:26)
77. Worship the Lord/call on the name of the Lord (Genesis 4:26)
78. Adam 930 years/Seth 912 years/ Enosh 905 years (Genesis 5:5, 8, 11)
79. 930 years (Genesis 5:5)
80. Jared/962 years old (Genesis 5:20)
81. Enoch (Genesis 5:24)
82. Methuselah (Genesis 5:27)
83. 969 years old (Genesis 5:27)
84. Lamech (Genesis 5:28–29)
85. Five hundred years old (Genesis 5:32)
86. Shem, Ham, and Japheth (Genesis 5:32)
87. One hundred twenty years (Genesis 6:3)
88. Nephilim (Genesis 6:4)
89. Human/men (Genesis 6:4)
90. Humankind (Genesis 6:6)
91. Noah (Genesis 6:8)
92. Cypress (Genesis 6:14)
93. Pitch/tar (Genesis 6:14)
94. Three—upper, middle, and lower (Genesis 6:16)
95. Two—a male and female (Genesis 6:19)

96. Seven (Genesis 7:2)
97. Two (Genesis 7:2)
98. Birds (Genesis 7:3)
99. Seven days (Genesis 7:4)
100. Forty days and nights (Genesis 7:4)
101. 600 years old (Genesis 7:6)
102. Eight (Genesis 7:13)
103. Twenty to twenty-three feet/fifteen cubits (Genesis 7:20)
104. 150 days (Genesis 7:24)
105. 150 days (Genesis 8:3)
106. Ararat (Genesis 8:4)
107. A window (Genesis 8:6)
108. Raven (Genesis 8:7)
109. Dove (Genesis 8:8–10)
110. Seven (Genesis 8:10)
111. An olive leaf (Genesis 8:11)
112. Three times (Genesis 8:8, 10, 12)
113. It did not return (Genesis 8:12)
114. 601 years old (Genesis 8:13)
115. Built an altar and offered a sacrifice (Genesis 8:20)
116. God (Genesis 8:21)
117. Everything that lives and moves/animals (Genesis 9:3)
118. Lifeblood (Genesis 9:4)
119. A flood (Genesis 9:11)
120. Rainbow (Genesis 9:13)
121. Ham (Genesis 9:18)
122. A vineyard (Genesis 9:20)
123. A tent (Genesis 9:21)
124. Ham (Genesis 9:22)
125. They covered him up (Genesis 9:23)
126. Canaan's (Genesis 9:25)
127. 350 years (Genesis 9:28)
128. 950 years (Genesis 9:28)
129. Nimrod (Genesis 10:8–9)
130. Genesis (Genesis 10:10–11)
131. Nimrod (Genesis 10:11)
132. Sodom and Gomorrah (Genesis 10:19)
133. Shinar/Babylonia (Genesis 11:2)
134. Brick (Genesis 11:3)
135. Tar (Genesis 11:3)
136. A city (Genesis 11:4)
137. Their language (Genesis 11:7)
138. Babel (Genesis 11:9)
139. Terah (Genesis 11:27)
140. Nahor and Haran (Genesis 11:27)
141. Lot (Genesis 11:27)
142. Sarai (Genesis 11:29)
143. Milcah (Genesis 11:29)
144. Ur of the Chaldeans (Genesis 11:31)
145. Canaan (Genesis 11:31)
146. Harran (Genesis 11:31)
147. Seventy-five years old (Genesis 12:4)
148. Harran (Genesis 12:4)
149. Sarai and Lot (Genesis 12:5)

150. Egypt (Genesis 12:10)

151. His sister (Genesis 12:13)

152. Pharaoh's officials (Genesis 12:15)

153. Sheep, cattle, donkeys, and camels (Genesis 12:16)

154. Pharaoh and his household (Genesis 12:17)

155. The herdsmen (Genesis 13:7)

156. Jordan (Genesis 13:11)

157. Sodom and Gomorrah (Genesis 13:10)

158. Dust (Genesis 13:16)

159. Mamre (Genesis 13:18)

160. The Salt Sea/Dead Sea (Genesis 14:3)

161. Tar pits (Genesis 14:10)

162. Lot (Genesis 14:12)

163. Abram (Genesis 14:13)

164. 318 (Genesis 14:14)

165. Priest (Genesis 14:18)

166. Salem (Genesis 14:18)

167. Bread and wine (Genesis 14:18)

168. A tenth (Genesis 14:20)

169. None (Genesis 14:23)

170. Eliezer of Damascus (Genesis 15:2)

171. The stars (Genesis 15:5)

172. Righteousness (Genesis 15:6)

173. Heifer, goat, ram, dove, and pigeon (Genesis 15:10)

174. Birds of prey/vultures (Genesis 15:11)

175. Four hundred years (Genesis 15:13)

176. A smoking firepot with a blazing torch (Genesis 15:17)

177. Hagar (Genesis 16:1)

178. Egypt (Genesis 16:1)

179. An angel (Genesis 16:7)

180. Ishmael (Genesis 16:12)

181. Beer Lahai Roi (Genesis 16:14)

182. Eighty-six years old (Genesis 16:16)

183. Nations (Genesis 17:5)

184. Circumcision (Genesis 17:10)

185. Eight days old (Genesis 17:12)

186. Nations (Genesis 17:16)

187. God (Genesis 17:19)

188. Laughs (Genesis 17:19)

189. Twelve (Genesis 17:20)

190. Ninety-nine years old (Genesis 17:24)

191. Thirteen years old (Genesis 17:25)

192. Mamre (Genesis 18:1)

193. Three (Genesis 18:2)

194. Bread (Genesis 18:6)

195. At the entrance of the tent (Genesis 18:9–10)

196. Laughing (Genesis 18:15)

197. Sodom and Gomorrah (Genesis 18:20–21)

198. Fifty (Genesis 18:24)

199. Ten (Genesis 18:32)

200. Evening (Genesis 19:1)

201. At the city gate (Genesis 19:1)

202. Have sex with them (Genesis 19:5)
203. His daughters (Genesis 19:8)
204. Blindness (Genesis 19:11)
205. His sons-in-law (Genesis 19:14)
206. Lot, his wife, and his two daughters (Genesis 19:16)
207. Zoar (Genesis 19:22)
208. Burning sulphur (Genesis 19:24)
209. The vegetation and animals (Genesis 19:25)
210. Lot's wife (Genesis 19:26)
211. Pillar of salt (Genesis 19:26)
212. Moab (Genesis 19:37)
213. Ben-Ammi (Genesis 19:38)
214. Moabites and Ammonites (Genesis 19:37–38)
215. Abimelech (Genesis 20:2)
216. A dream (Genesis 20:3)
217. He said she was his half sister, meaning they had the same father but different mothers (Genesis 20:12)
218. The women's wombs (Genesis 20:18)
219. One hundred (Genesis 21:5)
220. Laughter (Genesis 21:6)
221. Beersheba (Genesis 21:14)
222. A well of water (Genesis 21:19)
223. Archery (Genesis 21:20)
224. Egypt (Genesis 21:21)
225. A well (Genesis 21:25)
226. Tamarisk tree (Genesis 21:33)
227. Moriah (Genesis 22:2)
228. Burnt offering (Genesis 22:2)
229. Donkey (Genesis 22:3)
230. Two (Genesis 22:3)
231. Three days (Genesis 22:4)
232. The wood (Genesis 22:6)
233. The fire and the knife (Genesis 22:6)
234. The lamb (Genesis 22:7)
235. His hand (Genesis 22:10)
236. A ram (Genesis 22:13)
237. God will provide (Genesis 22:14)
238. Stars and sand (Genesis 22:17)
239. 127 (Genesis 23:1)
240. Hebron/Kiriath Arba (Genesis 23:2)
241. Machpelah near Mamre/Hebron (Genesis 23:9)
242. Ephron the Hittite (Genesis 23:10)
243. Four hundred pieces of silver (Genesis 23:15)
244. His chief servant (Genesis 24:2)
245. The Canaanites (Genesis 24:3)
246. Ten (Genesis 24:10)
247. Nahor (Genesis 24:10)
248. The local well (Genesis 24:11)
249. His camels (Genesis 24:14)
250. Rebekah (Genesis 24:15)
251. Bethuel (Genesis 24:15)
252. A gold nose ring and two gold bracelets (Genesis 24:22)
253. Laban (Genesis 24:29)

254. Ten (Genesis 24:55)

255. Keturah (Genesis 25:1)

256. Isaac (Genesis 25:5)

257. 175 years old (Genesis 25:7)

258. Cave of Machpelah (Genesis 25:9)

259. Nebaioth (Genesis 25:13)

260. Twelve (Genesis 25:13–16)

261. Egypt (Genesis 25:18)

262. Forty years old (Genesis 25:20)

263. Nations (Genesis 25:23)

264. The older would serve the younger (Genesis 25:23)

265. Red (Genesis 25:25)

266. Esau (Genesis 25:25)

267. Like a hairy garment (Genesis 25:25)

268. Esau's heel (Genesis 25:26)

269. Sixty years old (Genesis 25:27)

270. Hunting (Genesis 25:27)

271. Among the tents (Genesis 25:27)

272. Esau (Genesis 25:28)

273. Jacob (Genesis 25:28)

274. Red (Genesis 25:30)

275. Because he told Jacob to give him some of the red stew—*Edom* means "red." (Genesis 25:30)

276. Esau's birthright (Genesis 25:31)

277. His birthright (Genesis 25:33)

278. Lentil (Genesis 25:34)

279. Esau's birthright (Genesis 25:35)

280. A famine (Genesis 26:1)

281. Gerar (Genesis 26:1)

282. Egypt (Genesis 26:2)

283. His sister (Genesis 26:7)

284. Abimelech (Genesis 26:8)

285. Wells (Genesis 26:20–22, 33)

286. "The Lord has given us room" (Genesis 26:22)

287. Judith and Basemath (Genesis 26:34)

288. Wild game (Genesis 27:3)

289. Goatskin (Genesis 27:16)

290. His voice (Genesis 27:22)

291. Her brother Laban's house in Harran (Genesis 27:43)

292. Paddan Aram (Genesis 28:2)

293. Laban (Genesis 28:2)

294. Ishmael's (Genesis 28:9)

295. Mahalath (Genesis 28:9)

296. A stone (Genesis 28:11)

297. Angels (Genesis 28:12)

298. Bethel (Genesis 28:19)

299. Luz (Genesis 28:19)

300. A shepherdess (Genesis 29:9)

301. Cousin/daughter of his mother's brother (Genesis 29:10)

302. A well (Genesis 29:10)

303. Weak/delicate (Genesis 29:17)

304. Seven years (Genesis 29:18)

305. Zilpah (Genesis 29:24)

306. Leah (Genesis 29:25)

307. Seven years (Genesis 29:27)

308. One week (Genesis 29:28)

309. She was not loved (Genesis 29:31)

310. Reuben (Genesis 29:32)

311. Reuben (Genesis 29:32)

312. Simeon (Genesis 29:33)

313. Levi (Genesis 29:34)

314. Judah (Genesis 29:35)

315. Reuben, Simeon, Levi, Judah, Issachar, and Zebulun (Genesis 29:31–35; 30:18–20)

316. Dan and Naphtali (Genesis 30:4–8)

317. Dan (Genesis 30:6)

318. Naphtali (Genesis 30:8)

319. Gad and Asher (Genesis 30:9–13)

320. Gad (Genesis 30:11)

321. Asher (Genesis 30:13)

322. Mandrakes (Genesis 30:14)

323. Issachar (Genesis 30:18)

324. Zebulun (Genesis 30:20)

325. Dinah (Genesis 30:21)

326. Joseph and Benjamin (Genesis 30:24; 35:18)

327. Joseph (Genesis 30:24)

328. Sheep/lambs and goats (Genesis 30:32)

329. Poplar, almond, and plane (Genesis 30:37)

330. His household gods (Genesis 31:19)

331. Jacob (Genesis 31:24)

332. Twenty years (Genesis 31:38)

333. Galeed/Mizpah (Genesis 31:47)

334. Mahanaim (Genesis 32:2)

335. Four hundred men (Genesis 32:6)

336. Hip socket (Genesis 32:25)

337. Israel (Genesis 32:28)

338. “He struggles” (Genesis 32:28)

339. Peniel (Genesis 32:30)

340. The tendon of the hip (Genesis 32:32)

341. Sukkoth (Genesis 33:17)

342. Shechem (Genesis 34:2)

343. Hamor (Genesis 34:6)

344. Circumcision (Genesis 34:17)

345. Simeon and Levi (Genesis 34:25)

346. All their foreign gods (Genesis 35:2)

347. Benjamin (Genesis 35:18)

348. Ben-Oni (Genesis 35:18)

349. Bethlehem Ephrath (Genesis 35:19)

350. Reuben (Genesis 35:22)

351. Esau (Genesis 36)

352. Ishmael (Genesis 36:3)

353. Seir (Genesis 36:8)

354. Seventeen (Genesis 37:2)

355. Because he was born in his old age (Genesis 37:3)

356. A beautiful, ornate robe (Genesis 37:3)

357. Grain (Genesis 37:7)

358. Sun, moon, and stars (Genesis 37:9)

359. The Dreamer (Genesis 37:19)

360. A cistern (Genesis 37:20)
361. Reuben (Genesis 37:21)
362. Ishmaelites/Midianites (Genesis 37:25, 28)
363. Egypt (Genesis 37:25)
364. Judah (Genesis 37:26–27)
365. Twenty shekels of silver (Genesis 37:28)
366. Reuben (Genesis 37:29)
367. Goat (Genesis 37:31)
368. A ferocious animal devoured him (Genesis 37:33)
369. Potiphar (Genesis 37:36)
370. Captain of the palace guard (Genesis 37:36)
371. Er and Onan (Genesis 38:7, 10)
372. They were wicked (Genesis 38:7, 10)
373. His semen (Genesis 38:9)
374. Shelah (Genesis 38:14)
375. Tamar (Genesis 38:16)
376. A seal, his cord, and a staff (Genesis 38:18)
377. A scarlet cord (Genesis 38:28)
378. Perez and Zerah (Genesis 38:29–30)
379. Zerah (Genesis 38:30)
380. Pharaoh (Genesis 39:1)
381. His cloak (Genesis 39:13)
382. Rape (Genesis 39:14)
383. The jailer/warden (Genesis 39:21)
384. The chief cupbearer and chief baker (Genesis 40:2)
385. God (Genesis 40:8)
386. The cupbearer (Genesis 40:9–11)
387. The baker (Genesis 40:16–19)
388. Birds (Genesis 40:17)
389. Three days (Genesis 40:12, 18)
390. Pharaoh's birthday (Genesis 40:20)
391. He was impaled on a pole (Genesis 40:22)
392. Two years (Genesis 41:1)
393. The Nile (Genesis 41:1)
394. Ate them (Genesis 41:4)
395. Grain (Genesis 41:7)
396. Magicians and wise men (Genesis 41:8)
397. The cupbearer (Genesis 41:9)
398. Shaved and changed his clothes (Genesis 41:14)
399. Seven years (Genesis 41:26)
400. Seven years of abundance (Genesis 41:29)
401. Seven years of famine (Genesis 41:30)
402. One-fifth (Genesis 41:34)
403. His signet ring, robes, and a gold chain (Genesis 41:42)
404. Joseph (Genesis 41:45)
405. Asenath (Genesis 41:45)
406. Thirty years old (Genesis 41:46)
407. Manesseh and Ephraim (Genesis 41:51–52)
408. Manesseh (Genesis 41:51)
409. Ephraim (Genesis 41:52)

410. Ten (Genesis 42:3)

411. Benjamin (Genesis 42:4)

412. Spies (Genesis 42:9)

413. Simeon (Genesis 42:24)

414. Their silver (Genesis 42:35)

415. Reuben and Judah (Genesis 42:37; 43:9)

416. Eating with them (Genesis 43:32)

417. Five (Genesis 43:34)

418. A silver cup (Genesis 44:2)

419. Divination (Genesis 44:5)

420. Benjamin (Genesis 44:12)

421. Judah (Genesis 44:18)

422. "Is my father living?" (Genesis 45:3)

423. To save lives (Genesis 45:5)

424. Goshen (Genesis 45:10)

425. Five (Genesis 45:22)

426. Joseph (Genesis 46:4)

427. Sixty-six (Genesis 46:26)

428. Shepherding (Genesis 46:34)

429. Shepherding (Genesis 47:4)

430. 130 years old (Genesis 47:9)

431. Bless him (Genesis 47:10)

432. Livestock and land (Genesis 47:17–19)

433. A fifth (Genesis 47:26)

434. Seventeen years (Genesis 47:28)

435. 147 years old (Genesis 47:28)

436. Egypt (Genesis 47:29)

437. Joseph (Genesis 48:17)

438. Ephraim (Genesis 48:19)

439. Reuben (Genesis 49:4)

440. Simeon and Levi (Genesis 49:5)

441. Judah (Genesis 49:9)

442. The scepter/staff (Genesis 49:10)

443. Donkey and colt (Genesis 49:11)

444. Issachar (Genesis 49:14)

445. Dan (Genesis 49:16–17)

446. Joseph (Genesis 49:22)

447. Benjamin (Genesis 49:27)

448. Machpelah/his father's cave (Genesis 49:29–30)

449. Abraham, Sarah, Isaac, Rebekah, and Leah (Genesis 49:31)

450. Forty days (Genesis 50:3)

451. Canaan/the land promised to Abraham, Isaac, and Jacob (Genesis 50:24)

452. His bones (Genesis 50:25)

453. 110 years old (Genesis 50:26)

454. Joseph (Genesis 50:26)

Exodus

455. Seventy (Exodus 1:5)

456. Cities (Exodus 1:11)

457. Pithom and Ramses (Exodus 1:11)

458. Brick and mortar (Exodus 1:14)

459. In the fields (Exodus 1:14)

460. Midwives (Exodus 1:15)

461. Boys (Exodus 1:16)

462. That the Hebrew women gave birth before the midwives came (Exodus 1:19)

463. Families of their own (Exodus 1:21)

464. The Nile (Exodus 1:22)

465. Levi (Exodus 2:1)

466. Three months (Exodus 2:2)

467. Papyrus (Exodus 2:3)

468. Tar and pitch (Exodus 2:3)

469. His sister (Exodus 2:4)

470. Pharaoh's daughter (Exodus 2:5)

471. Moses' mother (Exodus 2:8)

472. Pharaoh's daughter (Exodus 2:10)

473. "Draw out [of the water]" (Exodus 2:10)

474. A Hebrew (Exodus 2:11)

475. In the sand (Exodus 2:12)

476. Pharaoh (Exodus 2:15)

477. Midian (Exodus 2:15)

478. A well/trough (Exodus 2:16–17)

479. Priest (Exodus 2:16)

480. Seven (Exodus 2:16)

481. Reuel (Exodus 2:18)

482. Zipporah (Exodus 2:21)

483. Gerhsom (Exodus 2:22)

484. That he had become a foreigner/sojourner in a foreign land (Exodus 2:22)

485. Jethro (Exodus 3:1; 2:18)

486. Jethro's (Exodus 3:1)

487. Mount Horeb (Exodus 3:1)

488. "Moses, Moses" (Exodus 3:4)

489. His sandals (Exodus 3:5)

490. Holy ground (Exodus 3:5)

491. Milk and honey (Exodus 3:8)

492. "I am who I am" (Exodus 3:14)

493. A snake (Exodus 4:3)

494. A staff (Exodus 4:4)

495. Leprosy (Exodus 4:6)

496. Pour water from the Nile on the ground and it would turn into blood (Exodus 4:9)

497. Speech and tongue (Exodus 4:10)

498. Aaron his brother (Exodus 4:14)

499. His wife and sons (Exodus 4:20)

500. He did not circumcise his son (Exodus 4:25)

501. Zipporah (Exodus 4:25)

502. Knife (Exodus 4:25)

503. Flint (Exodus 4:25)

504. The wilderness (Exodus 4:27)

505. Three days (Exodus 5:3)

506. Straw (Exodus 5:7)

507. Levi (Exodus 6:16)

508. Amram (Exodus 6:20)

509. Jochebed (Exodus 6:20)

510. Eighty years old (Exodus 7:7)

511. Eighty-three years old (Exodus 7:7)

512. Aaron's (Exodus 7:9)

513. Wise men, sorcerers, and magicians (Exodus 7:11)

514. Swallowed them up (Exodus 7:12)

515. The Nile (Exodus 7:17)

516. Fish (Exodus 7:21)

517. Turned the Nile to blood; frogs; and gnats (Exodus 7:20; 8:5; 8:16)

518. Aaron (Exodus 8:6)

519. Gnats (Exodus 8:18)

520. Flies (Exodus 8:21)

521. Flies and death of the firstborn (Exodus 8:28; 12:32)

522. Livestock (Exodus 9:3)

523. The Israelites (Exodus 9:4)

524. Soot from a furnace (Exodus 9:8)

525. Thunder and lightning (Exodus 9:23)

526. Flax and barley (Exodus 9:31)

527. Wheat and spelt (Exodus 9:32)

528. Locusts (Exodus 10:14)

529. Hail and locusts (Exodus 9:23; 10:13)

530. A strong west wind (Exodus 10:19)

531. The Red Sea (Exodus 10:19)

532. Three (Exodus 10:23)

533. Silver and gold (Exodus 11:2)

534. Midnight (Exodus 11:4)

535. Bark (Exodus 11:7)

536. The new year (Exodus 12:2)

537. The tenth day (Exodus 12:3)

538. One year old (Exodus 12:5)

539. Male (Exodus 12:5)

540. Sheep or goats (Exodus 12:5)

541. Fourteenth (Exodus 12:6)

542. Twilight (Exodus 12:6)

543. Sides and tops of the doorframes (Exodus 12:7)

544. Roasted over the fire (Exodus 12:8)

545. Bitter herbs and bread without yeast (Exodus 12:8)

546. Burn it (Exodus 12:10)

547. Cloak tucked into belt, sandals on feet, staff in hand (Exodus 12:11)

548. The animals (Exodus 12:12)

549. The blood (Exodus 12:13)

550. Seven days/a week (Exodus 12:15)

551. They were cut off (Exodus 12:15)

552. Hyssop (Exodus 12:22)

553. Death/the destroyer (Exodus 12:23)

554. Midnight (Exodus 12:29)

555. A prisoner (Exodus 12:29)

556. Silver, gold, and clothing (Exodus 12:35)

557. Six hundred thousand (Exodus 12:37)

558. 430 years (Exodus 12:41)

559. Joseph (Exodus 13:19)

560. Smoke/cloud (Exodus 13:21)

561. Fire (Exodus 13:21)

562. Six hundred (Exodus 14:7)

563. Hardened it (Exodus 14:8)

564. Graves (Exodus 14:11)

565. His staff and his hand (Exodus 14:16)

566. East (Exodus 14:21)

567. The Egyptians (Exodus 14:24)

568. Jammed the wheels (Exodus 14:25)

569. None (Exodus 14:28)

570. Moses (Exodus 15:1)

571. Miriam (Exodus 15:20)

572. Timbrel/tambourine (Exodus 15:20)

573. The water was bitter (Exodus 15:23)

574. A piece of wood (Exodus 15:25)

575. One month and a half (Exodus 16:1)

576. Meat (Exodus 16:3)

577. Enough for the day (Exodus 16:4)

578. Twice as much/two days' worth (Exodus 16:5)

579. Meat/quail and bread/manna (Exodus 16:12)

580. "What is it?" (Exodus 16:15)

581. An omer (Exodus 16:18)

582. Maggots (Exodus 16:20)

583. Two omers (Exodus 16:22)

584. White (Exodus 16:31)

585. Coriander (Exodus 16:31)

586. Honey (Exodus 16:31)

587. Generations to come (Exodus 16:33)

588. Forty (Exodus 16:35)

589. One-tenth (Exodus 16:36)

590. Horeb (Exodus 17:6)

591. They tested the Lord (Exodus 17:7)

592. They quarreled with the Lord (Exodus 17:7)

593. Amalekites (Exodus 17:8)

594. Joshua (Exodus 17:9)

595. Hold up his hands (Exodus 17:11)

596. A stone (Exodus 17:12)

597. Aaron and Hur (Exodus 17:12)

598. The Lord is my banner (Exodus 17:15)

599. Priest (Exodus 18:1)

600. Eliezer (Exodus 18:4)

601. "My God is helper" (Exodus 18:4)

602. Jethro (Exodus 18:5–6, 14)

603. Judges (Exodus 18:22)

604. Mount Sinai (Exodus 19:2–3)

605. Their clothes (Exodus 19:10)

606. The mountain (Exodus 19:12)

607. Arrow (Exodus 19:13)

608. Sexual relations (Exodus 19:15)

609. Aaron (Exodus 19:24)

610. Any other gods before God (Exodus 20:3)

611. Heaven above, earth beneath, waters below (Exodus 20:4)

612. Third and fourth (Exodus 20:5)

613. The name of God (Exodus 20:7)

614. Sabbath (Exodus 20:11)

615. God created the earth in six days and rested on the seventh (Exodus 20:11)

616. Our father and mother (Exodus 20:12)

617. Do not murder (Exodus 20:13)

618. Do not commit adultery (Exodus 20:14)

619. Do not steal (Exodus 20:15)

620. False testimony (Exodus 20:16)
621. Ox and donkey (Exodus 20:17)
622. Six years (Exodus 21:2)
623. His ear (Exodus 21:6)
624. An awl (Exodus 21:6)
625. Death (Exodus 21:15)
626. Death (Exodus 21:16)
627. Death (Exodus 21:17)
628. His loss of time (Exodus 21:18–19)
629. Death (Exodus 21:20)
630. Hand and foot (Exodus 21:24)
631. Eye and tooth (Exodus 21:26–27)
632. The animal was stoned to death and the meat not eaten (Exodus 21:28)
633. The animal was stoned to death and the owner killed (Exodus 21:29)
634. If he knew the bull was dangerous (Exodus 21:29)
635. Pay for the owner's loss and keep the dead animal (Exodus 21:33–34)
636. Pay the bride-price and marry her (Exodus 22:16)
637. Foreigners (Exodus 22:21)
638. The fatherless and widows (Exodus 22:22)
639. Interest (Exodus 22:25)
640. By sunset (Exodus 22:26)
641. Return it (Exodus 23:4)
642. Help it up (Exodus 23:5)
643. In Egypt (Exodus 23:9)
644. Ox, donkey, slave, and foreigner (Exodus 23:12)
645. Seven days (Exodus 23:15)
646. Three times a year (Exodus 23:17)
647. Its mother's milk (Exodus 23:19)
648. The hornet (Exodus 23:28)
649. The Book of the Covenant (Exodus 24:7)
650. Blue pavement (Exodus 24:10)
651. Forty days and nights (Exodus 24:18)
652. Acacia (Exodus 25:10)
653. Poles (Exodus 25:14)
654. Cherubim (Exodus 25:20)
655. The two tablets of the covenant law (Exodus 25:22)
656. Poles (Exodus 25:28)
657. Plates, dishes, pitchers, bowls, and bread (Exodus 25:29–30)
658. Seven (Exodus 25:37)
659. The curtains (Exodus 26:1)
660. Goat (Exodus 26:7)
661. Acacia wood (Exodus 26:15, 26)
662. Silver (Exodus 26:19)
663. The Most Holy Place (Exodus 26:33)
664. Acacia (Exodus 27:1)
665. Horns (Exodus 27:2)
666. Olive oil (Exodus 27:20)
667. Evening to morning (Exodus 27:21)
668. His sons—Nadab, Abihu, Eleazar, and Ithamar (Exodus 28:1, 4)
669. The sons of Israel (Exodus 28:9)
670. By birth (Exodus 28:10)
671. The tribes/sons of Israel (Exodus 28:21)

672. His heart (Exodus 28:30)
673. Decisions (Exodus 28:30)
674. Gold bells and pomegranates (Exodus 28:34)
675. Bells (Exodus 28:35)
676. "Holy to the Lord" (Exodus 28:36)
677. Linen (Exodus 28:42)
678. Their heads (Exodus 29:7)
679. Blood (Exodus 29:20)
680. Morning and twilight (Exodus 30:7–8)
681. Gold, frankincense, and myrrh (Exodus 30: 3, 23, 34)
682. A half shekel (Exodus 30:13)
683. Bronze (Exodus 30:18)
684. The priests (Exodus 30:30–32)
685. Bezalel and Oholiab (Exodus 31:2–6)
686. His finger (Exodus 31:18)
687. Gold earrings (Exodus 32:2)
688. Aaron (Exodus 32:4)
689. A calf (Exodus 32:4)
690. Killing them/wiping them out (Exodus 32:14)
691. On the front and back (Exodus 32:15)
692. Burned it, ground it to powder, put it in water, and made the people drink it (Exodus 32:20)
693. A calf jumped out (Exodus 32:24)
694. The Levites (Exodus 32:26–27)
695. Three thousand (Exodus 32:28)
696. A plague (Exodus 32:35)
697. Stood and worshiped (Exodus 33:10)
698. A friend (Exodus 33:11)
699. His face (Exodus 33:20)
700. In a cleft of the rock (Exodus 33:22)
701. His hand (Exodus 33:22)
702. His back (Exodus 33:23)
703. Moses (Exodus 34:1)
704. Treaties (Exodus 34:15)
705. Bread or water (Exodus 34:28)
706. Radiant (Exodus 34:29)
707. A veil (Exodus 34:33)
708. Blue, purple, and scarlet (Exodus 35:6, 25)
709. Giving any more (Exodus 36:6)
710. The lampstand (Exodus 37:17)
711. Gold (Exodus 37:2, 11, 17, 26)
712. Bronze (Exodus 38:3, 8, 10, 17, 19, 20)
713. The courtyard (Exodus 38:11–12)
714. Fifteen cubits long (Exodus 38:15)
715. Gold, silver, and bronze (Exodus 38:24, 25, 29)
716. Four rows of three (Exodus 39:10)
717. The twelve tribes (Exodus 39:14)
718. Pomegranate (Exodus 39:24)
719. Holy to the Lord (Exodus 39:30)
720. The cloud (Exodus 40:34–35)

Leviticus

721. Defect (Leviticus 1:3)

722. Aaron's (Leviticus 1:5)

723. Olive (Leviticus 2:1)

724. Yeast (Leviticus 2:11)

725. Salt (Leviticus 2:13)

726. The blood and the fat (Leviticus 3:17)

727. A bull (Leviticus 4:3)

728. The horns of the altar (Leviticus 4:7)

729. A bull (Leviticus 4:13)

730. A male goat (Leviticus 4:23)

731. Two doves or two young pigeons (Leviticus 5:7)

732. Choice flour (Leviticus 5:11)

733. A fifth (Leviticus 6:5)

734. Breast and thigh (Leviticus 7:34)

735. The burnt offering, the grain offering, the sin offering, the guilt offering, and the fellowship offering (Leviticus 7:37)

736. Tunic, sash, robe, ephod, waistband, breastpiece, and turban (Leviticus 8:7–9)

737. Seven times (Leviticus 8:11)

738. Lobe of right ear, thumb of right hand, and big toe of right foot (Leviticus 8:23)

739. Three (Leviticus 8:26)

740. The breast (Leviticus 8:29)

741. Blood and oil (Leviticus 8:30)

742. Seven days (Leviticus 8:33)

743. They would die (Leviticus 8:35)

744. Fire (Leviticus 9:24)

745. Nadab and Abihu (Leviticus 10:1)

746. Wine/fermented drink (Leviticus 10:9)

747. Split hoof completely divided, chews the cud (Leviticus 11:3)

748. Camel, hyrax/rock badger, rabbit, and pig (Leviticus 11:4–7)

749. It had fins and scales (Leviticus 11:9)

750. Locust, katydid, cricket, and grasshopper (Leviticus 11:22)

751. Break it (Leviticus 11:33)

752. Seven (Leviticus 12:2)

753. Eight days old (Leviticus 12:3)

754. Two weeks (Leviticus 12:5)

755. The priests/Aaron and his sons (Leviticus 13:2)

756. Seven days (Leviticus 13:4)

757. White (Leviticus 13:13, 16)

758. The hair (Leviticus 13:24, 31, 32)

759. Their clothes (Leviticus 13:34)

760. No (Leviticus 13:40)

761. Tear them (Leviticus 13:45)

762. "Unclean! Unclean!" (Leviticus 13:45)

763. Wool, linen, and leather (Leviticus 13:48, 59)

764. Burn it (Leviticus 13:57)

765. A priest (Leviticus 14:2–3)

766. Seven times (Leviticus 14:7)

767. Right ear, right thumb, and right big toe (Leviticus 14:14)

768. Doves and pigeons (Leviticus 14:30)

769. Mold (Leviticus 14:34–35)

770. A clay pot (Leviticus 15:12)

771. Day of Atonement (Leviticus 16:10)

772. The scapegoat (Leviticus 16:21–22)

773. The blood (Leviticus 17:11)

774. Seven days (Leviticus 18:19)

775. Any close relative (Leviticus 18:6)

776. Molech (Leviticus 18:21)

777. Grains and grapes on the edges, also called gleanings (Leviticus 19:9–10)

778. Deafness and blindness (Leviticus 19:14)

779. Animals, crops, and clothing (Leviticus 19:19)

780. Don't cut the sides of the head or clip the edges of the beard (Leviticus 19:27)

781. Stand in respect (Leviticus 19:32)

782. Both were put to death (Leviticus 20:10)

783. Stoning (Leviticus 20:27)

784. She must be a virgin (Leviticus 21:13)

785. Widow, divorced, or prostitute (Leviticus 21:14)

786. Eight days old (Leviticus 22:27)

787. Sabbath (Leviticus 23:3)

788. Passover (Leviticus 23:5)

789. Feast of Unleavened bread (Leviticus 23:6)

790. Feast of First Fruits (Leviticus 23:10)

791. Feast of Weeks (Leviticus 23:16)

792. Feast of Trumpets (Leviticus 23:24)

793. Day of Atonement (Leviticus 23:27)

794. Feast of Tabernacles/Booths (Leviticus 23:42)

795. Twelve (Leviticus 24:5)

796. A rest (Leviticus 25:4)

797. Year of Jubilee (Leviticus 25:11)

798. Israelite slaves (Leviticus 25:40–41)

799. Seven times (Leviticus 26:21)

800. Mount Sinai (Leviticus 26:46)

801. One-fifth (Leviticus 27:15, 19)

Numbers

802. A census (Numbers 1:1)

803. Two years (Numbers 1:1)

804. Twenty (Numbers 1:3)

805. The army (Numbers 1:20)

806. Judah with 74,600 (Numbers 1:26–27)

807. 600,000/603,550 (Numbers 1:46)

808. Levites (Numbers 1:51)

809. The Tabernacle (Numbers 1:53)

810. Their family banner (Numbers 2:2)

811. Gershonite, Kohathite, and Merarite (Numbers 3:18–20)

812. Gershonites (Numbers 3:25)

813. Kohathites (Numbers 3:31)

814. Merarite (Numbers 3:36)

815. Thirty to fifty (Numbers 4:30)

816. Barren (Numbers 5:27)

817. Wine/fermented drink/vinegar/grape juice (Numbers 6:3)

818. Grapes/raisins (Numbers 6:3)

819. Razor (Numbers 6:5)

820. Dead people (Numbers 6:6)

821. The fire (Numbers 6:18)

822. The Kohathites that carried the sacred objects (Numbers 7:9)

823. From between the two cherubim above the ark (Numbers 7:89)

824. Twenty-five to fifty years old (Numbers 8:24–25)

825. Fifty (Numbers 8:25)

826. An assistant (Numbers 8:26)

827. One month later (Numbers 9:11)

828. Trumpets (Numbers 10:2)

829. Silver (Numbers 10:2)

830. The leaders (Numbers 10:3)

831. The priests (Numbers 10:8)

832. Judah (Numbers 10:14)

833. Dan (Numbers 10:25)

834. Hobab (Numbers 10:29)

835. The outskirts (Numbers 11:1)

836. Taberah (Numbers 11:3)

837. Cucumbers, melons, leeks, onions, and garlic (Numbers 11:5)

838. A hand mill or mortar (Numbers 11:8)

839. Olive oil (Numbers 11:8)

840. A month (Numbers 11:20)

841. Nostrils (Numbers 11:20)

842. Seventy elders (Numbers 11:24–25)

843. Eldad and Medad (Numbers 11:26, 28)

844. Quail (Numbers 11:31)

845. Three feet or two cubits (Numbers 11:31)

846. A plague (Numbers 11:33)

847. Kibroth Hataavah (Numbers 11:34)

848. He had a Cushite wife and they wanted God to speak through them (Numbers 12:1–2)

849. Humility (Numbers 12:3)

850. Leprosy (Numbers 12:10)

851. Seven days (Numbers 12:14)

852. Twelve, one from each tribe (Numbers 13:3–15)

853. Judah (Numbers 13:6)

854. Ephraim (Numbers 13:8)

855. A single cluster of grapes (Numbers 13:23)

856. Pomegranates and figs (Numbers 13:23)

857. Forty days (Numbers 13:25)

858. Anak/Nephilim (Numbers 13:28)

859. Joshua and Caleb (Numbers 13:30)

860. Nephilim (Numbers 13:33)

861. Grasshoppers (Numbers 13:33)

862. Stone them (Numbers 14:10)

863. They didn't believe they could defeat the enemies in the Promised Land (Numbers 14:22–23)

864. Forty years (Numbers 14:33)

865. Twenty years old (Numbers 14:29)

866. One year for every day the spies were in the Promised Land (Numbers 14:34)

867. A plague (Numbers 14:37)

868. Collecting wood (Numbers 15:32)

869. The commands of the Lord (Numbers 15:39)

870. Korah, Dathan, and Abiram (Numbers 16:1)

871. 250 (Numbers 16:2)

872. Censers (Numbers 16:6–7)

873. Dathan and Abiram (Numbers 16:12)

874. The tents of Korah, Dathan, and Abiram (Numbers 16:26)

875. The earth (Numbers 16:32)

876. Fire (Numbers 16:35)

877. 250 (Numbers 16:35)

878. Eleazar (Numbers 16:36)

879. The altar (Numbers 16:38)

880. A plague (Numbers 16:46)

881. 14,700 (Numbers 16:49)

882. Twelve, one from each tribe (Numbers 17:1)

883. The leader of the tribe (Numbers 17:2)

884. The name of the leader (Numbers 17:2)

885. The ark of the covenant (Numbers 17:4)

886. Aaron's (Numbers 17:8)

887. Levites (Numbers 18:20)

888. A tenth (Numbers 18:26)

889. Red (Numbers 19:2)

890. Seven days (Numbers 19:11)

891. He struck it twice (Numbers 20:11)

892. He was barred from entering the Promised Land (Numbers 20:12)

893. Meribah (Numbers 20:13)

894. Edom (Numbers 20:18)

895. Hor (Numbers 20:25–28)

896. His priestly garments (Numbers 20:28)

897. Venomous snakes (Numbers 21:6)

898. Bronze (Numbers 21:9)

899. Look at the snake on the pole (Numbers 21:8)

900. Sihon (Numbers 21:23)

901. Heshbon (Numbers 21:26)

902. Og (Numbers 21:33)

903. Balak (Numbers 22:2)

904. Moab (Numbers 22:3)

905. Moab (Numbers 22:4)

906. Balaam (Numbers 22:5)

907. Beor (Numbers 22:5)

908. God (Numbers 22:12)

909. All his silver and gold (Numbers 22:18)

910. Two (Numbers 22:22)

911. An angel (Numbers 22:22)

912. A sword (Numbers 22:23)

913. His foot (Numbers 22:25)

914. Three (Numbers 22:28)

915. His sword (Numbers 22:29)

916. Kill him (Numbers 22:33)

917. Bamoth Baal (Numbers 22:41)

918. Seven (Numbers 23:1)

919. Three times (Numbers 23:1, 13, 29)

920. Three (Numbers 24:10)

921. A star (Numbers 24:17)

922. Baal (Numbers 25:3)

923. Phineas (Numbers 25:7-8)

924. A spear (Numbers 25:8)

925. It stopped (Numbers 25:8)

926. 24,000 (Numbers 25:9)

927. Judah (Numbers 26:22)

928. Less—601,730 compared to 603,550 (Numbers 26:51)

929. Zelophehad (Numbers 27:1)

930. Joshua (Numbers 27:19-20)

931. Eleazar (Numbers 27:22)

932. The fourteenth day (Numbers 28:16)

933. Seventh (Numbers 29:1, 7, 12)

934. Her father or husband (Numbers 30:5, 8)

935. Twelve thousand—one thousand from each tribe (Numbers 31:4)

936. Five (Numbers 31:8)

937. A sword (Numbers 31:8)

938. Reubenites, Gadites, and the half tribe of Manesseh (Numbers 32:1, 33)

939. Battle with every Israelite until the land subdued (Numbers 32:18-19)

940. 123 years old (Numbers 33:39)

941. The Mediterranean Sea (Numbers 34:6)

942. Mount Hor (Numbers 34:7)

943. The Jordan River (Numbers 34:12)

944. A city of refuge (Numbers 35:6)

945. Forty-eight (Numbers 35:7)

946. Two (Numbers 35:30)

947. Jericho (Numbers 36:13)

Deuteronomy

948. Deuteronomy

949. Eleven days (Deuteronomy 1:2)

950. The fortieth year (Deuteronomy 1:3)

951. The Anakites (Deuteronomy 2:10)

952. The Rephaites (Deuteronomy 2:11)

953. The Anakites (Deuteronomy 2:20-21)

954. Sixty cities (Deuteronomy 3:4)

955. Og, king of Bashan (Deuteronomy 3:11)

956. The Dead Sea (Deuteronomy 3:17)

957. Joshua (Deuteronomy 3:28)

958. A nation (Deuteronomy 4:34)

959. The Ten Commandments (Deuteronomy 5:6–21)

960. The third and fourth generations (Deuteronomy 5:9)

961. The ox and donkey (Deuteronomy 5:14)

962. The most important commandment (Deuteronomy 6:4–5, Matthew 22:37–38)

963. Their hands and foreheads (Deuteronomy 6:8)

964. The doorframes and gates (Deuteronomy 6:9)

965. Asherah (Deuteronomy 7:5)

966. They were more numerous (Deuteronomy 7:7)

967. Every word from the mouth of God (Deuteronomy 8:3)

968. Their clothes and sandals (Deuteronomy 8:4, 29:5)

969. Their feet (Deuteronomy 8:4)

970. Iron and copper (Deuteronomy 8:9)

971. The Anakites (Deuteronomy 9:2)

972. Two (Deuteronomy 9:9, 18)

973. Taberah, Massah, Kibroth-hattaavah, and Kadesh-barnea (Deuteronomy 9:22–23)

974. A wooden ark (Deuteronomy 10:1)

975. The Levites (Deuteronomy 10:8)

976. Rain (Deuteronomy 11:13–14)

977. The Euphrates River to the Mediterranean Sea (Deuteronomy 11:24)

978. Their sons and daughters (Deuteronomy 12:31)

979. He must be put to death (Deuteronomy 13:2–5)

980. They must be put to death (Deuteronomy 13:6–9)

981. Chew the cud and have a divided hoof (Deuteronomy 14:6)

982. Camel, rabbit, hyrax, and pig (Deuteronomy 14:7–8)

983. It has fins and scales (Deuteronomy 14:9)

984. Goat (Deuteronomy 14:21)

985. One-tenth (Deuteronomy 14:22–23)

986. Cancel it (Deuteronomy 15:1–2)

987. None (Deuteronomy 15:6)

988. Set him free (Deuteronomy 15:12)

989. Earlobe (Deuteronomy 15:17)

990. An awl (Deuteronomy 15:17)

991. Seven days (Deuteronomy 16:3)

992. Evening/twilight as the sun goes down (Deuteronomy 16:6)

993. Hold an assembly and no work (Deuteronomy 16:8)

994. Seven weeks (Deuteronomy 16:9)

995. Seven days (Deuteronomy 16:13)

996. How much God had blessed them (Deuteronomy 16:17)

997. The witnesses (Deuteronomy 17:7)

998. Horses, wives, and wealth/silver/gold (Deuteronomy 17:16–18)

999. The law (Deuteronomy 17:18)

1000. What they spoke about in the future actually comes true (Deuteronomy 18:22)

1001. An ax (Deuteronomy 19:5)

1002. The priest (Deuteronomy 20:2)

1003. Peace (Deuteronomy 20:10)

1004. Women, children, and livestock (Deuteronomy 20:14)

1005. The fruit trees (Deuteronomy 20:19)

1006. The town closest to the crime scene (Deuteronomy 21:1–3)

1007. Double (Deuteronomy 21:17)

1008. Have him stoned (Deuteronomy 21:20–21)

1009. Take the body down and bury it (Deuteronomy 21:23)

1010. Ox, sheep, or donkey (Deuteronomy 22:1–3)

1011. A cloak (Deuteronomy 22:3)

1012. Men's clothes (Deuteronomy 22:5)

1013. A parapet/a short border wall (Deuteronomy 22:8)

1014. Ox and donkey (Deuteronomy 22:10)

1015. Wool and linen (Deuteronomy 22:11)

1016. Tassels (Deuteronomy 22:12)

1017. The town elders with the young woman's father and mother (Deuteronomy 22:15)

1018. The cloth (Deuteronomy 22:17)

1019. One hundred shekels of silver (Deuteronomy 22:19)

1020. She was stoned to death (Deuteronomy 22:20)

1021. At the door of her father's house (Deuteronomy 22:21)

1022. Ammonite and Moabite (Deuteronomy 23:3)

1023. Edomite and Egyptian (Deuteronomy 23:7–8)

1024. Outside the camp (Deuteronomy 23:12)

1025. A sickle (Deuteronomy 23:25)

1026. War (Deuteronomy 24:5)

1027. Forty lashes (Deuteronomy 25:3)

1028. Muzzle the ox (Deuteronomy 25:4)

1029. It was cut off (Deuteronomy 25:11–12)

1030. The Levite, the foreigner, the fatherless, and the widow (Deuteronomy 26:12)

1031. Plaster (Deuteronomy 27:2)

1032. Mount Ebal (Deuteronomy 27:4)

1033. The basket and kneading trough (Deuteronomy 28:17)

1034. Locusts (Deuteronomy 28:42)

1035. Afterbirth (Deuteronomy 28:57)

1036. Wine or fermented drink (Deuteronomy 29:6)

1037. The Reubenites, Gadites, and the half tribe of Manasseh (Deuteronomy 29:8)

1038. They were blotted out (Deuteronomy 29:20)

1039. The heavens and the sea (Deuteronomy 30:12–13)

1040. 120 years old (Deuteronomy 31:2)

1041. Joshua (Deuteronomy 31:7)

1042. Seven years (Deuteronomy 31:10–11)

1043. Festival of the Tabernacles (Deuteronomy 31:10)

1044. Poison (Deuteronomy 32:32)

1045. Mount Nebo (Deuteronomy 32:50)

1046. Mount Hor (Deuteronomy 32:50)

1047. Simeon (Deuteronomy 33)

1048. Joseph (Deuteronomy 33:17)

1049. Dan (Deuteronomy 33:22)

1050. God (Deuteronomy 34:6)

1051. Moab in a place no one knows (Deuteronomy 34:6)

1052. 120 years old (Deuteronomy 34:7)

1053. His sight/eyes (Deuteronomy 34:7)

1054. Thirty days (Deuteronomy 34:8)

1055. He laid his hands on him (Deuteronomy 34:9)

Joshua

1056. The Jordan River (Joshua 1:2)

1057. Be strong and courageous (Joshua 1:6, 7, 9, 18)

1058. The Book of the Law (Joshua 1:8)

1059. Two (Joshua 2:1)

1060. Rahab (Joshua 2:1)

1061. On the roof under stalks of flax (Joshua 2:6)

1062. The city wall (Joshua 2:15)

1063. A scarlet cord/rope (Joshua 2:18)

1064. The Levitical priests (Joshua 2:3)

1065. About a thousand yards/three thousand feet/two thousand cubits (Joshua 3:4)

1066. The ark of the covenant (Joshua 3:11)

1067. It stopped flowing upstream (Joshua 3:13)

1068. Adam (Joshua 3:16)

1069. In the middle of the river (Joshua 3:17)

1070. Twelve stones (Joshua 4:8)

1071. 40,000 men (Joshua 4:13)

1072. Gilgal (Joshua 4:20)

1073. They got circumcised (Joshua 5:2)

1074. Passover (Joshua 5:10)

1075. Manna (Joshua 5:12)

1076. Neither (Joshua 5:14)

1077. The commander of the Lord's army (Joshua 5:14)

1078. Once a day (Joshua 6:3)

1079. Seven days (Joshua 6:4)

1080. Trumpets of ram's horns (Joshua 6:4)

1081. Seven times (Joshua 6:4)

1082. Seven priests (Joshua 6:13)

1083. Shouting and horn blowing (Joshua 6:16)

1084. The devoted things/idols (Joshua 6:18)

1085. Gold, silver, bronze, and iron (Joshua 6:19)

1086. Cattle, sheep, and donkeys (Joshua 6:21)

1087. Her mother, father, brothers, and sisters (Joshua 6:23)

1088. Rebuild it (Joshua 6:26)

1089. Their first and last born son (Joshua 6:26)

1090. Achan (Joshua 7:1)

1091. Judah (Joshua 7:1)

1092. Ai (Joshua 7:4)

1093. Three thousand men (Joshua 7:4)

1094. Thirty-six men (Joshua 7:4)

1095. Amorites (Joshua 7:7)

1096. A robe, gold, and silver (Joshua 7:21)

1097. Babylonia (Joshua 7:21)

1098. Two hundred shekels (Joshua 7:21)

1099. Fifty shekels (Joshua 7:21)

1100. In the ground under his tent (Joshua 7:21)

1101. The valley of Achor (Joshua 7:24)

1102. Stoned them (Joshua 7:25)

1103. The goods and cattle (Joshua 8:2)

1104. A javelin (Joshua 8:18)

1105. The king (Joshua 8:23)

1106. The law of Moses (Joshua 8:32)

1107. The Gibeonites (Joshua 9:6)

1108. Bread (Joshua 9:12)

1109. They did not consult the Lord (Joshua 9:14)

1110. Woodcutters and water carriers (Joshua 9:23)

1111. Large hailstones (Joshua 10:11)

1112. God stopped the sun in the sky (Joshua 10:13)

1113. Five kings (Joshua 10:16)

1114. A cave (Joshua 10:16)

1115. The horses (Joshua 11:6)

1116. Their chariots (Joshua 11:6)

1117. Thirty-one kings (Joshua 12:24)

1118. Old (Joshua 13:1)

1119. Nine and a half tribes (Joshua 14:2)

1120. Two and a half tribes (Joshua 14:3)

1121. The Levite tribe (Joshua 14:3–4)

1122. Forty years old (Joshua 14:7)

1123. Eighty-five years old (Joshua 14:10)

1124. The Anakites (Joshua 14:12)

1125. Hebron (Joshua 14:13)

1126. Achsah (Joshua 15:16)

1127. Othniel (Joshua 15:17)

1128. Jerusalem (Joshua 15:63)

1129. The Jebusites (Joshua 15:63)

1130. Luz (Joshua 16:2)

1131. Makir (Joshua 17:1)

1132. Canaanites (Joshua 17:13)

1133. Three men (Joshua 18:4)

1134. Casting lots (Joshua 18:10)

1135. Benjamin (Joshua 18:28)

1136. Simeon (Joshua 19:9)

1137. A town called Timnath Serah (Joshua 19:50)

1138. The elders (Joshua 20:4)

1139. Forty-eight (Joshua 21:41)

1140. An altar (Joshua 22:11–12)

1141. Burt offerings or sacrifices (Joshua 22:26)

1142. An altar (Joshua 22:34)

1143. Thorns (Joshua 23:13)

1144. He and his house (Joshua 24:15)

1145. 110 years old (Joshua 24:29)

1146. Joseph's bones (Joshua 24:32)

Judges

1147. His thumbs and big toes (Judges 1:7)

1148. Judah (Judges 1:8)

1149. Othniel (Judges 1:12)

1150. Luz (Judges 1:23)

1151. They didn't drive out all the former inhabitants (Judges 1:27–33)

1152. Bokim (Judges 2:5)

1153. Baal and Ashtoreth (Judges 2:13)

1154. They returned to their corrupt ways (Judges 2:19)

1155. Caleb (Judges 3:9)

1156. City of Palms/Jericho (Judges 3:13)

1157. Moab (Judges 3:14)

1158. He was left handed (Judges 3:15)

1159. Benjamin (Judges 3:15)

1160. To his right thigh (Judges 3:16)

1161. He was fat (Judges 3:17)

1162. "I have a secret message from God for you" (Judges 3:20)

1163. His belly (Judges 3:21)

1164. Relieving himself (Judges 3:24)

1165. Ten thousand (Judges 3:29)

1166. Oxgoad (Judges 3:31)

1167. Jabin (Judges 4:2)

1168. Sisera (Judges 4:2)

1169. Chariots (Judges 4:3)

1170. Lappidoth (Judges 4:4)

1171. Barak (Judges 4:6)

1172. Jael (Judges 4:17)

1173. Heber (Judges 4:17)

1174. Milk (Judges 4:19)

1175. A tent peg (Judges 4:21)

1176. Barak (Judges 5:1)

1177. When the crops were planted (Judges 6:3)

1178. Joash the Abiezrite (Judges 6:11)

1179. A winepress (Judges 6:11)

1180. Manasseh (Judges 6:15)

1181. The Midianites (Judges 6:16)

1182. Goat (Judges 6:19)

1183. Set it on fire (Judges 6:21)

1184. A staff (Judges 6:21)

1185. The Lord is peace (Judges 6:24)

1186. Baal (Judges 6:28)

1187. Asherah (Judges 6:28)

1188. His father, Joash (Judges 6:30–31)

1189. Jerubbaal/Jerub-Baal (Judges 6:32)

1190. Jezreel (Judges 6:33)

1191. A trumpet (Judges 6:34)

1192. A wool fleece (Judges 6:37)

1193. Fleece (Judges 6:37)

1194. A bowlful (Judges 6:38)

1195. He asked all that were afraid to leave (Judges 7:3)

1196. Those that brought the water to their mouths (Judges 7:6)

1197. Three hundred men (Judges 7:6)

1198. Purah (Judges 7:10)

1199. A round loaf of barley bread (Judges 7:13)

1200. Trumpets, jars, and torches (Judges 7:16)

1201. Oreb and Zeeb (Judges 7:25)

1202. Sukkoth (Judges 8:5)

1203. Zebah and Zalmunna (Judges 8:10)

1204. Briers and thorns (Judges 8:7)

1205. Peniel (Judges 8:8)

1206. A tower (Judges 8:9)

1207. Jether (Judges 8:20)

1208. Their earrings (Judges 8:24)

1209. An ephod (Judges 8:27)

1210. Abimelech (Judges 8:31)

1211. Shechem (Judges 9:3)

1212. Seventy sons (Judges 9:5)

1213. Jotham (Judges 9:5)

1214. The trees (Judges 9:8)

1215. Shechem (Judges 9:23)

1216. Gaal (Judges 9:26)

1217. Shechem (Judges 9:49)

1218. A millstone (Judges 9:53)

1219. A sword (Judges 9:54)

1220. His servant/armor-bearer (Judges 9:54)

1221. Issachar (Judges 10:1)

1222. Thirty sons (and thirty donkeys) (Judges 10:5)

1223. Gilead (Judges 11:1)

1224. A prostitute (Judges 11:1)

1225. Ammonites (Judges 11:6)

1226. That he would sacrifice the first thing that came out of his door when he returned home (Judges 11:31)

1227. His daughter (Judges 11:34)

1228. Two months (Judges 11:37)

1229. That she never married (Judges 11:37)

1230. Ephraim (Judges 12:1)

1231. Shibboleth (Judges 12:6)

1232. Thirty daughters (Judges 12:8)

1233. Seventy donkeys (Judges 12:14)

1234. Zorah (Judges 13:2)

1235. Manoah (Judges 13:2)

1236. Dan (Judges 13:2)

1237. Wine/fermented drink, unclean foods, and a razor to cut his hair (Judges 13:4–5)

1238. Three times (Judges 13:3, 9, 13)

1239. A flame (Judges 13:20)

1240. Timnah (Judges 14:1–2)

1241. Philistine (Judges 14:1)

1242. A lion (Judges 14:6)

1243. Bees (Judges 14:8)

1244. Honey (Judges 14:9)

1245. Thirty linen garments and thirty sets of clothes (Judges 14:12)

1246. "Out of the eater, something to eat: out of the strong, something sweet" (Judges 14:14)

1247. Seven days (Judges 14:17)

1248. He stripped thirty men from Ashkelon of their clothes (Judges 14:19)

1249. Gave her away (Judges 15:2)

1250. Three hundred foxes (Judges 15:4)

1251. Torches (Judges 15:4)

1252. The Philistine fields, vineyards, and olive groves (Judges 15:5)

1253. Burned them to death (Judges 15:6)

1254. Judah (Judges 15:11)

1255. A thousand men (Judges 15:15)

1256. A donkey (Judges 15:15)

1257. A prostitute (Judges 16:1)

1258. Gaza (Judges 16:1–3)

1259. A hill facing Hebron (Judges 16:3)

1260. Valley of Sorek (Judges 16:4)

1261. Eleven hundred shekels each (Judges 16:5)

1262. He needed to be tied with seven fresh bowstrings (Judges 16:7)

1263. He needed to be tied with new unused ropes (Judges 16:11)

1264. He needed seven braids of his hair weaved into a loom and tightened with a pin (Judges 16:13)

1265. Nagging (Judges 16:16)

1266. He told her the truth the fourth time (Judges 16:15–17)

1267. No razor had touched his head (Judges 16:17)

1268. They gouged out his eyes (Judges 16:21)

1269. Bronze shackles (Judges 16:21)

1270. Grind grain (Judges 16:21)

1271. Dagon (Judges 16:23)

1272. The Philistine temple (Judges 16:26)

1273. Three thousand (Judges 16:27)

1274. The pillars (Judges 16:29–30)

1275. His father Manoah (Judges 16:31)

1276. Twenty years (Judges 16:31)

1277. Micah (Judges 17:4)

1278. An ephod and some household gods (Judges 17:5)

1279. Levi (Judges 17:12)

1280. Dan (Judges 18:1)

1281. Ephraim (Judges 18:2)

1282. Micah (Judges 18:15–17)

1283. Dan (Judges 18:27–28)

1284. Shiloh (Judges 18:31)

1285. Levi (Judges 19:1–2)

1286. Jerusalem (Judges 19:10)

1287. An old man (Judges 19:16)

1288. Gibeah (Judges 19:16)

1289. Raped her (Judges 19:25)

1290. Twelve parts (Judges 19:29)

1291. Benjamin (Judges 20:12)

1292. They were left handed (Judges 20:16)

1293. A hair (Judges 20:16)

1294. Three days (Judges 20:30)

1295. Their daughters (Judges 21:1, 7, 18)

1296. Benjamin (Judges 21:3)

1297. Jabesh Gilead and Shiloh (Judges 21:12, 21)

1298. Whatever they saw fit (Judges 21:25)

Ruth

1299. The judges (Ruth 1:1)

1300. Bethlehem (Ruth 1:1)

1301. Moab (Ruth 1:1)

1302. A famine (Ruth 1:1)

1303. Elimelech (Ruth 1:2)

1304. Mahlon and Kilion (Ruth 1:2)

1305. Ruth and Orpah (Ruth 1:4)

1306. Moab (Ruth 1:4)

1307. They all died (Ruth 1:3–5)

1308. Bethlehem (Ruth 1:19)

1309. Mara/bitter (Ruth 1:20)

1310. Boaz (Ruth 2:3)

1311. Gleaning (Ruth 2:7, 17)

1312. Barley (Ruth 2:17)

1313. Boaz (Ruth 2:20)

1314. Naomi (Ruth 3:3)

1315. Wash, perfume, put on new clothes (Ruth 3:3)

1316. His feet (Ruth 3:8)

1317. The threshing floor (Ruth 3:14)

1318. Barley (Ruth 3:15)

1319. Ten (Ruth 4:2)

1320. A sandal (Ruth 4:7)

1321. Obed (Ruth 4:17)

1322. Jesse (Ruth 4:17)

1323. David (Ruth 4:17)

1324. David (Ruth 4:22)

1 Samuel

1325. A Zuphite (1 Samuel 1:1)

1326. Peninnah and Hannah (1 Samuel 1:2)

1327. Hophni and Phinehas (1 Samuel 1:3)

1328. Because he loved her (1 Samuel 1:5)

1329. Eli (1 Samuel 1:3)

1330. She was unable to have a child (1 Samuel 1:5)

1331. A razor (1 Samuel 1:11)

1332. Drunk (1 Samuel 1:12)

1333. Wine or beer (1 Samuel 1:15)

1334. Samuel (1 Samuel 1:20)

1335. "Because I asked for him/heard by God" (1 Samuel 1:20)

1336. Shiloh (1 Samuel 1:24)

1337. Three-year-old bull, an ephah of flour, and a skin of wine (1 Samuel 1:24)

1338. A little robe (1 Samuel 2:18)

1339. Three sons and two daughters (1 Samuel 2:21)

1340. Sleeping with the women that worked at the entrance of the tent of meeting (1 Samuel 2:22)

1341. The choice parts of every offering (1 Samuel 2:29)

1342. On the same day (1 Samuel 2:34)

1343. The Lord (1 Samuel 3:6)

1344. Eli (1 Samuel 3:5)

1345. Four times (1 Samuel 3:8, 10)

1346. The ark (1 Samuel 4:11)

1347. Hophni and Phineas (1 Samuel 4:11)

1348. Eli (1 Samuel 4:18)

1349. Ninety-eight years old (1 Samuel 4:15)

1350. He fell off his chair and broke his neck (1 Samuel 4:18)

1351. He was heavy (1 Samuel 4:18)

1352. Ichabod (1 Samuel 4:21)

1353. "No glory/the glory of the Lord has left" (1 Samuel 4:21)

1354. Ashdod (1 Samuel 5:1)

1355. Dagon (1 Samuel 5:2)

1356. Face down before the ark (1 Samuel 5:3)

1357. His head and hands (1 Samuel 5:4)

1358. The threshold (1 Samuel 5:5)

1359. Tumors (1 Samuel 5:6)

1360. Gath (1 Samuel 5:8)

1361. Ekron (1 Samuel 5:10)

1362. Seven months (1 Samuel 6:1)

1363. Five gold tumors and five gold rats (1 Samuel 6:4)

1364. Beth Shemesh (1 Samuel 6:9)

1365. Five rulers/cities hit by plagues (1 Samuel 6:17)

1366. They looked inside the ark (1 Samuel 6:19)

1367. Seventy men that looked inside the ark (1 Samuel 6:19)

1368. Abinadab (1 Samuel 7:1)

1369. Twenty years (1 Samuel 7:2)

1370. Baal and Ashtoreth (1 Samuel 7:4)

1371. Ebenezer (1 Samuel 7:12)

1372. "God helps us/stone of help" (1 Samuel 7:12)

1373. Ramah (1 Samuel 7:17)

1374. Joel and Abijah (1 Samuel 8:2)

1375. A king (1 Samuel 8:5)

1376. They wanted to be like all the other nations (1 Samuel 8:20)

1377. Kish (1 Samuel 9:1)

1378. Benjamin (1 Samuel 9:1–2)

1379. He was a head taller (1 Samuel 9:2)

1380. Donkeys (1 Samuel 9:3, 20)

1381. Seers (1 Samuel 9:9)

1382. The tribe was the smallest of all the others (1 Samuel 9:21)

1383. Flask of olive oil (1 Samuel 10:1)

1384. Near the tomb of Rachel (1 Samuel 10:2)

1385. Prophets (1 Samuel 10:10)

1386. Prophesying (1 Samuel 10:11)

1387. In the supplies/baggage (1 Samuel 10:22)

1388. Nahash (1 Samuel 11:1)

1389. Gouge out their right eye (1 Samuel 11:2)

1390. Thunder and rain (1 Samuel 12:18)

1391. Thirty years old (1 Samuel 13:1)

1392. Forty-two years (1 Samuel 13:1)

1393. Jonathan (1 Samuel 13:2)

1394. Samuel (1 Samuel 13:8)

1395. He sacrificed a burnt offering before Samuel arrived (1 Samuel 13:12)

1396. Samuel (1 Samuel 13:14)

1397. The Philistines (1 Samuel 13:20)

1398. Plow points, mattocks, axes, sickles, and forks (1 Samuel 13:20–21)

1399. A sword/spear (1 Samuel 13:22)

1400. Jonathan (1 Samuel 14:4–14)

1401. Jonathan (1 Samuel 14:27–28)

1402. Honey (1 Samuel 14:29)

1403. Cast lots (1 Samuel 14:42)

1404. Three (1 Samuel 14:49)

1405. Michal (1 Samuel 14:49)

1406. Ahinoam (1 Samuel 14:50)

1407. Abner (1 Samuel 14:50)

1408. Agag, king of the Amalekites (1 Samuel 15:3, 8–9)

1409. The bleating of sheep (1 Samuel 15:14)

1410. Samuel (1 Samuel 15:33)

1411. He regretted it (1 Samuel 15:35)

1412. Bethlehem (1 Samuel 16:1)

1413. Seven (1 Samuel 16:10)

1414. Tending sheep (1 Samuel 16:11)

1415. Oil (1 Samuel 16:13)

1416. An evil spirit (1 Samuel 16:14–16)

1417. The harp/lyre (1 Samuel 16:18)

1418. His armor-bearer (1 Samuel 16:21)

1419. Valley of Elah (1 Samuel 17:2)

1420. Gath (1 Samuel 17:4)

1421. Nine feet tall (1 Samuel 17:4)

1422. Five thousand shekels—about 125 pounds (1 Samuel 17:6)

1423. A weaver's rod (1 Samuel 17:7)

1424. Six hundred shekels—about fifteen pounds (1 Samuel 17:7)

1425. Eliab (1 Samuel 17:13)

1426. Forty days (1 Samuel 17:16)

1427. Food (1 Samuel 17:17)

1428. Great wealth, his daughter in marriage, and tax exemption (1 Samuel 17:25)

1429. Lion and bear (1 Samuel 17:34)

1430. Tunic, coat of armor, and a bronze helmet (1 Samuel 17:38)

1431. Five stones (1 Samuel 17:40)

1432. The stream (1 Samuel 17:40)

1433. Staff, shepherd's bag, and sling (1 Samuel 17:40)

1434. A dog (1 Samuel 17:43)

1435. Sword, spear, and javelin (1 Samuel 17:45)

1436. The forehead (1 Samuel 17:49)

1437. He cut off Goliath's head (1 Samuel 17:51)

1438. Goliath's sword (1 Samuel 17:51)

1439. To Jerusalem (1 Samuel 17:54)

1440. In his tent (1 Samuel 17:54)

1441. Abner (1 Samuel 17:55)

1442. Robe, tunic, sword, bow, and belt (1 Samuel 18:4)

1443. Tens of thousands (1 Samuel 18:7)

1444. An evil spirit (1 Samuel 18:10)

1445. A spear (1 Samuel 18:11)

1446. Merab (1 Samuel 18:19)

1447. Adriel of Meholah (1 Samuel 18:19)

1448. Michal (1 Samuel 18:20)

1449. One hundred Philistine foreskins (1 Samuel 18:25)

1450. Two hundred (1 Samuel 18:27)

1451. Kill David (1 Samuel 19:1)

1452. Three (1 Samuel 18:11; 19:10)

1453. Michal (1 Samuel 19:11–12)

1454. An idol, covered with a garment and goat's hair (1 Samuel 19:13)

1455. Prophesying (1 Samuel 19:21)

1456. Kindness/love (1 Samuel 20:15)

1457. The New Moon festival (1 Samuel 20:18)

1458. He fired arrows at a target (1 Samuel 20:21–22)

1459. Nob (1 Samuel 21:1)

1460. Bread (1 Samuel 21:3, 6)

1461. Doeg the Edomite (1 Samuel 21:7)

1462. Goliath's sword (1 Samuel 21:9)

1463. The ephod (1 Samuel 21:9)

1464. Achish (1 Samuel 21:10)

1465. A madman (1 Samuel 21:13)

1466. Made marks on the doors and let saliva run down his beard (1 Samuel 21:13)

1467. Doeg the Edomite (1 Samuel 22:9, 18)

1468. Eighty-five priests (1 Samuel 22:18)

1469. Nob (1 Samuel 22:19)

1470. Abiathar (1 Samuel 22:20)

1471. The ephod (1 Samuel 23:6)

1472. En Gedi (1 Samuel 24:1–3)

1473. Relieving himself (1 Samuel 24:3)

1474. His robe (1 Samuel 24:4)

1475. Nabal (1 Samuel 25:2–3, 11)

1476. Abigail (1 Samuel 25:3)

1477. Abigail (1 Samuel 25:18, 23–24)

1478. "Fool" (1 Samuel 25:25)

1479. A banquet (1 Samuel 25:36–37)

1480. It failed him (1 Samuel 25:37)

1481. He married her (1 Samuel 25:43)

1482. Ahimoam (1 Samuel 25:43)

1483. Paltiel (1 Samuel 25:44)

1484. Abishai (1 Samuel 26:6)

1485. His spear and water jug (1 Samuel 26:12)

1486. Abner (1 Samuel 26:14–15)

1487. Ziklag (1 Samuel 27:6)

1488. Ramah (1 Samuel 28:3)

1489. Spiritists and mediums (1 Samuel 28:3)

1490. Dreams, Urim, or prophets (1 Samuel 28:6)

1491. Endor (1 Samuel 28:7)

1492. Samuel (1 Samuel 28:11)

1493. An old man wearing a robe (1 Samuel 28:14)

1494. Saul and his sons (1 Samuel 28:19)

1495. The Philistine commanders (1 Samuel 29:3, 9)

1496. The Amalekites (1 Samuel 30:1–2)

1497. Abiathar, son of Ahimelech (1 Samuel 30:7)

1498. Two hundred (1 Samuel 30:10)

1499. An Egyptian slave (1 Samuel 30:13)

1500. Philistines (1 Samuel 31:2)

1501. Jonathan, Abinadab, and Malki-Shua (1 Samuel 31:2)

1502. Archers (1 Samuel 31:3)

1503. His armor-bearer (1 Samuel 31:4)

1504. He fell on his sword (1 Samuel 31:4)

1505. Ashtoreth (1 Samuel 31:10)

1506. Beth Shan (1 Samuel 31:10)

1507. Jabesh Gilead (1 Samuel 31:11–12)

1508. Tamarisk (1 Samuel 31:13)

2 Samuel

1509. Amalekite (2 Samuel 1:8)
1510. He said he killed Saul when he found him lying on his sword (2 Samuel 1:10)
1511. His crown and his band on his arm (2 Samuel 1:10)
1512. He had him killed (2 Samuel 1:15)
1513. Hebron (2 Samuel 2:4)
1514. Jabesh Gilead (2 Samuel 2:4)
1515. Abner (2 Samuel 2:8)
1516. Ish-Bosheth (2 Samuel 2:8–9)
1517. Ephraim, Benjamin, and all Israel (2 Samuel 2:9)
1518. Two years (2 Samuel 2:10)
1519. Seven years and six months (2 Samuel 2:11)
1520. Gibeon (2 Samuel 2:13)
1521. Twelve (2 Samuel 2:15)
1522. Joab, Abishai, and Asahel (2 Samuel 2:18)
1523. Asahel (2 Samuel 2:18)
1524. Abner (2 Samuel 2:21)
1525. A spear (2 Samuel 2:23)
1526. Nineteen (2 Samuel 2:30)
1527. 360 men (2 Samuel 2:31)
1528. Amnon (2 Samuel 3:2)
1529. Ahinoam (2 Samuel 3:2)
1530. Kileab (2 Samuel 3:3)
1531. Abigail (2 Samuel 3:3)
1532. Absalom (2 Samuel 3:3)
1533. Ahimoam, Abigail, Maakah, Haggith, Abital, and Eglah (2 Samuel 3:2–5)
1534. Eglah (2 Samuel 3:5)
1535. Michal (2 Samuel 3:14)
1536. Paltiel (2 Samuel 3:15)
1537. Abner (2 Samuel 3:17–18)
1538. Joab (2 Samuel 3:27, 30)
1539. A nurse (2 Samuel 4:4)
1540. Saul and Jonathan were dead (2 Samuel 4:4)
1541. Mephibosheth (2 Samuel 4:4)
1542. Recab and Baanah (2 Samuel 4:6)
1543. In bed (2 Samuel 4:7)
1544. Ish-Bosheth's head (2 Samuel 4:8)
1545. He had them killed (2 Samuel 4:12)
1546. Thirty years old (2 Samuel 5:4)
1547. Forty years (2 Samuel 5:4)
1548. Seven and a half years (2 Samuel 5:5)
1549. Thirty-three years (2 Samuel 5:5)
1550. The Jebusites (2 Samuel 5:6)
1551. The City of David (2 Samuel 5:9)
1552. Tyre (2 Samuel 5:11)
1553. Hiram (2 Samuel 5:11)
1554. A new cart (2 Samuel 6:3)
1555. Abinadab (2 Samuel 6:3)
1556. Uzzah (2 Samuel 6:7–8)
1557. The oxen (2 Samuel 6:6)
1558. Obed-Edom (2 Samuel 6:11)

1559. Linen ephod (2 Samuel 6:14)

1560. His wife Michal (2 Samuel 6:16)

1561. Loaf of bread, cake of raisins, and cake of dates (2 Samuel 6:19)

1562. She didn't have any more children (2 Samuel 6:23)

1563. Nathan (2 Samuel 7:2)

1564. In a tent (2 Samuel 7:2)

1565. His house, kingdom, and throne (2 Samuel 7:16)

1566. Every two would die, but the third would live (2 Samuel 8:2)

1567. Head of the army (2 Samuel 8:16)

1568. Priests (2 Samuel 8:17)

1569. Ziba (2 Samuel 9:2)

1570. Mephibosheth (2 Samuel 9:6)

1571. His son (2 Samuel 9:6)

1572. He restored his land and allowed him to eat at the king's table (2 Samuel 9:7)

1573. A dead dog (2 Samuel 9:8)

1574. Mika (2 Samuel 9:12)

1575. He was lame in both feet (2 Samuel 9:13)

1576. Hanun (2 Samuel 10:4)

1577. Shaved off half their beards and cut off their garments at the buttocks (2 Samuel 10:4)

1578. Jericho (2 Samuel 10:5)

1579. The Arameans (2 Samuel 10:6, 19)

1580. The spring (2 Samuel 11:1)

1581. The Ammonites (2 Samuel 11:1)

1582. Bathsheba (2 Samuel 11:3)

1583. Uriah the Hittite (2 Samuel 11:3)

1584. She was pregnant (2 Samuel 11:5)

1585. His master's servants (2 Samuel 11:9)

1586. Get him drunk (2 Samuel 11:13)

1587. Joab (2 Samuel 11:16)

1588. Got married (2 Samuel 11:27)

1589. Nathan (2 Samuel 12:1)

1590. A lamb/ewe (2 Samuel 12:4)

1591. The sword (2 Samuel 12:10)

1592. He died (2 Samuel 12:18)

1593. Solomon (2 Samuel 12:24)

1594. Jedidah (2 Samuel 12:25)

1595. Tamar (2 Samuel 13:1)

1596. Amnon, her half brother (2 Samuel 13:1)

1597. Sick (2 Samuel 13:5)

1598. Absalom (2 Samuel 13:28)

1599. All his sons (2 Samuel 13:30)

1600. Joab (2 Samuel 14:2)

1601. Tekoa (2 Samuel 14:2)

1602. Five pounds (2 Samuel 14:26)

1603. Tamar (2 Samuel 14:27)

1604. Joab (2 Samuel 14:30)

1605. The side of the road to the city gates (2 Samuel 15:2)

1606. Absalom (2 Samuel 15:10)

1607. Hebron (2 Samuel 15:10)

1608. The ark (2 Samuel 15:25)

1609. Ziba (2 Samuel 16:3)

1610. Shimei (2 Samuel 16:5–6)

1611. Absalom (2 Samuel 16:8)

1612. Abishai (2 Samuel 16:9)

1613. David's concubines (2 Samuel 16:22)

1614. Ahithophel (2 Samuel 16:23)

1615. Hushai (2 Samuel 17:14)

1616. A well (2 Samuel 17:18)

1617. Hung himself (2 Samuel 17:23)

1618. Amasa (2 Samuel 17:25)

1619. Joab, Abishai, and Ittai (2 Samuel 18:2)

1620. Absalom (2 Samuel 18:9)

1621. Oak (2 Samuel 18:9)

1622. A mule (2 Samuel 18:9)

1623. Joab (2 Samuel 18:14)

1624. Ahimaaz and a Cushite (2 Samuel 18:19)

1625. Joab (2 Samuel 19:5–7)

1626. Shimei (2 Samuel 19:18–20)

1627. Ziba (Samuel 19:26–27)

1628. Barzillai (2 Samuel 19:31–32)

1629. Sheba (2 Samuel 20:1)

1630. Amasa (2 Samuel 20:10)

1631. Joab (2 Samuel 20:15)

1632. A wise woman (2 Samuel 20:16)

1633. His head (2 Samuel 20:22)

1634. The Gibeonites (2 Samuel 21:1–2)

1635. Seven male descendants from Saul (2 Samuel 21:6)

1636. Mephibosheth, son of Jonathan (2 Samuel 21:7)

1637. The bones of Saul and Jonathan (2 Samuel 21:13)

1638. Elhanan (2 Samuel 21:19)

1639. Twenty-four digits, six on each hand and foot (2 Samuel 21:20–21)

1640. Rapha (2 Samuel 21:22)

1641. His righteousness (2 Samuel 22:21)

1642. David's (2 Samuel 23:1)

1643. Eight hundred men (2 Samuel 23:8)

1644. Eleazar (2 Samuel 23:10)

1645. Water from a well (2 Samuel 23:15)

1646. Abishai (2 Samuel 23:18–19)

1647. Benaiah (2 Samuel 23:20–21)

1648. Uriah the Hittite (2 Samuel 23:39)

1649. Thirty-seven (2 Samuel 23:39)

1650. He counted his troops (2 Samuel 24:1, 10)

1651. Gad (2 Samuel 24:11)

1652. Three years of famine, three months of fleeing from enemies, and three days of plague (2 Samuel 24:13)

1653. The plague (2 Samuel 24:15)

1654. Seventy thousand (2 Samuel 24:15)

1655. An angel of the Lord (2 Samuel 24:16–17)

1656. A threshing floor (2 Samuel 24:18)

1657. An altar (2 Samuel 24:21)

1 Kings

1658. Abishag (1 Kings 1:3)

1659. Adonijah (1 Kings 1:5)

1660. Joab and Abiathar (1 Kings 1:7)

1661. Nathan (1 Kings 1:11–12)

1662. Bathsheba (1 Kings 1:11)

1663. Zadok (1 Kings 1:38)

1664. Adonijah (1 Kings 1:50)

1665. Joab (1 King 2:5–6)

1666. Abner and Amasa (1 Kings 2:5)

1667. The City of David (1 Kings 2:10)

1668. Thirty-three years (1 Kings 2:11)

1669. Forty years (1 Kings 2:11)

1670. Abishag (1 Kings 2:17)

1671. His mother, Bathsheba (1 Kings 2:19)

1672. Death (1 Kings 2:25)

1673. Abiathar (1 Kings 2:26)

1674. Benaiah (1 Kings 2:25, 34, 46)

1675. Adonijah, Joab, and Shimei (1 Kings 2:25, 34, 46)

1676. Joab (1 Kings 2:28)

1677. Benaiah (1 Kings 2:35)

1678. Zadok (1 Kings 2:35)

1679. Shimei (1 Kings 2:46)

1680. Pharaoh, king of Egypt (1 Kings 3:1)

1681. Gibeon (1 Kings 3:5)

1682. A wise/discerning heart (1 Kings 3:9)

1683. Wealth, long life, and death of enemies (1 Kings 3:11)

1684. Prostitutes (1 Kings 3:16)

1685. A sword (1 Kings 3:24)

1686. Cut the child in half (1 Kings 3:25)

1687. Give the child to the other (1 Kings 3:26)

1688. Four thousand stalls (1 Kings 4:26)

1689. His wisdom and breadth of understanding (1 Kings 4:29)

1690. The east and Egypt (1 Kings 4:30)

1691. Three thousand proverbs (1 King 4:32)

1692. 1,005 songs (1 Kings 4:32)

1693. Hyssop that grows out of walls (1 Kings 4:33)

1694. Animals, birds, reptiles, and fish (1 Kings 4:33)

1695. Hiram (1 Kings 5:1)

1696. Cedars of Lebanon (1 Kings 5:6)

1697. Mediterranean Sea (1 Kings 5:9)

1698. Juniper/pine logs (1 Kings 5:10)

1699. Thirty thousand laborers (1 Kings 5:13)

1700. One out of every three months (1 Kings 5:14)

1701. Seventy thousand carriers (1 Kings 5:15)

1702. Eighty thousand stonecutters (1 Kings 5:15)

1703. 3,300 foremen (1 Kings 5:16)

1704. Byblos (1 Kings 5:18)

1705. 480 years (1 Kings 6:1)

1706. Four years (1 Kings 6:1)

1707. The quarry (1 Kings 6:7)

1708. Hammer, chisel, or any iron tool (1 Kings 6:7)

1709. Cedar (1 Kings 6:10, 14)

1710. Gold (1 Kings 6:21)

1711. Olive wood (1 Kings 6:23–24)

1712. Seven years (1 Kings 6:38)

1713. Thirteen years (1 Kings 7:1)

1714. The Hall of Justice (1 Kings 7:7)

1715. Pharaoh's daughter (1 Kings 7:8)

1716. Huram (1 Kings 7:13)

1717. Pillars (1 Kings 7:21)

1718. The two stone tablets (1 Kings 8:9)

1719. Sheep and goats (1 Kings 8:63)

1720. Fourteen days (1 Kings 8:65)

1721. The temple (1 Kings 9:6–8)

1722. Twenty towns in Galilee (1 Kings 9:11)

1723. Gold (1 Kings 9:26)

1724. Queen of Sheba (1 Kings 10:1)

1725. Spices (1 Kings 10:10)

1726. Almugwood (1 Kings 10:12)

1727. 666 talents (1 Kings 10:14)

1728. Gold (1 Kings 10:16–17)

1729. Gold and ivory (1 Kings 10:18)

1730. Lions (1 Kings 10:19–20)

1731. Silver (1 Kings 10:21)

1732. Apes and baboons (1 Kings 10:22)

1733. Silver (1 Kings 10:27)

1734. Horses (1 Kings 10:26, 28)

1735. Seven hundred wives (1 Kings 11:3)

1736. Three hundred concubines (1 Kings 11:3)

1737. Ashtoreth, Molek, and Chemosh (1 Kings 11:5, 7)

1738. Ashtoreth (1 Kings 11:5)

1739. Chemosh (1 Kings 11:7)

1740. Molech (1 Kings 11:7)

1741. Hadad (1 Kings 11:14)

1742. Rezon (1 Kings 11:25)

1743. Jeroboam (1 Kings 11:28)

1744. Ahijah (1 Kings 11:29)

1745. A cloak (1 Kings 11:30–31)

1746. The ten tribes Jeroboam would lead (1 Kings 11:31)

1747. Egypt (1 Kings 11:40)

1748. Shishak (1 Kings 11:40)

1749. Forty years (1 Kings 11:42)

1750. Rehoboam (1 Kings 12:1)

1751. Young men he grew up with (1 Kings 12:8)

1752. Scorpions (1 Kings 12:11)

1753. Judah and Benjamin (1 Kings 12:21)

1754. Shemaiah (1 Kings 12:22)

1755. Two golden calves (1 Kings 12:28)

1756. Dan and Bethel (1 Kings 12:29)

1757. Josiah (1 Kings 13:2)

1758. It shriveled up (1 Kings 13:4)

1759. Ashes (1 Kings 13:5)

1760. A lion (1 Kings 13:24)

1761. The lion and his donkey (1 Kings 13:24)

1762. Jeroboam's wife (1 Kings 14:2)

1763. Blindness (1 Kings 14:4)

1764. He died (1 Kings 14:17)

1765. Nadab (1 Kings 14:20)

1766. Naamah, an Ammonite (1 Kings 14:21)

1767. Egypt (1 Kings 14:25–26)

1768. Shishak (1 Kings 14:25–26)

1769. Shields (1 Kings 14:26–27)

1770. Abijah, his son (1 Kings 14:31)

1771. Uriah the Hittite (1 Kings 15:5)

1772. Asa (1 Kings 15:11)

1773. Maakah, his grandmother (1 Kings 15:13)

1774. Remove the high places (1 Kings 15:14)

1775. Baasha (1 Kings 15:16)

1776. Ben-Hadad, grandson of the king of Aram (1 Kings 15:18)

1777. His feet (1 Kings 15:23)

1778. Baasha (1 Kings 15:28–29)

1779. Jehu (1 Kings 16:7)

1780. Elah (1 Kings 16:8)

1781. Zimri (1 Kings 16:10)

1782. Zimri (1 Kings 16:15)

1783. Set it on fire (1 Kings 16:18)

1784. Omri (1 Kings 16:23)

1785. Samaria (1 Kings 16:24)

1786. Ahab (1 Kings 16:28)

1787. Twenty-two years (1 Kings 16:29)

1788. Jezebel (1 Kings 16:31)

1789. Sidon, meaning she was a Sidonian (1 Kings 16:31)

1790. Jericho (1 Kings 16:34)

1791. Joshua (1 Kings 16:34)

1792. Elijah from Tishbe (1 Kings 17:1)

1793. Drought/no dew or rain (1 Kings 17:1)

1794. Ravens (1 Kings 17:4)

1795. Bread and meat (1 Kings 17:6)

1796. Zarephath (1 Kings 17:10)

1797. Sticks (1 Kings 17:12)

1798. Flour and oil (1 Kings 17:14)

1799. The son of the widow (1 Kings 17:17, 22)

1800. Three times (1 Kings 17:21)

1801. Obadiah (1 Kings 18:3, 7)

1802. One hundred prophets (1 Kings 18:4)

1803. Two caves, fifty prophets in each (1 Kings 18:4)

1804. Mount Carmel (1 Kings 18:19)

1805. 850 total prophets (1 Kings 18:19)

1806. Baal (1 Kings 18:19)

1807. Asherah (1 Kings 18:19)

1808. A bull (1 Kings 18:23)

1809. Deep in thought, busy, traveling, or asleep (1 Kings 18:27)

1810. Swords and spears (1 Kings 18:28)

1811. Twelve (1 Kings 18:31)

1812. Three times (1 Kings 18:34)

1813. Kishon Valley (1 Kings 18:40)

1814. Seven times (1 Kings 18:43)

1815. Jezreel (1 Kings 18:46)

1816. Jezebel (1 Kings 19:2–3)

1817. A broom tree (1 Kings 19:4)

1818. Bread and water (1 Kings 19:6)

1819. Horeb (1 Kings 19:8)

1820. Wind, earthquake, and fire (1 Kings 19:11–12)

1821. Hazael, king of Aram; Jehu, king of Israel; and Elisha, his successor (1 Kings 19:15–16)

1822. Seven thousand (1 Kings 19:18)

1823. Twelve yoke of oxen (1 Kings 19:19)

1824. His cloak/mantle (1 Kings 19:19)

1825. He slaughtered his oxen and burned his farming equipment (1 Kings 19:21)

1826. The junior officers (1 Kings 20:14)

1827. Ben-Hadad (1 Kings 20:30, 32)

1828. A lion (1 Kings 20:36)

1829. Naboth (1 Kings 21:1)

1830. A vegetable garden (1 Kings 21:2)

1831. Jezebel (1 Kings 21:9–10)

1832. God and the king (1 Kings 21:13)

1833. Dogs (1 Kings 21:19)

1834. Dogs (1 Kings 21:23)

1835. He humbled himself (1 Kings 21:29)

1836. Ramoth Gilead (1 Kings 22:3)

1837. Four hundred prophets (1 Kings 22:6)

1838. Micaiah (1 Kings 22:8)

1839. A lying/deceiving spirit (1 Kings 22:22)

1840. Zedekiah (1 Kings 22:24)

1841. A random arrow (1 Kings 22:34)

1842. Prostitutes (1 Kings 22:38)

1843. Dogs (1 Kings 22:38)

1844. A fleet of trading ships (1 Kings 22:48)

1845. Jehoram (1 Kings 22:50)

1846. Ahaziah (1 Kings 22:51)

2 Kings

1847. Ahaziah (2 King 1:2)

1848. Ball-Zebub (2 Kings 1:3)

1849. Elijah (2 Kings 1:8)

1850. Three companies (2 Kings 1:9–13)

1851. Fire from heaven (2 Kings 1:12)

1852. Jehoram (2 Kings 1:17)

1853. Bethel, Jericho, the Jordan (2 Kings 2:2, 4, 6)

1854. A company of prophets (2 Kings 2:3, 5, 7)

1855. Jordan river (2 Kings 2:8)

1856. His cloak (2 Kings 2:8)

1857. It parted in two (2 Kings 2:8)

1858. A double portion (2 Kings 2:9)

1859. A chariot of fire (2 Kings 2:11)

1860. Horses of fire (2 Kings 2:11)

1861. He tore it in two (2 Kings 2:12)

1862. It parted in two (2 Kings 2:14)

1863. Fifty prophets (2 Kings 2:16)

1864. Salt (2 Kings 2:21)

1865. Baldy (2 Kings 2:23)

1866. Bears (2 Kings 2:24)

1867. Two (2 Kings 2:24)

1868. Forty-two boys (2 Kings 2:24)

1869. Israel, Judah, and Edom (2 Kings 3:9)

1870. Water (2 Kings 3:9)

1871. Shaphat (2 Kings 3:11)

1872. A harp (2 Kings 3:15)

1873. Blood (2 Kings 3:22)

1874. Olive oil (2 Kings 4:1–7)

1875. Prophet (2 Kings 4:1)

1876. A bed, table, chair, and lamp (2 Kings 4:10)

1877. Gehazi (2 Kings 4:12)

1878. A son (2 Kings 4:16)

1879. His head (2 Kings 4:19)

1880. His staff (2 Kings 4:31)

1881. He lay across him (2 Kings 4:35)

1882. Seven times (2 Kings 4:35)

1883. It was poisoned (2 Kings 4:40)

1884. Flour (2 Kings 4:41)

1885. Elisha (2 Kings 4:44)

1886. Barley (2 Kings 4:42)

1887. Naaman (2 Kings 5:1, 14–15)

1888. Leprosy (2 Kings 5:1)

1889. Aram (2 Kings 5:1)

1890. Seven times (2 Kings 5:14)

1891. The Jordan River (2 Kings 5:14)

1892. Nothing (2 Kings 5:16)

1893. Gehazi (2 Kings 5:20)

1894. Leprosy (2 Kings 5:27)

1895. An ax head made of iron (2 Kings 6:6)

1896. A stick (2 Kings 6:6)

1897. Horses and chariots of fire (2 Kings 6:17)

1898. Blindness (2 Kings 6:18)

1899. Into Samaria, the territory of Israel (2 Kings 6:20)

1900. Prepare a great feast (2 Kings 6:22–23)

1901. A donkey's head (2 Kings 6:25)

1902. Leprosy (2 Kings 7:3)

1903. Chariots and horses (2 Kings 7:6)

1904. Seven years (2 King 8:1)

1905. Hazael (2 Kings 8:7)

1906. Hazael (2 Kings 8:13–14)

1907. Suffocated him with thick cloth soaked with water over his mouth (2 Kings 8:15)

1908. Ahaziah (2 Kings 8:26)

1909. Jehu (2 Kings 9:2–3)

1910. Run (2 Kings 9:3)

1911. Ahab/Jezebel (2 Kings 9:7–8)

1912. Joram and Ahaziah (2 Kings 9:21, 24, 27)

1913. Eye makeup (2 Kings 9:30)

1914. Eunuchs (2 Kings 9:32–33)

1915. Her skull, her feet, and her hands (2 Kings 9:35)

1916. Dogs (2 Kings 9:36)

1917. Seventy sons (2 Kings 10:1)

1918. Jehu (2 Kings 10:7)

1919. Put into baskets and sent to Jehu (2 Kings 10:7)

1920. Baal (2 King 10:19)

1921. A latrine (2 Kings 10:27)

1922. Athaliah (2 Kings 11:1)

1923. Joash (2 Kings 11:2)

1924. Jehoiada (2 Kings 11:15)

1925. Joash (2 Kings 11:21)

1926. Seven years old (2 Kings 11:21)

1927. Zibiah (2 Kings 12:1)

1928. Remove the high places (2 Kings 12:3)

1929. The census, personal vows, money brought voluntarily (2 Kings 12:4)

1930. To repair the temple (2 Kings 12:5)

1931. It has not been repaired (2 Kings 12:6)

1932. Carpenters, builders, masons, and stonecutters (2 Kings 12:11–12)

1933. Hazael (2 Kings 12:17)

1934. The sacred objects and gold found in the temple treasuries (2 Kings 12:18)

1935. His officials, Jozabad and Jehozabad (2 Kings 12:20–21)

1936. Beth Millo (2 Kings 12:20)

1937. Amaziah, king of Judah (2 Kings 12:21)

1938. Aram (2 Kings 13:7)

1939. An illness (2 Kings 13:14)

1940. An arrow (2 Kings 13:16–17)

1941. Three times (2 Kings 13:18)

1942. He came to life (2 Kings 13:21)

1943. Jehoash, king of Israel (2 Kings 14:13–14)

1944. Azariah, king of Judah (2 Kings 14:21)

1945. Azariah, king of Judah (2 Kings 15:5)

1946. Shallum, king of Israel (2 Kings 15:10, 13–14)

1947. Menachem, king of Israel (2 Kings 15:19–20)

1948. Pul, king of Assyria (2 Kings 15:19–20)

1949. Pekah, king of Israel (2 Kings 15:29)

1950. Tiglath-Pileser (2 Kings 15:29)

1951. Hoshea (2 Kings 15:30)

1952. His son (2 Kings 16:3)

1953. Assyria (2 Kings 16:7)

1954. Assyria (2 Kings 16:7)

1955. Silver and gold from the temple (2 Kings 16:8)

1956. An altar (2 Kings 16:10)

1957. Hoshea (2 Kings 17:1)

1958. Shalmaneser (2 Kings 17:3–5)

1959. Egypt (2 Kings 17:4)

1960. Egypt (2 Kings 17:4)

1961. Deported them to Assyria (2 Kings 17:6)

1962. Lions (2 Kings 17:25)

1963. Gods worshiped by nations (2 Kings 17:29–31)

1964. The bronze snake (2 Kings 18:4)

1965. Nehushtan (2 Kings 18:4)

1966. Hezekiah (2 Kings 18:9)

1967. Sennacherib (2 Kings 18:13)

1968. The temple (2 Kings 18:16)

1969. Isaiah (2 Kings 19:2)

1970. He went to the temple and prayed (2 Kings 19:14–15)

1971. 185,000 (2 Kings 19:35)

1972. Nineveh (2 Kings 18:36)

1973. Sennacherib (2 Kings 19:37)

1974. Nisroch (2 Kings 19:37)

1975. Adrammelech and Sharezer (2 Kings 19:37)

1976. His son, Esarhaddon (2 Kings 19:37)

1977. Isaiah (2 Kings 20:1, 5)

1978. The wall (2 Kings 20:2)

1979. Fifteen more years (2 Kings 20:6)

1980. Assyria (2 Kings 20:6)

1981. Figs (2 Kings 20:7)

1982. The shadow on the steps would move backwards (2 Kings 20:9)

1983. Ten steps (2 Kings 20:9)

1984. Babylon (2 Kings 20:12–13)

1985. Baladan (2 Kings 20:12)

1986. Marduk-Baladan (2 Kings 20:12)

1987. Silver, gold, spices, fine oil, armory, and treasure (2 Kings 20:13)

1988. Isaiah (2 Kings 20:16)

1989. A pool and tunnel (2 Kings 20:20)

1990. Manasseh (2 Kings 20:21)

1991. Twelve years old (2 Kings 21:1)

1992. Baal, Asherah, and the starry hosts (2 Kings 21:3)

1993. Asherah (2 Kings 21:7)

1994. Amon (2 Kings 21:18)

1995. His officials (2 Kings 21:23)

1996. Josiah (2 Kings 22:1)

1997. Eight years old (2 Kings 22:1)

1998. Hilkiah (2 Kings 22:8)

1999. Shaphan (2 Kings 22:10)

2000. His robes (2 Kings 22:11)

2001. King Solomon (2 Kings 23:13)

2002. Ashtoreth (2 Kings 23:13)

2003. Chemosh (2 Kings 23:13)

2004. Molek (2 Kings 23:13)

2005. Human bones (2 Kings 23:14)

2006. Passover (2 Kings 23:23)

2007. Josiah (2 Kings 23:25)

2008. Pharaoh Necho, king of Egypt (2 Kings 23:29)

2009. Megiddo (2 Kings 23:29)

2010. Jehoahaz (2 Kings 23:31)

2011. Jehoahaz (2 Kings 23:33)

2012. Jehoiakim/Eliakim (2 Kings 23:34)

2013. Nebuchadnezzar (2 Kings 24:1)

2014. Jehoiakim (2 Kings 24:1)

2015. Jehoiachin (2 Kings 24:12)

2016. The treasures and the gold articles Solomon made (2 Kings 24:13)

2017. The poorest (2 Kings 24:14)

2018. Seven thousand (2 Kings 24:16)

2019. Mattaniah/Zedekiah (2 Kings 24:17)

2020. He was Jehoiachin's uncle (2 Kings 24:17)

2021. Laid siege to it (2 Kings 25:2)

2022. His sons (2 Kings 25:7)

2023. Put out Zedekiah's eyes and shackled him (2 Kings 25:7)

2024. Nebuzaradan (2 Kings 25:8–9)

2025. Gedaliah (2 Kings 25:22)

2026. Egypt (2 Kings 25:26)

2027. Awel-Marduk (2 Kings 25:27)

2028. Jehoiachin (2 Kings 25:27–29)

1 Chronicles

2029. Adam (1 Chronicles 1:1)

2030. Seth (1 Chronicles 1:1)

2031. The Philistines (1 Chronicles 1:12)

2032. Er (1 Chronicles 2:3)

2033. Seven (1 Chronicles 2:13)

2034. Two, Zeruiah, and Abigail (1 Chronicles 2:16)

2035. Amnon (1 Chronicles 3:1)

2036. Ahinoam (1 Chronicles 3:1)

2037. Daniel (1 Chronicles 3:1)

2038. Abigail (1 Chronicles 3:1)

2039. Absalom (1 Chronicles 3:2)

2040. Six (1 Chronicles 3:4)

2041. Tamar (1 Chronicles 3:9)

2042. One, Rehoboam (1 Chronicles 3:10)

2043. Jabez (1 Chronicles 4:9–10)

2044. Reuben (1 Chronicles 5:1)

2045. Joseph (1 Chronicles 5:2)

2046. Pul/Tiglath-Pileser, king of Assyria (1 Chronicles 5:26)

2047. Gershon, Kohath, and Merari (1 Chronicles 6:1–48)

2048. Kohath (1 Chronicles 6:2–3)

2049. Cities of refuge (1 Chronicles 6:57, 67)

2050. Zelophehad (1 Chronicles 7:15)

2051. Ephraim (1 Chronicles 7:26)

2052. Benjamin (1 Chronicles 8:33)

2053. Kish (1 Chronicles 8:33)

2054. Mephibosheth (1 Chronicles 8:34)

2055. Levi (1 Chronicles 9:17–18)

2056. Jonathan, Abinadab, and Malki-Shua (1 Chronicles 10:2)

2057. The Philistines (1 Chronicles 10:2)

2058. His armor-bearer (1 Chronicles 10:4)

2059. They fell on their swords (1 Chronicles 10:4–5)

2060. Dagon (1 Chronicles 10:10)

2061. A medium (1 Chronicles 10:13)

2062. Jerusalem (1 Chronicles 11:4)

2063. Joab (1 Chronicles 11:6)

2064. The City of David (1 Chronicles 11:7)

2065. Three thousand men (1 Chronicles 11:11)

2066. Water (1 Chronicles 11:17)

2067. Abishai (1 Chronicles 11:20)

2068. A lion (1 Chronicles 11:22)

2069. Egypt (1 Chronicles 11:23)

2070. Benjamin (1 Chronicles 12:2)

2071. Gad (1 Chronicles 12:8)

2072. Uzzah (1 Chronicles 13:9)

2073. The oxen (1 Chronicles 13:9)

2074. Perez Uzzah (1 Chronicles 13:11)

2075. Obed-Edom the Gittite (1 Chronicles 13:13)

2076. God blessed the house (1 Chronicles 13:14)

2077. Hiram (1 Chronicles 14:1)

2078. Baal Perazim (1 Chronicles 14:11)

2079. The Levites weren't carrying it (1 Chronicles 15:13)

2080. On their shoulders with poles (1 Chronicles 15:15)

2081. Michal (1 Chronicles 15:29)

2082. A tent (1 Chronicles 16:1)

2083. Load of bread, cake of dates, and cake of raisins (1 Chronicles 16:3)

2084. Asaph (1 Chronicles 16:5, 37)

2085. Cedar (1 Chronicles 17:1)

2086. His love (1 Chronicles 17:13)

2087. Nathan (1 Chronicles 17:15)

2088. Chariots (1 Chronicles 18:3–4)

2089. The Ammonites (1 Chronicles 19:2)

2090. Jericho (1 Chronicles 19:5)

2091. The Ammonites (1 Chronicles 19:6)

2092. Arameans (1 Chronicles 19:6–7)

2093. Help them (1 Chronicles 19:19)

2094. Going off to war (1 Chronicles 20:1)

2095. Elhanan, son of Jair (1 Chronicles 20:5)

2096. Lahmi (1 Chronicles 20:5)

2097. Twenty-four digits, six on each hand and foot (1 Chronicles 20:6–7)

2098. Rapha in Gath (1 Chronicles 20:8)

2099. Satan (1 Chronicles 21:1)

2100. Gad (1 Chronicles 21:9–10)

2101. Three years of famine, three months of enemy attack, and three days of plague (1 Chronicles 21:12)

2102. Seventy thousand men (1 Chronicles 21:14)

2103. Araunah the Jebusite (1 Chronicles 21:20–22)

2104. Six hundred shekels (1 Chronicles 21:25)

2105. An altar (1 Chronicles 21:26)

2106. The temple (1 Chronicles 22:1)

2107. His son Solomon (1 Chronicles 22:5–6)

2108. He had shed too much blood (1 Chronicles 22:8)

2109. Thirty years and older (1 Chronicles 23:3)

2110. Twenty years old or more (1 Chronicles 23:24)

2111. Zadok (1 Chronicles 24:3)

2112. Sons of Asaph (1 Chronicles 25:1)

2113. The temple (1 Chronicles 26:27)

2114. Twenty-four thousand men (1 Chronicles 27:1)

2115. One month a year (1 Chronicles 27:1–2)

2116. The royal army (1 Chronicles 27:34)

2117. The Spirit (1 Chronicles 28:12)

2118. A shadow (1 Chronicles 29:15)

2119. Zadok (1 Chronicles 29:22)

2120. Forty years (1 Chronicles 29:27)

2121. Seven in Hebron and thirty-three in Jerusalem (1 Chronicles 29:27)

2122. Samuel, Nathan, and Gad (1 Chronicles 29:29)

2 Chronicles

2123. Gibeon (2 Chronicles 1:3)

2124. A thousand burnt offerings (2 Chronicles 1:6)

2125. Wisdom and knowledge (2 Chronicles 1:10)

2126. Wealth, riches, and honor (2 Chronicles 1:12)

2127. Stones (2 Chronicles 1:15)

2128. Hiram, king of Tyre (2 Chronicles 2:3, 7)

2129. Huram-Abi (2 Chronicles 2:13)

2130. They floated rafts down the sea (2 Chronicles 2:16)

2131. 153,600 workers (2 Chronicles 2:18)

2132. Mount Moriah (2 Chronicles 3:1)

2133. A threshing floor (2 Chronicles 3:1)

2134. Jakin and Boaz (2 Chronicles 3:17)

2135. Ten each (2 Chronicles 4:6–8)

2136. The poles (2 Chronicles 5:9)

2137. The two tablets from Moses (2 Chronicles 5:10)

2138. The cloud of the glory of the Lord (2 Chronicles 5:14)

2139. The temple (2 Chronicles 6:29–30)

2140. Fire (2 Chronicles 7:1)

2141. Humble themselves, pray, seek God's face, and turn from their wicked ways (2 Chronicles 7:14)

2142. Israelites (2 Chronicles 8:9)

2143. Spices, gold, and precious stones (2 Chronicles 9:1)

2144. Algumwood (2 Chronicles 9:11)

2145. 666 talents (2 Chronicles 9:13)

2146. Lion (2 Chronicles 9:18–19)

2147. Apes and baboons (2 Chronicles 9:21)

2148. Silver (2 Chronicles 9:27)

2149. Egypt (2 Chronicles 9:28)

2150. Forty years (2 Chronicles 9:30)

2151. Egypt (2 Chronicles 10:2)

2152. His friends he grew up with (2 Chronicles 10:8)

2153. Scorpions (2 Chronicles 10:14)

2154. Rehoboam (2 Chronicles 10:18–19)

2155. Judah and Benjamin (2 Chronicles 11:1)

2156. Shemaiah (2 Chronicles 11:2)

2157. The Levites (2 Chronicles 11:14)

2158. Maakah (2 Chronicles 11:21)

2159. Shishak (2 Chronicles 12:2)

2160. Naamah, an Ammonite (2 Chronicles 12:13)

2161. Abijah, his son (2 Chronicles 12:16)

2162. Maakah (2 Chronicles 13:2)

2163. Abijah (2 Chronicles 13:18–19)

2164. Asa, his son (2 Chronicles 14:1)

2165. The Cushites (2 Chronicles 14:9)

2166. Azariah (2 Chronicles 15:8)

2167. Ephraim, Manasseh, and Simeon (2 Chronicles 15:9)

2168. Maakah (2 Chronicles 15:16)

2169. The Kidron Valley (2 Chronicles 15:16)

2170. Baasha (2 Chronicles 16:1)

2171. Ben-Hadad, king of Aram (2 Chronicles 16:4)

2172. Aram (2 Chronicles 16:7)

2173. His feet (2 Chronicles 16:12)

2174. Jehoshaphat (2 Chronicles 17:1)

2175. To teach them the law (2 Chronicles 17:9)

2176. King Ahab (2 Chronicles 18:1)

2177. King Ahab (2 Chronicles 18:3)

2178. Micaiah (2 Chronicles 18:7)

2179. A deceiving spirit (2 Chronicles 18:22)

2180. A disguise (2 Chronicles 18:29)

2181. The king of Israel/Ahab (2 Chronicles 18:30)

2182. Between the breastplate and the scale armor (2 Chronicles 18:33)

2183. A random person (2 Chronicles 18:33)

2184. Judges (2 Chronicles 19:5, 8)

2185. The Moabites and Ammonites (2 Chronicles 20:23)

2186. Trading ships (2 Chronicles 20:36)

2187. His brothers (2 Chronicles 21:4)

2188. King Ahab of Israel (2 Chronicles 21:6)

2189. Elijah (2 Chronicles 21:12)

2190. His bowels (2 Chronicles 21:18)

2191. Jehu (2 Chronicles 22:9)

2192. Joash (2 Chronicles 22:10–11)

2193. Jehosheba, the daughter of King Jehoram (2 Chronicles 22:11)

2194. Jehoiada, the priest (2 Chronicles 22:11)

2195. The temple (2 Chronicles 22:12)

2196. Six years (2 Chronicles 22:12)

2197. Athaliah (2 Chronicles 22:12)

2198. Jehoiada (2 Chronicles 23:11)

2199. Athaliah (2 Chronicles 23:15)

2200. Seven years old (2 Chronicles 24:1)

2201. A chest (2 Chronicles 24:11–12)

2202. Zechariah (2 Chronicles 24:20–21)

2203. The Arameans (2 Chronicles 24:23–24)

2204. In his bed (2 Chronicles 24:25)

2205. Amaziah (2 Chronicles 25:14)

2206. Beth Shemesh (2 Chronicles 25:23)

2207. Israel (2 Chronicles 25:23)

2208. Sixteen years old (2 Chronicles 26:1)

2209. Zechariah (2 Chronicles 26:5)

2210. Arrows and stones (2 Chronicles 26:15)

2211. Azariah (2 Chronicles 26:17)

2212. Leprosy (2 Chronicles 26:19)

2213. Jotham (2 Chronicles 27:1, 6)

2214. His children (2 Chronicles 27:3)

2215. Aram, Israel, Assyria, Edom, and Philistia (2 Chronicles 28:5, 16, 17, 20)

2216. Pekah (2 Chronicles 28:6)

2217. Oded (2 Chronicles 28:9)

2218. Fellow Israelites they had taken as prisoner (2 Chronicles 28:11)

2219. Assyria (2 Chronicles 28:16)

2220. Tiglath-Pileser (2 Chronicles 28:20)

2221. The temple (2 Chronicles 28:24)

2222. On every street corner (2 Chronicles 28:24)

2223. Hezekiah (2 Chronicles 29:1–3)

2224. Opened the temple (2 Chronicles 29:3)

2225. David and Asaph (2 Chronicles 29:30)

2226. Passover (2 Chronicles 30:3)

2227. Couriers (2 Chronicles 30:5–6)

2228. He prayed for them (2 Chronicles 30:18)

2229. Seven more days (2 Chronicles 30:23)

2230. Their tithes (2 Chronicles 31:6)

2231. Sennacherib (2 Chronicles 32:1)

2232. God (2 Chronicles 32:17)

2233. Isaiah (2 Chronicles 32:20)

2234. In the temple of his god (2 Chronicles 32:21)

2235. His own sons (2 Chronicles 32:21)

2236. Hezekiah (2 Chronicles 32:31)

2237. Isaiah (2 Chronicles 32:32)

2238. Manasseh (2 Chronicles 32:33)

2239. Twelve years old (2 Chronicles 33:1)

2240. Assyria (2 Chronicles 33:11)

2241. Prayed/repented (2 Chronicles 33:13)

2242. Amon (2 Chronicles 33:21)

2243. Humble himself (2 Chronicles 33:23)

2244. His officials (2 Chronicles 33:24)

2245. Eight years old (2 Chronicles 34:1)

2246. The bones of the priests that sacrificed on those altars (2 Chronicles 34:5)

2247. Hilkiah (2 Chronicles 34:9)

2248. The Book of the Law (2 Chronicles 34:14)

2249. Huldah (2 Chronicles 34:22)

2250. Asaph (2 Chronicles 35:15)

2251. Samuel (2 Chronicles 35:18)

2252. Necho (2 Chronicles 35:20)

2253. Megiddo (2 Chronicles 35:22)

2254. He was shot by archers (2 Chronicles 35:23)

2255. Jeremiah (2 Chronicles 35:25)

2256. Jehoahaz, Josiah's son (2 Chronicles 36:3)

2257. Eliakim, Jehoahaz's brother (2 Chronicles 36:4)

2258. Jehoiakim (2 Chronicles 36:4)

2259. Took him to Egypt (2 Chronicles 36:4)

2260. Nebuchadnezzar (2 Chronicles 36:6)

2261. The temple articles (2 Chronicles 36:7)

2262. Three months and ten days (2 Chronicles 36:9)

2263. Jehoiachin (2 Chronicles 36:10)

2264. Zedekiah (2 Chronicles 36:10)

2265. Zedekiah was his uncle (2 Chronicles 36:10)

2266. Jeremiah (2 Chronicles 36:12)

2267. The temple and the palaces (2 Chronicles 36:19)

2268. A Sabbath rest (2 Chronicles 36:21)

2269. Seventy years (2 Chronicles 36:21)

2270. Jeremiah (2 Chronicles 36:21)

2271. Cyrus (2 Chronicles 36:22)

2272. Jeremiah (2 Chronicles 36:22)

2273. The temple in Jerusalem (2 Chronicles 36:23)

Ezra

2274. Ezra and Nehemiah

2275. Jeremiah, Haggai, and Zechariah (Ezra 1:1; 5:1)

2276. King Cyrus (Ezra 1:1)

2277. Jeremiah (Ezra 1:1)

2278. Judah, Benjamin, and the Levites (Ezra 1:5)

2279. Nebuchadnezzar (Ezra 1:7)

2280. 5,400 articles (Ezra 1:11)

2281. Unclean (Ezra 2:62)

2282. The altar (Ezra 3:2)

2283. The laying of the foundation (Ezra 3:12)

2284. Joy and weeping (Ezra 3:13)

2285. Esarhaddon (Ezra 4:2)

2286. Cyrus, Darius, Xerxes, and Artaxerxes (Ezra 4:5–7)

2287. Aramaic (Ezra 4:7)

2288. Taxes, tributes, and duties (Ezra 4:13)

2289. A troublesome/rebellious city (Ezra 4:15)

2290. Darius (Ezra 4:24)

2291. Haggai and Zechariah (Ezra 5:1)

2292. Zerubbabel and Joshua (Ezra 5:2)

2293. Tattenai (Ezra 5:7)

2294. Sheshbazzar (Ezra 5:14)

2295. King Darius (Ezra 6:1, 7)

2296. Ninety feet by ninety feet (Ezra 6:3)

2297. The royal Persian treasury (Ezra 6:4)

2298. They would be impaled on the beam (Ezra 6:11)

2299. Turn to rubble (Ezra 6:11)

2300. Levi (Ezra 7:1–5)

2301. King Artaxerxes (Ezra 7:11)

2302. Priests, Levites, and temple workers (Ezra 7:24)

2303. Soldiers (Ezra 8:22)

2304. The people had intermarried with foreigners (Ezra 9:2–3)

2305. Married foreign women (Ezra 10:18, 44)

Nehemiah

2306. Susa in Babylon (Nehemiah 1:1)

2307. Hanani (Nehemiah 1:2)

2308. Jerusalem (Nehemiah 1:2)

2309. The walls and the gates (Nehemiah 1:3)

2310. Cupbearer (Nehemiah 1:11)

2311. King Artaxerxes (Nehemiah 2:1)

2312. Wine (Nehemiah 2:1)

2313. He looked sad (Nehemiah 2:1)

2314. Trans-Euphrates (Nehemiah 2:7)

2315. Asaph (Nehemiah 2:8)

2316. Valley, Jackal, Dung, and Fountain (Nehemiah 2:13–14)

2317. Sanballat, Tobiah, and Geshem (Nehemiah 2:19)

2318. Sanballat (Nehemiah 2:19)

2319. Tobiah (Nehemiah 2:19)

2320. Geshem (Nehemiah 2:19)

2321. The gates around Jerusalem (Nehemiah 3)

2322. A fox (Nehemiah 4:3)

2323. A weapon (Nehemiah 4:17)

2324. Interest (Nehemiah 5:11)

2325. Governor (Nehemiah 5:14)

2326. Food (Nehemiah 5:14)

2327. A revolt (Nehemiah 6:6)

2328. Noadiah (Nehemiah 6:14)

2329. Fifty-two days (Nehemiah 6:15)

2330. Hanani, his brother (Nehemiah 7:2)

2331. Ezra, chapter 2 (Nehemiah 7)

2332. Ezra (Nehemiah 8:2)

2333. From daybreak to noon (Nehemiah 8:3)

2334. Branches (Nehemiah 8:14, 16)

2335. Dust (Nehemiah 9:1)

2336. Nehemiah (Nehemiah 10:1)

2337. Those people that lived around them (Nehemiah 10:30)

2338. The Sabbath (Nehemiah 10:31)

2339. One out of every ten (Nehemiah 11:1)

2340. Choirs (Nehemiah 12:31)

2341. Rejoicing (Nehemiah 12:43)

2342. Ammonite and Moabite (Nehemiah 13:1)

2343. In the temple courts (Nehemiah 13:7)

2344. Work, such as treading the winepress, bringing in grain (Nehemiah 13:15)

2345. Ashdod (Nehemiah 13:24)

2346. Beat them and pulled out their hair (Nehemiah 13:25)

2347. Solomon (Nehemiah 13:26)

Esther

2348. Xerxes (Esther 1:1)

2349. 127 provinces (Esther 1:1)

2350. India to Cush (Esther 1:1)

2351. Susa (Esther 1:2)

2352. 180 days (Esther 1:4)

2353. Seven days (Esther 1:5)

2354. Vashti (Esther 1:9)

2355. The women in the royal palace (Esther 1:9)

2356. She refused the king's request (Esther 1:11–12)

2357. Other women/wives (Esther 1:17)

2358. Hegai (Esther 2:3)

2359. Benjamin (Esther 2:5)

2360. Hadassah (Esther 2:7)

2361. Cousin (Esther 2:7)

2362. Her nationality (Esther 2:10)

2363. Mordecai (Esther 2:10)

2364. Twelve months (Esther 2:12)

2365. Abihail (Esther 2:15)

2366. Bigthana and Teresh (Esther 2:21)

2367. Esther (Esther 2:22)

2368. Haman (Esther 3:2)

2369. Pur or Lot (Esther 3:7)

2370. His signet ring (Esther 3:12)

2371. All the Jews (Esther 3:13)

2372. The thirteenth day of the twelfth month of Adar (Esther 3:13)

2373. Sackcloth (Esther 4:2)

2374. Clothes (Esther 4:4)

2375. They were put to death (Esther 4:11)

2376. His gold scepter (Esther 4:11)

2377. Up to half the kingdom (Esther 5:3)

2378. To hold a banquet (Esther 5:4)

2379. Xerxes and Haman (Esther 5:4)

2380. Another banquet (Esther 5:8)

2381. To tell the king what she really desired (Esther 5:8)

2382. Zeresh (Esther 5:14)

2383. Seventy-five feet high (Esther 5:14)

2384. Haman's wife Zeresh (Esther 5:14)

2385. He couldn't sleep (Esther 6:1)

2386. A royal robe (Esther 6:8)

2387. On the head of the horse that was ridden (Esther 6:8)

2388. A horse (Esther 6:11)

2389. Molesting her (Esther 7:8)

2390. Haman (Esther 7:10)

2391. Mordecai (Esther 8:2)

2392. Assemble and protect themselves (Esther 8:11)

2393. Blue and white (Esther 8:15)

2394. Jews (Esther 8:17)

2395. Five hundred men (Esther 9:6)

2396. Ten (Esther 9:13)

2397. The plunder (Esther 9:15)

2398. 75,000 (Esther 9:16)

2399. Mordecai (Esther 9:20)

2400. Adar (Esther 9:21)

2401. Feasting, giving presents to one another, and giving to the poor (Esther 9:22)

2402. "Lot" (Esther 9:24)

2403. Purim (Esther 9:26)

2404. Two days (Esther 9:27)

2405. Second in charge (Esther 10:3)

2406. Esther

Job

2407. Job (Job 1:1)

2408. Uz (Job 1:1)

2409. Ten, seven sons and three daughters (Job 1:2)

2410. Job (Job 1:3)

2411. Birthdays (Job 1:4)

2412. Purify them through sacrifice (Job 1:5)

2413. Roaming through the earth, going back and forth on it (Job 1:7)

2414. A hedge (Job 1:10)

2415. Job's body (Job 1:12)

2416. The Sabeans (Job 1:15)

2417. Fire falling from the sky (Job 1:16)

2418. The Chaldeans (Job 1:17)

2419. A mighty wind (Job 1:19)

2420. Job (Job 1:21)

2421. From roaming throughout the earth, going back and forth on it (Job 2:2)

2422. His flesh and bones (Job 2:5)

2423. Painful sores (Job 2:7)

2424. From the soles of his feet to the crown of his head (Job 2:7)

2425. A piece of broken pottery (Job 2:8)

2426. Job's wife (Job 2:9)

2427. The trouble (Job 2:10)

2428. Eliphaz, Bildad, and Zophar (Job 2:11)

2429. Temanite, Shuhite, and Naamathite (Job 2:11)

2430. Their robes (Job 2:12)

2431. Dust (Job 2:12)

2432. Seven days and nights (Job 2:13)

2433. The day of his birth (Job 3:1)

2434. Eliphaz (Job 4:1)

2435. A spirit (Job 4:15)

2436. Hardship and trouble (Job 5:6)

2437. Scales (Job 6:2)

2438. Worms and scabs (Job 7:5)

2439. Return (Job 7:9)

2440. Bildad (Job 8:1)

2441. A spider's web (Job 8:14)

2442. The Bear, Orion, and the Pleiades (Job 9:9)

2443. Soap and a cleansing powder (Job 9:30)

2444. A lion (Job 10:16)

2445. The grave (Job 10:19)

2446. Human (Job 11:12)

2447. A laughingstock (Job 12:4)

2448. Animals, birds, the earth, and fish (Job 12:7–8)

2449. God/the Almighty (Job 13:3)

2450. Job (Job 13:15)

2451. Moths (Job 13:28)

2452. A tree (Job 14:7)

2453. His sins (Job 14:16–17)

2454. Born (Job 15:7)

2455. Long winded (Job 16:3)

2456. The grave (Job 17:13)

2457. Cattle (Job 18:3)

2458. His breath (Job 19:17)

2459. "By the skin of my teeth" (Job 19:20)

2460. Dung (Job 20:7)

2461. His liver (Job 20:25)

2462. The bulls/calves (Job 21:10)

2463. God (Job 22:17)

2464. The north, south, east, and west (Job 23:8–9)

2465. Midnight (Job 24:17)

2466. Bildad (Job 25)

2467. Water (John 26:8)

2468. His integrity/innocence (Job 27:5–6)

2469. Cocoon (John 27:18)

2470. Wisdom (Job 28:10–12)

2471. Righteousness (Job 29:14)

2472. Owls (Job 30:29)

2473. His arm would fall from his shoulder (Job 31:21–22)

2474. Because he was righteous in his own eyes (Job 32:1)

2475. Elihu (Job 32:2)

2476. A Buzite (Job 32:2)

2477. They could not refute Job (Job 32:3)

2478. He was younger (Job 32:4)

2479. God speaks to them (Job 33:14–16)

2480. Scorn (Job 34:7)

2481. Dust (Job 34:14–15)

2482. Job (Job 35:16)

2483. Rain, thunder, and lightning (Job 36:26–30)

2484. Ice (Job 37:10)

2485. A storm (Job 38:1)

2486. The earth's foundation (Job 38:4)

2487. The morning stars (Job 38:6–7)

2488. The sea (Job 38:8)

2489. The morning (Job 38:12)

2490. Gates of death and the gates of deep darkness (Job 38:17)

2491. Snow and hail (Job 38:22)

2492. Rain and dew (Job 38:28)

2493. Orion's belt (Job 38:31)

2494. Pleiades, Orion, and the Bear (Job 38:31–32)

2495. The ibis and the rooster (Job 38:36)

2496. The mountain goat and the doe (Job 39:1)

2497. The ostrich (Job 39:13, 17)

2498. The ostrich (Job 39:18)

2499. The horse (Job 39:20)

2500. The horse (Job 39:22)

2501. Twice (Job 40:5)

2502. His voice (Job 40:9)

2503. Behemoth (Job 40:15–18)

2504. Grass (Job 40:15)

2505. A cedar (Job 40:17)

2506. A lotus plant (Job 40:21)

2507. Leviathan (Job 41:1)

2508. Fire and smoke (Job 41:20–21)

2509. Sword, spear, dart, javelin, arrows, slingstones, club, and lance (Job 41:26–29)

2510. Eliphaz (Job 42:7)

2511. Make sacrifices and have Job pray for them (Job 42:8)

2512. Twice as much (Job 42:10)

2513. Piece of silver and a gold ring (Job 42:11)

2514. Seven sons and three daughters (Job 42:13)

2515. Jemimah, Keziah, and Keren-Happuch (Job 42:14)

2516. 140 years (Job 42:16)

2517. Four generations (Job 42:16)

Psalms

2518. Psalms (150 chapters)

2519. The wicked (Psalm 1:1)

2520. The sinners (Psalm 1:1)

2521. Mockers (Psalm 1:1)

2522. The law (Psalm 1:2)

2523. Chaff (Psalm 1:4)

2524. Iron (Psalm 2:9)

2525. Their teeth (Psalm 3:7)

2526. Sin (Psalm 4:4)

2527. His requests (Psalm 5:3)

2528. Their throats (Psalm 5:9)

2529. His bones (Psalm 6:2)

2530. A lion (Psalm 7:2)

2531. His wrath (Psalm 7:11)

2532. Human beings (Psalm 8:4–5)

2533. The pit they have dug (Psalm 9:15)

2534. God (Psalm 10:11)

2535. The fatherless and the oppressed (Psalm 10:18)

2536. His holy temple, his heavenly throne (Psalm 11:4)

2537. Their neighbor (Psalm 12:2)

2538. His face (Psalm 13:1)

2539. God (Psalm 14:1)

2540. Interest (Psalm 15:5)

2541. The grave/the realm of the dead (Psalm 16:10)

2542. Wings (Psalm 17:8)

2543. Lion (Psalm 17:12)

2544. Deliverer (Psalm 18:2)

2545. Deer (Psalm 18:33)

2546. The heavens and the skies (Psalm 19:1)

2547. Horses and chariots (Psalm 20:7)

2548. A bow (Psalm 21:12)

2549. Psalm 22 (Psalm 22)

2550. Psalm 22 (Psalm 22:1)

2551. A worm (Psalm 22:6)

2552. Insults (Psalm 22:7)

2553. Bulls, lions, and dogs (Psalm 22:12,13,16)

2554. Water (Psalm 22:14)

2555. Bones (Psalm 22:14)

2556. His hands and feet (Psalm 22:16)

2557. His bones (Psalm 22:17)

2558. His clothes/garments (Psalm 22:18)

2559. Green pastures (Psalm 23:2)

2560. The valley of the shadow of death/the darkest valley (Psalm 23:4)

2561. His rod and staff (Psalm 23:4)

2562. A table (Psalm 23:5)

2563. Oil (Psalm 23:5)

2564. My cup (Psalm 23:5)

2565. The house of the Lord (Psalm 23:6)

2566. The gates and doors (Psalm 24:7)

2567. His youth (Psalm 25:7)

2568. His heart and mind (Psalm 26:2)

2569. In the house of the Lord (Psalm 27:4)

2570. The beauty of the Lord (Psalm 27:4)

2571. His heart (Psalm 28:7)

2572. His voice (Psalm 29:3–5)

2573. Calf (Psalm 29:6)

2574. The pit/grave (Psalm 30:3)

2575. Dancing (Psalm 30:11)

2576. His spirit (Psalm 31:5)

2577. On the cross (Psalm 31:5/ Luke 23:46)

2578. His sins (Psalm 32:2)

2579. A horse and a mule (Psalm 32:9)

2580. Jars (Psalm 33:7)

2581. That the Lord is good (Psalm 34:8)

2582. Bones (Psalm 34:20)

2583. Lions (Psalm 35:17)

2584. Wings (Psalm 36:7)

2585. The desires of our heart (Psalm 37:4)

2586. The land/earth (Psalm 37:11)

2587. Sin (Psalm 38:3)

2588. Hearing and speech (Psalm 38:13–14)

2589. Breath (Psalm 39:5)

2590. A new song (Psalm 40:3)

2591. His sins (Psalm 40:12)

2592. Bread (Psalm 41:9)

2593. Deer (Psalm 42:1)

2594. Tears (Psalm 42:3)

2595. His soul (Psalm 43:11)

2596. Bow and sword (Psalm 44:6)

2597. God's robe (Psalm 45:8)

2598. The mountains (Psalm 46:2)

2599. And know that He is God (Psalm 46:10)

2600. All the nations (Psalm 47:1)

2601. The temple (Psalm 48:9)

2602. Sheep (Psalm 49:14)

2603. A thousand (Psalm 50:10)

2604. Hyssop (Psalm 51:7)

2605. Heart (Psalm 51:10)

2606. The Holy Spirit (Psalm 51:11)

2607. Broken, contrite (Psalm 51:17)

2608. An olive tree (Psalm 52:8)

2609. Not even one (Psalm 53:3)

2610. Zion (Psalm 53:6)

2611. God (Psalm 54:3)

2612. Evening, morning, and noon (Psalm 55:17)

2613. Butter and oil (Psalm 55:21)

2614. Our cares (Psalm 55:22)

2615. His tears (Psalm 56:8)

2616. Spears, arrows, and swords (Psalm 57:4)

2617. A net and a pit (Psalm 57:6)

2618. His faithfulness (Psalm 57:10)

2619. A slug (Psalm 58:8)

2620. Dogs (Psalm 59:6, 14)

2621. Judah (Psalm 60:7)

2622. Edom (Psalm 60:8)

2623. The rock (Psalm 61:2)

2624. Wings (Psalm 61:4)

2625. Fortress (Psalm 62:2, 6)

2626. Life (Psalm 63:3)

2627. Deadly arrows (Psalm 64:3)

2628. Calm them (Psalm 65:7)

2629. All the earth (Psalm 66:1)

2630. God's face (Psalm 67:1)

2631. Widows (Psalm 68:5)

2632. Chariots (Psalm 68:17)

2633. Your house/God's house or temple (Psalm 69:9)

2634. Gall (Psalm 69:21)

2635. The book of life (Psalm 69:28)

2636. His life (Psalm 70:2)

2637. Harp and lyre (Psalm 71:22)

2638. Lips and tongue (Psalm 71:23–24)

2639. The sun and the moon (Psalm 72:5)

2640. Sheba (Psalm 72:15)

2641. A necklace (Psalm 73:6)

2642. Leviathan (Psalm 74:14)

2643. Cup mixed with wine (Psalm 75:8)

2644. Salem (Psalm 76:2)

2645. The parting of the Red Sea (Psalm 77:15–20)

2646. Parables (Psalm 78:2)

2647. Judah (Psalm 78:68)

2648. His wrath (Psalm 79:6)

2649. Tears (Psalm 80:5)

2650. New Moon festival (Psalm 81:3)

2651. Honey (Psalm 81:16)

2652. The gods (Psalm 82:5)

2653. Israel's (Psalm 83:4)

2654. A thousand (Psalm 84:10)

2655. Kiss (Psalm 85:10)

2656. Undivided (Psalm 86:11)

2657. Zion (Psalm 87:2)

2658. Darkness (Psalm 88:18)

2659. The throne (Psalm 89:36, 44)

2660. A day (Psalm 90:4)

2661. Seventy to eighty years (Psalm 90:10)

2662. Feathers (Psalm 91:4)

2663. Lion and cobra/serpent (Psalm 91:13)

2664. His faithfulness (Psalm 92:2)

2665. The seas (Psalm 93:3)

2666. The widow, the foreigner, and the fatherless (Psalm 94:5–6)

2667. Meribah and Massah (Psalm 95:8)

2668. Forty years (Psalm 95:10)

2669. A new song (Psalm 96:1)

2670. Wax (Psalm 97:5)

2671. God's righteousness (Psalm 97:6)

2672. The rivers (Psalm 98:8)

2673. The mountains (Psalm 98:8)

2674. Moses, Aaron, and Samuel (Psalm 99:6)

2675. Through all generations (Psalm 100:5)

2676. Deceit (Psalm 101:7)

2677. Smoke (Psalm 102:3)

2678. Ashes (Psalm 102:9)

2679. Love (Psalm 103:8)

2680. East from west (Psalm 103:12)

2681. Dust (Psalm 103:14)

2682. Grass (Psalm 103:15)

2683. Light (Psalm 104:2)

2684. The earth (Psalm 104:5)

2685. Plague on livestock, boils (Psalm 105:27–36)

2686. Moses and Aaron (Psalm 106:16)

2687. Righteousness (Psalm 106:30–31)

2688. False gods (Psalm 106:37)

2689. Drunkards (Psalm 107:27)

2690. Quieting the storm (Psalm 107:29)

2691. They are practically the same word for word (Psalm 108:6–13)

2692. A widow (Psalm 109:9)

2693. A footstool (Psalm 110:1)

2694. Melchizedek (Psalm 110:4)

2695. The fear of the Lord (Psalm 111:8)

2696. Bad news (Psalm 112:7)

2697. The poor and the needy (Psalm 113:7)

2698. The mountains (Psalm 114:4)

2699. Idols (Psalm 115:6)

2700. His faithful servants (Psalm 116:15)

2701. Psalm 117

2702. Two verses (Psalm 117)

2703. Humans/princes (Psalm 118:8–9)

2704. The capstone (Psalm 118:22)

2705. Name (Psalm 118:26)

2706. Psalm 119

2707. His word (Psalm 119:11)

2708. His soul (Psalm 119:81)

2709. The elders (Psalm 119:100)

2710. God's word (Psalm 119:105)

2711. Pure gold (Psalm 119:127)

2712. Seven times a day (Psalm 119:164)

2713. Sheep (Psalm 119:176)

2714. 176

2715. Lips and tongue (Psalm 120:2)

2716. To the mountains (Psalm 121:1)

2717. Jerusalem (Psalm 122:6)

2718. The master (Psalm 123:2)

2719. A bird (Psalm 124:7)

2720. Zion (Psalm 125:1)

2721. Songs of joy (Psalm 126:5)

2722. The Lord (Psalm 127:1)

2723. The watchmen/guards (Psalm 127:1)

2724. Children (Psalm 127:3)

2725. Arrows (Psalm 127:4)

2726. His quiver (Psalm 127:5)

2727. Your wife (Psalm 128:3)

2728. Your children (Psalm 128:3)

2729. On the roof (Psalm 129:6)

2730. His word (Psalm 130:5)

2731. A weaned child (Psalm 131:2)

2732. On the throne (Psalm 132:12)

2733. Zion (Psalm 132:13–14)

2734. A horn/a king (Psalm 132:17)

2735. God's people/Brothers (Psalm 133:1)

2736. The temple (Psalm 134:1)

2737. Clouds, lightning, rain, and wind (Psalm 135:7)

2738. Sihon, king of the Amorites; and Og, king of Bashan (Psalm 135:11; 136:19, 20)

2739. His love endures forever (Psalm 136)

2740. Babylon (Psalm 137:1)

2741. His holy temple (Psalm 138:2)

2742. His mother's womb (Psalm 139:13)

2743. Fearfully and wonderfully (Psalm 139:14)

2744. All his days (Psalm 139:16)

2745. Heart (Psalm 139:23)

2746. Serpents (Psalm 140:3)

2747. Coals (Psalm 140:10)

2748. His prayers (Psalm 141:2)

2749. His mouth (Psalm 141:3)

2750. His prison (Psalm 142:7)

2751. A parched land (Psalm 143:6)

2752. Battle (Psalm 144:1)

2753. Ten strings (Psalm 144:9)

2754. Food (Psalm 145:15)

2755. Princes/human beings (Psalm 146:3)

2756. The brokenhearted (Psalm 147:3)

2757. The stars (Psalm 147:4)

2758. Praise God (Psalm 148)

2759. A double-edged sword (Psalm 149:6)

2760. Trumpet, harp, lyre, tambourine/timbrel, strings, flute, and cymbals (Psalm 150:3–5)

2761. Praise the Lord (Psalm 150:6)

Proverbs

2762. Solomon (Proverbs 1:1)

2763. The fear of the Lord (Proverbs 1:7)

2764. Father and mother (Proverbs 1:8)

2765. Birds (Proverbs 1:17)

2766. Wisdom (Proverbs 1:20)

2767. Silver (Proverbs 2:4)

2768. Wisdom (Proverbs 2:12)

2769. Adulterous (Proverbs 2:16)

2770. An adulteress (Proverbs 2:18)

2771. His life (Proverbs 3:1–2)

2772. Love and faithfulness (Proverbs 3:3)

2773. Our understanding (Proverbs 3:5)

2774. Our bones (Proverbs 3:7–8)

2775. Our barns and our vats (Proverbs 3:9–10)

2776. Those he loves (Proverbs 3:12)

2777. Gold, silver, and rubies (Proverbs 3:14–15)

2778. Riches and honor (Proverbs 3:16)

2779. Wisdom (Proverbs 3:19)

2780. Goodness (Proverbs 3:27)

2781. Our neighbor (Proverbs 3:28)

2782. The wicked (Proverbs 3:33)

2783. Wisdom (Proverbs 4:6)

2784. A garland of grace (Proverbs 4:9)

2785. Wickedness (Proverbs 4:17)

2786. Our heart (Proverbs 4:23)

2787. Honey (Proverbs 5:3)

2788. Gall (Proverbs 5:4)

2789. The grave (Proverbs 5:5)

2790. The door (Proverbs 5:8)

2791. Strangers (Proverbs 5:10)

2792. Water (Proverbs 5:15)

2793. Doe/deer (Proverbs 5:19)

2794. Ant (Proverbs 6:6)

2795. A commander or ruler (Proverbs 6:7–8)

2796. Poverty (Proverbs 6:11)

2797. Seven (Proverbs 6:16)

2798. A prostitute (Proverbs 6:26)

2799. On our fingers (Proverbs 7:3)

2800. Myrrh, aloes, and cinnamon (Proverbs 7:17)

2801. An ox (Proverbs 7:22)

2802. Silver and gold (Proverbs 8:11)

2803. Before the world came to be (Proverbs 8:23)

2804. Seven (Proverbs 9:1)

2805. A mocker (Proverbs 9:7)

2806. The wise (Proverbs 9:8)

2807. Folly (Proverbs 9:13–14)

2808. Sweet (Proverbs 9:17)

2809. Grief (Proverbs 10:1)

2810. Love (Proverbs 10:12)

2811. A rod (Proverbs 10:13)

2812. Vinegar (Proverbs 10:26)

2813. Guidance (Proverbs 11:14)

2814. A gold ring (Proverbs 11:22)

2815. Wind (Proverbs 11:29)

2816. Knowledge (Proverbs 12:1)

2817. Crown (Proverbs 12:4)

2818. Bones (Proverbs 12:4)

2819. Animals (Proverbs 12:10)

2820. Anxiety (Proverbs 12:25)

2821. A kind word (Proverbs 12:25)

2822. A sluggard (Proverbs 13:4)

2823. Great wealth (Proverbs 13:7)

2824. The heart (Proverbs 13:12)

2825. The rod (Proverbs 13:24)

2826. Ox (Proverbs 14:4)

2827. Death (Proverbs 14:12)

2828. Life (Proverbs 14:27)

2829. Envy (Proverbs 14:30)

2830. Their maker (Proverbs 14:31)

2831. Wrath (Proverbs 15:1)

2832. The soothing tongue (Proverbs 15:4)

2833. Vegetables (Proverbs 15:17)

2834. Advisers (Proverbs 15:22)

2835. House (Proverbs 15:25)

2836. Gold (Proverbs 16:16)

2837. Pride (Proverbs 16:18)

2838. Death (Proverbs 16:25)

2839. Gray hair (Proverbs 16:31)

2840. Strife (Proverbs 17:1)

2841. The heart (Proverbs 17:3)

2842. Cubs (Proverbs 17:12)

2843. A dam (Proverbs 17:14)

2844. A brother (Proverbs 17:17)

2845. Good medicine (Proverbs 17:22)

2846. A beating (Proverbs 18:6)

2847. Tower (Proverbs 18:10)

2848. The tongue (Proverbs 18:21)

2849. A wife (Proverbs 18:22)

2850. A friend (Proverbs 18:24)

2851. Wealth (Proverbs 19:4)

2852. A king's rage (Proverbs 19:12)

2853. A prudent wife (Proverbs 19:14)

2854. Their death (Proverbs 19:18)

2855. The Lord's purpose (Proverbs 19:21)

2856. A dish (Proverbs 19:24)

2857. Brawler (Proverbs 20:1)

2858. A lion (Proverbs 20:2)

2859. Ears that hear and eyes that see (Proverbs 20:12)

2860. Knowledge (Proverbs 20:15)

2861. Sweet (Proverbs 20:17)

2862. Gravel (Proverbs 20:17)

2863. Gray hair (Proverbs 20:29)

2864. The heart (Proverbs 21:2)

2865. The corner of the roof and the desert (Proverbs 21:9, 19)

2866. A gift (Proverbs 21:14)

2867. Wine and olive oil (Proverbs 21:17)

2868. The horse (Proverbs 21:31)

2869. A child (Proverbs 22:6)

2870. The borrower (Proverbs 22:7)

2871. A lion (Proverbs 22:13)

2872. A deep pit (Proverbs 22:14)

2873. An ancient boundary stone (Proverbs 22:28)

2874. A knife (Proverbs 23:2)

2875. Wine (Proverbs 23:32)

2876. A ship (Proverbs 23:34)

2877. A house (Proverbs 24:3–4)

2878. Advisers (Proverbs 24:6)

2879. Knowledge (Proverbs 24:13–14)

2880. Your enemy (Proverbs 24:17)

2881. A kiss on the lips (Proverbs 24:26)

2882. Your house (Proverbs 24:27)

2883. A bandit/thief (Proverbs 24:33–34)

2884. Apples (Proverbs 25:11)

2885. Honey (Proverbs 25:16)

2886. Your neighbor's (Proverbs 25:17)

2887. Burning coals (Proverbs 25:22)

2888. Good news (Proverbs 25:25)

2889. Self-control (Proverbs 25:28)

2890. A rod (Proverbs 25:3)

2891. A proverb (Proverbs 26:7)

2892. His vomit (Proverbs 26:11)

2893. A lion (Proverbs 26:13)

2894. His bed (Proverbs 26:14)

2895. Gossip (Proverbs 26:20)

2896. You'll fall in it (Proverbs 26:27)

2897. Jealousy (Proverbs 27:4)

2898. Kisses (Proverbs 27:6)

2899. Iron (Proverbs 27:17)

2900. His heart (Proverbs 27:19)

2901. Crops (Proverbs 28:3)

2902. A ruler (Proverbs 28:15)

2903. Bread (Proverbs 28:21)

2904. The righteous (Proverbs 28:28)

2905. Nets (Proverbs 29:5)

2906. Mockers (Proverbs 29:8)

2907. Peace (Proverbs 29:17)

2908. Revelation (Proverbs 29:18)

2909. Agur (Proverbs 30:1)

2910. His teeth and jaws (Proverbs 30:14)

2911. "Give, give" (Proverbs 30:15)

2912. The grave, a barren womb, dry land, and fire (Proverbs 30:16)

2913. Ravens (Proverbs 30:17)

2914. He stores up food in the summer (Proverbs 30:25)

2915. Crags (Proverbs 30:26)

2916. King (Proverbs 30:27)

2917. The king's palace (Proverbs 30:28)

2918. Lemuel (Proverbs 31:1)

2919. Beer and wine (Proverbs 31:4)

2920. Those perishing and in anguish (Proverbs 31:6, 7)

2921. Rubies (Proverbs 31:10)

2922. Her husband (Proverbs 31:11)

2923. Wool and flax (Proverbs 31:13)

2924. A merchant ship (Proverbs 31:14)

2925. Her lamp (Proverbs 31:18)

2926. A distaff and spindle (Proverbs 31:19)

2927. The poor and needy (Proverbs 31:20)

2928. Scarlet (Proverbs 31:21)

2929. Purple (Proverbs 31:22)

2930. At the city gate (Proverbs 31:23)

2931. Sashes (Proverbs 31:24)

2932. She laughs (Proverbs 31:25)

2933. Idleness (Proverbs 31:27)

2934. Her children and husband (Proverbs 31:28)

2935. Charm and beauty (Proverbs 31:30)

2936. She fears the Lord (Proverbs 31:30)

Ecclesiastes

2937. David (Ecclesiastes 1:1)

2938. Meaningless (Ecclesiastes 1:2)

2939. Wind (Ecclesiastes 1:6)

2940. The sun (Ecclesiastes 1:9)

2941. King of Israel (Ecclesiastes 1:12)

2942. Grief/sorrow (Ecclesiastes 1:18)

2943. Houses, vineyards, gardens, parks, and reservoirs (Ecclesiastes 2:4–5)

2944. Wind (Ecclesiastes 2:11)

2945. Wisdom (Ecclesiastes 2:13)

2946. Die (Ecclesiastes 3:2)

2947. Heal (Ecclesiastes 3:3)

2948. Laugh (Ecclesiastes 3:4)

2949. Dance (Ecclesiastes 3:4)

2950. Give up (Ecclesiastes 3:6)

2951. Mend (Ecclesiastes 3:7)

2952. Speak (Ecclesiastes 3:7)

2953. Hate (Ecclesiastes 3:8)

2954. Peace (Ecclesiastes 3:8)

2955. Eternity (Ecclesiastes 3:11)

2956. Animals (Ecclesiastes 3:19)

2957. To the dust (Ecclesiastes 3:20)

2958. The dead (Ecclesiastes 4:2)

2959. One not even born (Ecclesiastes 4:3)

2960. A friend (Ecclesiastes 4:10)

2961. Strands (Ecclesiastes 4:12)

2962. King (Ecclesiastes 4:13)

2963. Words (Ecclesiastes 5:2)

2964. Money (Ecclesiastes 5:10)

2965. Sleeping (Ecclesiastes 5:12)

2966. Naked (Ecclesiastes 5:15)

2967. A stillborn child (Ecclesiastes 6:3)

2968. Mouth (Ecclesiastes 6:7)

2969. A good name (Ecclesiastes 7:1)

2970. Feasting (Ecclesiastes 7:2)

2971. Fool (Ecclesiastes 7:7)

2972. Ten (Ecclesiastes 7:19)

2973. Wisdom (Ecclesiastes 8:1)

2974. A righteous person (Ecclesiastes 8:14)

2975. Lion (Ecclesiastes 9:4)

2976. White (Ecclesiastes 9:8)

2977. A city (Ecclesiastes 9:15)

2978. Wisdom (Ecclesiastes 9:18)

2979. Perfume (Ecclesiastes 10:1)

2980. Slaves (Ecclesiastes 10:7)

2981. He'll fall into it (Ecclesiastes 10:8)

2982. Strength or skill (Ecclesiastes 10:10)

2983. Rafters (Ecclesiastes 10:18)

2984. Grain/Bread (Ecclesiastes 11:1)

2985. Wind and clouds (Ecclesiastes 11:4)

2986. The path of wind and a body formed in the womb (Ecclesiastes 11:5)

2987. Our creator (Ecclesiastes 12:1)

2988. Nails or goads (Ecclesiastes 12:11)

2989. Books (Ecclesiastes 12:12)

2990. Fear God and keep his commandments (Ecclesiastes 12:11)

Song of Songs

2991. Wine (Song of Songs 1:2)

2992. Perfume (Song of Songs 1:3)

2993. Kedar (Song of Songs 1:5)

2994. Dark (Song of Songs 1:6)

2995. A mare (Song of Songs 1:9)

2996. Earrings (Song of Songs 1:11)

2997. Myrrh (Song of Songs 1:13)

2998. Doves (Song of Songs 1:15)

2999. A rose (Song of Songs 2:1)

3000. An apple (Song of Songs 2:3)

3001. Love (Song of Songs 2:7)

3002. Stag (Song of Songs 2:9)

3003. Foxes (Song of Songs 2:15)

3004. Lilies (Song of Songs 2:16)

3005. The watchmen (Song of Songs 3:3)

3006. Her mother's (Song of Songs 3:4)

3007. Solomon's carriage (Song of Songs 3:7)

3008. His mother (Song of Songs 3:11)

3009. Goats (Song of Songs 4:1)

3010. Her teeth (Song of Songs 4:2)

3011. Her temples (Song of Songs 4:3)

3012. Her neck (Song of Songs 4:4)

3013. Her breasts (Song of Songs 4:5)

3014. Milk and honey (Song of Songs 4:11)

3015. Myrrh (Song of Songs 5:5)

3016. The watchmen (Song of Songs 5:7)

3017. A raven (Song of Songs 5:11)

3018. A dove (Song of Songs 5:12)

3019. Lilies (Song of Songs 5:13)

3020. Gold (Song of Songs 5:14)

3021. Marble (Song of Songs 5:15)

3022. Goats (Song of Songs 6:5)

3023. Sixty queens (Song of Songs 6:8)

3024. Shulammite (Song of Songs 6:13)

3025. Jewels (Song of Songs 7:1)

3026. Her navel (Song of Songs 7:2)

3027. Her eyes (Song of Songs 7:4)

3028. Her nose (Song of Songs 7:4)

3029. Apples (Song of Songs 7:8)

3030. An apple tree (Songs of Songs 8:5)

3031. Their sister (Songs of Songs 8:8)

Isaiah

3032. Judah and Jerusalem (Isaiah 1:1)

3033. Amoz (Isaiah 1:1)

3034. Uzziah, Jotham, Ahaz, and Hezekiah (Isaiah 1:1)

3035. The ox and donkey (Isaiah 1:3)

3036. Sodom and Gomorrah (Isaiah 1:9)

3037. Bulls, lambs, and goats (Isaiah 1:11)

3038. The New Moon feast/festival (Isaiah 1:14)

3039. Scarlet/red/crimson (Isaiah 1:18)

3040. Snow and wool (Isaiah 1:18)

3041. The City of Righteousness and the Faithful City (Isaiah 1:26)

3042. All nations (Isaiah 2:2)

3043. Plowshares (Isaiah 2:4)

3044. Pruning hooks (Isaiah 2:4)

3045. Rodents/moles and bats (Isaiah 2:20)

3046. A boy/children/youth (Isaiah 3:4)

3047. Make them bald (Isaiah 3:17)

3048. Seven (Isaiah 4:1)

3049. Holy (Isaiah 4:3)

3050. A vineyard (Isaiah 5:7)

3051. Good (Isaiah 5:20)

3052. Drinking wine and mixing drinks (Isaiah 5:22)

3053. Uzziah (Isaiah 6:1)

3054. God's robe (Isaiah 6:1)

3055. Six wings (Isaiah 6:2)

3056. Covering faces, covering feet, and flying (Isaiah 6:2)

3057. The doorposts and thresholds (Isaiah 6:4)

3058. His lips (Isaiah 6:5)

3059. Tongs (Isaiah 6:6)

3060. A live coal (Isaiah 6:7)

3061. His guilt was taken away and his sins atoned for (Isaiah 6:7)

3062. "Here I am. Send me." (Isaiah 6:8)

3063. King Rezin and King Pekah (Isaiah 7:1)

3064. Aram and Israel (Isaiah 7:1)

3065. Isaiah 7:14

3066. Immanuel (Isaiah 7:14)

3067. Flies and bees (Isaiah 7:18)

3068. Maher-Shalal-Hash-Baz, means "swift is the booty, speedy is the prey" (Isaiah 8:1 NASB)

3069. The Assyrians (Isaiah 8:4)

3070. A stone (Isaiah 8:14)

3071. Spiritists and mediums (Isaiah 8:19)

3072. The government (Isaiah 9:6)

3073. Wonderful Counselor, Mighty God, Everlasting Father, Prince of Peace (Isaiah 9:6)

3074. The government and peace (Isaiah 9:7)

3075. Assyria (Isaiah 10:5)

3076. Jesse (Isaiah 11:1)

3077. Righteousness the belt and faithfulness the sash (Isaiah 11:5)

3078. The lamb (Isaiah 11:6)

3079. The goat (Isaiah 11:6)

3080. A little child (Isaiah 11:6)

3081. Straw (Isaiah 11:7)

3082. A viper/cobra/snake (Isaiah 11:8)

3083. A banner (Isaiah 11:10–12)

3084. Angry (Isaiah 12:1)

3085. The stars, constellations, sun, and moon (Isaiah 13:10)

3086. The Medes (Isaiah 13:17)

3087. Jackals (Isaiah 13:21–22)

3088. The morning star, son of the dawn (Isaiah 14:12)

3089. Moab (Isaiah 15:1–2)

3090. Blood (Isaiah 15:9)

3091. Three years (Isaiah 16:14)

3092. Damascus (Isaiah 17:1)

3093. Cush (Isaiah 18:2)

3094. The Nile (Isaiah 19:7)

3095. Assyria (Isaiah 19:23)

3096. Sargon (Isaiah 20:1)

3097. Three years (Isaiah 20:3)

3098. Horses, donkeys, and camels (Isaiah 21:7)

3099. Their hair (Isaiah 22:12)

3100. Eliakim (Isaiah 22:20-21)

3101. Tarshish (Isaiah 23:1, 14)

3102. Seventy (Isaiah 23:15)

3103. The earth (Isaiah 24:3, 6, 22)

3104. Death (Isaiah 25:8)

3105. Wind (Isaiah 26:18)

3106. Leviathan (Isaiah 27:1)

3107. Zion (Isaiah 28:16)

3108. Hearts (Isaiah 29:13)

3109. The potter (Isaiah 29:16)

3110. Egypt (Isaiah 30:7)

3111. Egypt (Isaiah 31:1)

3112. Their horses (Isaiah 31:3)

3113. Assyria (Isaiah 31:8)

3114. Women (Isaiah 32:9)

3115. Straw (Isaiah 33:11)

3116. Blood (Isaiah 34:3)

3117. The desert owl, screech owl, and the great owl (Isaiah 34:11)

3118. Blindness, deafness, lameness, and muteness (Isaiah 35:5–6)

3119. Sennacherib (Isaiah 36:1)

3120. Hezekiah (Isaiah 36:1)

3121. Egypt (Isaiah 36:6)

3122. Aramaic (Isiah 36:11)

3123. Hebrew (Isaiah 36:13)

3124. Sackcloth (Isaiah 37:1)

3125. Egypt/Cush (Isaiah 37:9)

3126. 185,000 (Isaiah 37:36)

3127. Nisrok (Isaiah 37:38)

3128. His sons Adrammeleck and Sharezer (Isaiah 37:38)

3129. Esarhaddon, his son (Isaiah 37:38)

3130. Hezekiah (Isaiah 38:1–3)

3131. Fifteen years (Isaiah 38:5)

3132. Assyria (Isaiah 38:6)

3133. The sun's shadow moved back ten steps (Isaiah 38:8)

3134. A poultice of figs (Isaiah 38:21)

3135. Marduk-Baladan, son of the king of Babylon (Isaiah 39:1)

3136. Babylon (Isaiah 39:2)

3137. A voice (Isaiah 40:3)

3138. Grass and flowers (Isaiah 40:8)

3139. A bucket (Isaiah 40:15)

3140. An eagle (Isaiah 40:31)

3141. Pools of water (Isaiah 41:18)

3142. A bruised reed (Isaiah 42:3)

3143. A smoldering wick (Isaiah 42:3)

3144. Gentiles (Isaiah 42:6)

3145. Our sins/transgressions (Isaiah 43:25)

3146. Idols (Isaiah 44:9)

3147. Cedar, cypress, oak, and pine (Isaiah 44:14)

3148. Cyrus (Isaiah 45:1)

3149. Bronze and iron (Isaiah 45:2)

3150. Clay (Isaiah 45:9)

3151. Sabeans (Isaiah 45:14)

3152. Idol makers (Isaiah 45:16)

3153. Bel and Nebo (Isaiah 46:1)

3154. Babylon (Isaiah 47:5)

3155. Astrologers and stargazers (Isaiah 47:13)

3156. Wooden images/metal gods (Isaiah 48:5)

3157. A river (Isaiah 48:18)

3158. The wicked (Isaiah 48:22)

3159. The Gentiles (Isaiah 49:6)

3160. Flesh (Isaiah 49:26)

3161. Pull out his beard (Isaiah 50:6)

3162. Mock and spit on him (Isaiah 50:6)

3163. Eden (Isaiah 51:3)

3164. God's wrath (Isaiah 51:17)

3165. Good news (Isaiah 52:7)

3166. Shoot (Isaiah 53:2)

3167. Beauty or majesty (Isaiah 53:2)

3168. People (Isaiah 53:3)

3169. Suffering/pain (Isaiah 53:3)

3170. Transgressions (Isaiah 53:5)

3171. Peace (Isaiah 53:5)

3172. Healed (Isaiah 53:5)

3173. Sheep (Isaiah 53:6)

3174. Our iniquity (Isaiah 53:6)

3175. Lamb (Isaiah 53:7)

3176. Shearers (Isaiah 53:7)

3177. The land of the living (Isaiah 53:8)

3178. The wicked and the rich (Isaiah 53:9)

3179. Any deceit (Isaiah 53:9)

3180. A barren woman (Isaiah 54:1)

3181. The mountains/hills (Isaiah 54:10)

3182. Weapon (Isaiah 54:17)

3183. The word from his mouth (Isaiah 55:11)

3184. Prayer (Isaiah 56:7)

3185. Dogs (Isaiah 56:10–11)

3186. Sorceress, adulterers, and prostitutes (Isaiah 57:3)

3187. Molech (Isaiah 57:9)

3188. The wicked (Isaiah 57:20)

3189. The wicked (Isaiah 57:21)

3190. Fasting (Isaiah 58:4)

3191. His arm (Isaiah 59:1)

3192. Sin (Isaiah 59:7)

3193. The breastplate of righteousness and the helmet of salvation (Isaiah 59:17)

3194. Foreigners (Isaiah 60:10)

3195. The Lord (Isaiah 60:20)

3196. Jesus (Isaiah 61:1–2; Luke 4:18–30)

3197. Jerusalem (Isaiah 62:6)

3198. Red (Isaiah 63:2)

3199. Blood (Isaiah 63:3)

3200. The Holy Spirit (Isaiah 63:10)

3201. Filthy rags (Isaiah 64:6)

3202. Our sins (Isaiah 64:9)

3203. Heaven and earth (Isaiah 65:17)

3204. Weeping and crying (Isaiah 65:19)

3205. Straw (Isaiah 65:25)

3206. Dust (Isaiah 65:25)

3207. Footstool (Isaiah 66:1)

3208. A river (Isaiah 66:12)

3209. Archers (Isaiah 66:19)

3210. The worm (Isaiah 66:24)

Jeremiah

3211. Hilkiah (Jeremiah 1:1)

3212. Priest (Jeremiah 1:1)

3213. Josiah, Jehoiakim, and Zedekiah (Jeremiah 1:2–3)

3214. "I'm too young" (Jeremiah 1:7)

3215. An almond tree (Jeremiah 1:11)

3216. Boiling (Jeremiah 1:13)

3217. Their gods (Jeremiah 2:11)

3218. Cisterns (Jeremiah 2:13)

3219. The Nile and the Euphrates (Jeremiah 2:18)

3220. Their father (Jeremiah 2:27)

3221. Judah (Jeremiah 3:8)

3222. Stone and wood (Jeremiah 3:9)

3223. Judah (Jeremiah 3:11)

3224. The ark of the covenant (Jeremiah 3:16)

3225. Backsliding (Jeremiah 3:22)

3226. Eagles (Jeremiah 4:13)

3227. Their hearts (Jeremiah 4:14)

3228. One person (Jeremiah 5:1)

3229. Stone (Jeremiah 5:3)

3230. Lion, wolf, and leopard (Jeremiah 5:6)

3231. Another man's wife (Jeremiah 5:8)

3232. Their quivers (Jeremiah 5:16)

3233. Birds (Jeremiah 5:27)

3234. The north (Jeremiah 6:22)

3235. Robbers (Jeremiah 7:11)

3236. Shiloh (Jeremiah 7:12)

3237. The Queen of Heaven (Jeremiah 7:18)

3238. Their sons and daughters (Jeremiah 7:31)

3239. Valley of Slaughter (Jeremiah 7:32)

3240. Gildead (Jeremiah 8:22)

3241. Lies (Jeremiah 9:3)

3242. Jackals (Jeremiah 9:11)

3243. Death (Jeremiah 9:21)

3244. Idols (Jeremiah 10:5)

3245. Towns (Jeremiah 11:13)

3246. Streets (Jeremiah 11:13)

3247. Anathoth (Jeremiah 11:21)

3248. Thorns (Jeremiah 12:13)

3249. Linen (Jeremiah 13:1)

3250. Water (Jeremiah 13:1)

3251. In a crevice in the rocks (Jeremiah 13:4)

3252. His skin (Jeremiah 13:23)

3253. A leopard (Jeremiah 13:23)

3254. A drought (Jeremiah 14:1, 3, 4)

3255. Moses and Samuel (Jeremiah 15:1)

3256. Sword, dogs, birds, and wild animals (Jeremiah 15:3)

3257. Manasseh (Jeremiah 15:4)

3258. Marry or have kids (Jeremiah 16:2)

3259. Mourn or show sympathy (Jeremiah 16:5)

3260. Sit down to eat or drink (Jeremiah 16:8)

3261. Psalm 1 (Jeremiah 17:8; Psalm 1:3)

3262. Carry a load (Jeremiah 17:21, 22, 24, 27)

3263. The potter's house (Jeremiah 18:2)

3264. A clay jar (Jeremiah 19:1, 10)

3265. Judah and Jerusalem (Jeremiah 19:11)

3266. Pashur (Jeremiah 20:1–2)

3267. Babylon (Jeremiah 20:4)

3268. Zedekiah (Jeremiah 21:1–2)

3269. Surrendering (Jeremiah 21:9)

3270. Cedar (Jeremiah 22:14–15)

3271. Jehoiakim (Jeremiah 22:18–19)

3272. A signet ring (Jeremiah 22:24)

3273. The shepherds (Jeremiah 23:1)

3274. A righteous branch (Jeremiah 23:5)

3275. Figs (Jeremiah 24:2)

3276. The exiles to Babylon (Jeremiah 24:5)

3277. King Zedekiah, his officials, and the survivors from Jerusalem (Jeremiah 24:8)

3278. Twenty-three years (Jeremiah 25:3)

3279. Seventy years (Jeremiah 25:11)

3280. The king of Babylon and his nation (Jeremiah 25:12)

3281. Wrath (Jeremiah 25:15)

3282. Micah (Jeremiah 26:18)

3283. Uriah (Jeremiah 26:20)

3284. A yoke (Jeremiah 27:2)

3285. King of Babylon/Nebuchadnezzar (Jeremiah 27:12)

3286. The temple (Jeremiah 27:21–22)

3287. Hananiah (Jeremiah 28:10)

3288. Iron (Jeremiah 28:13)

3289. The wild animals (Jeremiah 28:14)

3290. Plans to prosper, not to harm, to give hope and a future (Jeremiah 29:11)

3291. Shemaiah (Jeremiah 29:24)

3292. David (Jeremiah 30:9)

3293. Jacob's (Jeremiah 30:18)

3294. Rachel (Jeremiah 31:15)

3295. Ramah (Jeremiah 31:15)

3296. The children (Jeremiah 31:29)

3297. On their hearts (Jeremiah 31:33)

3298. Zedekiah (Jeremiah 32:3)

3299. A field (Jeremiah 32:7)

3300. A righteous branch (Jeremiah 33:15)

3301. The king of Babylon (Jeremiah 34:3)

3302. Peaceful (Jeremiah 34:5)

3303. The Hebrew slaves (Jeremiah 34:9)

3304. Zedekiah (Jeremiah 34:21)

3305. Rekabites (Jeremiah 35:2)

3306. Wine (Jeremiah 35:5)

3307. Baruch (Jeremiah 36:4)

3308. In the temple (Jeremiah 36:5)

3309. Cut them with a knife and threw them in the fire (Jeremiah 36:23)

3310. Zedekiah (Jeremiah 37:1)

3311. Egypt (Jeremiah 37:5)

3312. He was arrested (Jeremiah 37:13–14)

3313. Jonathan (Jeremiah 37:15)

3314. A cistern (Jeremiah 38:6)

3315. Ebed-Melek (Jeremiah 38:7)

3316. Surrender to Babylon (Jeremiah 38:17)

3317. About a year and a half (Jeremiah 39:1–2)

3318. Jericho (Jeremiah 39:5)

3319. His sons (Jeremiah 39:6)

3320. His eyes (Jeremiah 39:7)

3321. Nebuzaradan (Jeremiah 39:9)

3322. The poor people (Jeremiah 39:10)

3323. Ebed-Melek (Jeremiah 39:16–17)

3324. Nebuzaradan, commander of the Babylonian army (Jeremiah 40:4)

3325. Stay behind in Jerusalem (Jeremiah 40:5–6)

3326. Gedaliah (Jeremiah 40:5)

3327. Ishmael (Jeremiah 41:2)

3328. Into a cistern (Jeremiah 41:7)

3329. Egypt (Jeremiah 42:19)

3330. Tahpanhes (Jeremiah 43:7)

3331. Egypt (Jeremiah 43:12)

3332. Heaven (Jeremiah 44:19)

3333. Cakes (Jeremiah 44:19)

3334. Hophra (Jeremiah 44:30)

3335. Baruch, his secretary (Jeremiah 45:1–5)

3336. Necho (Jeremiah 46:2)

3337. Carchemish (Jeremiah 46:2)

3338. The sword (Jeremiah 46:10)

3339. Amon (Jeremiah 46:25)

3340. The Philistines (Jeremiah 47:4–5)

3341. Moab (Jeremiah 48:9, 25)

3342. Molech (Jeremiah 49:1)

3343. Strip it bare since grape pickers and thieves always leave something behind (Jeremiah 49:9–10)

3344. In labor (Jeremiah 49:24)

3345. Bel and Marduk (Jeremiah 50:2)

3346. Babylon (Jeremiah 51:7)

3347. Medes (Jeremiah 51:11)

3348. The temple (Jeremiah 51:11)

3349. Seraiah (Jeremiah 51:60–61)

3350. The Euphrates river (Jeremiah 51:63)

3351. Nebuzaradan (Jeremiah 52:12)

3352. To work the vineyards and fields (Jeremiah 52:16)

3353. 4,600 (Jeremiah 52:30)

3354. Jehoiachin (Jeremiah 52:31–33)

3355. Evil-Merodach/Awel-Marduk (Jeremiah 52:31)

Lamentations

3356. Jerusalem (Lamentations 1:7–8)

3357. A yoke (Lamentations 1:14)

3358. Dust (Lamentations 2:10)

3359. Children and infants (Lamentations 2:11)

3360. Prophets (Lamentations 2:14)

3361. Faithfulness (Lamentations 3:22–23)

3362. A cloud (Lamentations 3:44)

3363. Ostrich (Lamentations 4:3)

3364. Sodom (Lamentations 4:6)

3365. By famine (Lamentations 4:9)

3366. Their children (Lamentations 4:10)

3367. Egypt and Assyria (Lamentations 5:6)

3368. Mourning (Lamentations 5:15)

Ezekiel

3369. Kebar (Ezekiel 1:1)

3370. Babylon (Ezekiel 1:3)

3371. Priest (Ezekiel 1:3)

3372. Four (Ezekiel 1:5)

3373. Four of each (Ezekiel 1:6)

3374. Man, lion, ox, and eagle (Ezekiel 1:10)

3375. A wheel/rim (Ezekiel 1:15)

3376. Eyes (Ezekiel 1:18)

3377. Rushing waters (Ezekiel 1:24)

3378. Metal (Ezekiel 1:27)

3379. Son of man (Ezekiel 2:1)

3380. The Israelites (Ezekiel 2:3)

3381. A scroll (Ezekiel 3:1)

3382. Sweet like honey (Ezekiel 3:3)

3383. Stone/flint (Ezekiel 3:9)

3384. Seven days (Ezekiel 3:15)

3385. A block of clay (Ezekiel 4:1)

3386. A siege/ramps (Ezekiel 4:2)

3387. 390 days (Ezekiel 4:5)

3388. Forty days (Ezekiel 4:6)

3389. Ropes (Ezekiel 4:8)

3390. Wheat, barley, beans, lentils, millet, and spelt (Ezekiel 4:9)

3391. Twenty shekels (Ezekiel 4:10)

3392. Water (Ezekiel 4:11)

3393. Human excrement (Ezekiel 4:12)

3394. Cow dung (Ezekiel 4:15)

3395. A sharp sword (Ezekiel 5:1)

3396. His hair (Ezekiel 5:2)

3397. Plague, famine, the sword, scattering them all over, and wild beasts (Ezekiel 5:12, 17)

3398. Idols (Ezekiel 6:4)

3399. Urine (Ezekiel 7:17)

3400. Their silver (Ezekiel 7:19)

3401. His hair (Ezekiel 8:3)

3402. Jerusalem (Ezekiel 8:3)

3403. Idol worship (Ezekiel 8:3, 10, 14, 16)

3404. Tammuz (Ezekiel 8:12)

3405. A writing kit (Ezekiel 9:2)

3406. Their foreheads (Ezekiel 9:4)

3407. Burning coals (Ezekiel 10:2)

3408. Eyes (Ezekiel 10:12)

3409. A cherub, a human, a lion, and an eagle (Ezekiel 10:14)

3410. By the Kebar river (Ezekiel 10:15)

3411. The glory of the Lord (Ezekiel 10:18)

3412. Human hands (Ezekiel 10:21)

3413. Meat (Ezekiel 11:7)

3414. He died (Ezekiel 11:13)

3415. Babylonia (Ezekiel 11:24)

3416. A wall (Ezekiel 12:5)

3417. Whitewash (Ezekiel 13:15)

3418. Magic charms (Ezekiel 13:18)

3419. Noah, Daniel, Job (Ezekiel 14:14, 20)

3420. Sword, famine, wild beasts, and plague (Ezekiel 14:21)

3421. Fire (Ezekiel 15:5–6)

3422. A prostitute (Ezekiel 16:13–15)

3423. Payment/she did it for free (Ezekiel 16:31)

3424. Sodom and Samaria (Ezekiel 16:49, 51)

3425. Eagle (Ezekiel 17:3, 7)

3426. Babylon (Ezekiel 17:12)

3427. A cedar (Ezekiel 17:22)

3428. Grapes (Ezekiel 18:2)

3429. The parent (Ezekiel 18:20)

3430. A lion (Ezekiel 19:1–9)

3431. Hand, arm (Ezekiel 20:33)

3432. A sword (Ezekiel 21:1-3)

3433. A scepter (Ezekiel 21:13)

3434. The liver (Ezekiel 21:21)

3435. The dross (Ezekiel 22:18)

3436. Copper, tin, iron, lead, and silver (Ezekiel 22:20)

3437. Samaria and Jerusalem (Ezekiel 23:4)

3438. Oholah and Oholibah (Ezekiel 23:4)

3439. Assyria and Babylon (Ezekiel 23:9, 15, 17)

3440. Egypt (Ezekiel 23:27)

3441. A pot (Ezekiel 24:11)

3442. His wife (Ezekiel 24:16, 18)

3443. Mourn or weep (Ezekiel 24:23)

3444. Camels and sheep (Ezekiel 25:5)

3445. Tyre (Ezekiel 26–28)

3446. Nebuchadnezzar, king of Babylon (Ezekiel 26:7)

3447. Trading (Ezekiel 27:12–23)

3448. Daniel (Ezekiel 28:3)

3449. King of Tyre (Ezekiel 28:12–13)

3450. Its beauty (Ezekiel 28:17)

3451. The Nile (Ezekiel 29:9)

3452. Egypt (Ezekiel 29:12–13)

3453. Tyre (Ezekiel 29:18)

3454. Egypt (Ezekiel 30:14–18)

3455. Pharaoh (Ezekiel 30:22)

3456. The king of Babylon (Ezekiel 30:24)

3457. A cedar (Ezekiel 31:3)

3458. The realm of the dead (Ezekiel 32:21, 27)

3459. Ezekiel (Ezekiel 33:7)

3460. Sheep (Ezekiel 34:2, 30–31)

3461. Shepherds (Ezekiel 34:2, 8–9)

3462. David (Ezekiel 34:23)

3463. Edom (Ezekiel 35:15)

3464. Flesh (Ezekiel 36:26)

3465. Bones (Ezekiel 37:1)

3466. A vast army (Ezekiel 37:10)

3467. Israel (Ezekiel 37:11)

3468. Sticks (Ezekiel 37:15–16)

3469. Judah and Israel/Joseph and Ephraim (Ezekiel 37:15–16)

3470. Magog (Ezekiel 38:1)

3471. The weapons of the fallen army (Ezekiel 39:10)

3472. A measuring rod (Ezekiel 40:5)

3473. A new temple (Ezekiel 40–43)

3474. One hundred cubits long (Ezekiel 41:13)

3475. A man and a lion (Ezekiel 41:19)

3476. Five hundred cubits long (Ezekiel 42:16–20)

3477. The east (Ezekiel 43:2)

3478. Zadok (Ezekiel 44:15)

3479. Linen (Ezekiel 44:17)

3480. It made them perspire (Ezekiel 44:18)

3481. Widowed or divorced women (Ezekiel 44:22)

3482. A priest (Ezekiel 44:22)

3483. A tenth (Ezekiel 45:11)

3484. Twenty gerahs (Ezekiel 45:12)

3485. A mina (Ezekiel 45:12)

3486. The gate opposite from which they entered (Ezekiel 46:9)

3487. Water/a river (Ezekiel 47:1)

3488. The Dead Sea (Ezekiel 47:8)

3489. Fresh water (Ezekiel 47:8)

3490. Fruit trees (Ezekiel 47:12)

3491. Healing (Ezekiel 47:12)

3492. The Mediterranean (Ezekiel 47:20)

3493. The Zadokites (Ezekiel 48:11)

3494. The tribes of Israel (Ezekiel 48:31)

3495. The Lord is there (Ezekiel 48:35)

Daniel

3496. Nebuchadnezzar (Daniel 1:1)

3497. Jehoiakim (Daniel 1:2)

3498. Articles from the temple (Daniel 1:2)

3499. Ashpenaz (Daniel 1:3)

3500. The language and the literature of the Babylonians (Daniel 1:4)

3501. Food and wine (Daniel 1:5)

3502. Three years (Daniel 1:5)

3503. Hananiah, Mishael, and Azariah (Daniel 1:6)

3504. Shadrach, Meshach, and Abednego (Daniel 1:7)

3505. Belteshazzar (Daniel 1:7)

3506. Ten days (Daniel 1:12)

3507. Vegetables (Daniel 1:12)

3508. Literature and learning (Daniel 1:17)

3509. Understanding visions and dreams (Daniel 1:17)

3510. Ten times better (Daniel 1:20)

3511. King Cyrus (Daniel 1:21)

3512. Magicians, enchanters, sorcerers, and astrologers (Daniel 2:2)

3513. Cut them into pieces and turn their houses into rubble (Daniel 2:5)

3514. Arioch (Daniel 2:14)

3515. Gold, silver, bronze, and iron (Daniel 2:32–33)

3516. A rock (Daniel 2:34)

3517. The first part of the statute–the head (Daniel 2:38)

3518. Kingdoms that will rule one after another (Daniel 2:39–40)

3519. Ruler of the province and in charge of the wise men (Daniel 2:48)

3520. Administrators over the province of Babylon (Daniel 2:49)

3521. Ninety feet tall or sixty cubits (Daniel 3:1)

3522. Gold (Daniel 3:1)

3523. They must fall down and worship the image of gold (Daniel 3:5)

3524. Shadrach, Meshach, and Abednego (Daniel 3:12)

3525. A fiery furnace (Daniel 3:17)

3526. Seven times hotter (Daniel 3:19)

3527. The soldiers that threw Daniel's friends into the fire (Daniel 3:22)

3528. Four (Daniel 3:25)

3529. A son of the gods (Daniel 3:25)

3530. Fire/smoke (Daniel 3:27)

3531. A god Nebuchadnezzar worshiped (Daniel 4:8)

3532. A tree (Daniel 4:10)

3533. Nebuchadnezzar (Daniel 4:22)

3534. The roof of his royal palace (Daniel 4:29)

3535. Ox/cattle (Daniel 4:33)

3536. Dew (Daniel 4:33)

3537. Grass (Daniel 4:33)

3538. His sanity was restored (Daniel 4:36)

3539. King Belshazzar (Daniel 5:1)

3540. The gold and silver goblets (Daniel 5:2)

3541. The fingers of a human hand (Daniel 5:5)

3542. They would be clothed in purple, have a gold chain around their neck, and be promoted to the third highest ruler (Daniel 5:7)

3543. The queen (Daniel 5:10)

3544. Nebuchadnezzar (Daniel 5:11)

3545. Mene, tekel, and parsin (Daniel 5:25)

3546. Medes and Persians (Daniel 5:28)

3547. He was slain (Daniel 5:30)

3548. Darius the Mede (Daniel 5:31)

3549. The king (Daniel 6:7)

3550. Thirty days (Daniel 6:7)

3551. The person was thrown into a lions' den (Daniel 6:7)

3552. Three times a day (Daniel 6:13)

3553. King Darius (Daniel 6:15–16)

3554. His signet ring (Daniel 6:17)

3555. An angel (Daniel 6:22)

3556. Daniel's accusers, their wives, and their children (Daniel 6:24)

3557. Darius and Cyrus (Daniel 6:28)

3558. Belshazzar (Daniel 7:1)

3559. Beasts (Daniel 7:3)

3560. An eagle (Daniel 7:4)

3561. Three ribs (Daniel 7:5)

3562. Four heads and four wings (Daniel 7:6)

3563. Iron (Daniel 7:7)

3564. Ten (Daniel 7:7)

3565. Boastfully (Daniel 7:8)

3566. Clouds of heaven (Daniel 7:13)

3567. Four kings/kingdoms (Daniel 7:17)

3568. Ten kings that come from the fourth kingdom (Daniel 7:24)

3569. Belshazzar (Daniel 8:1)

3570. A ram and a goat (Daniel 8:3, 5)

3571. The goat (Daniel 8:7)

3572. Four (Daniel 8:8)

3573. Gabriel (Daniel 8:16)

3574. The kings of Media and Persia (Daniel 8:20)

3575. The king of Greece (Daniel 8:21)

3576. Four kingdoms that came from this one nation (Daniel 8:22)

3577. Darius (Daniel 9:1)

3578. Jeremiah (Daniel 9:2)

3579. Gabriel (Daniel 9:21)

3580. Seventy sevens (Daniel 9:24)

3581. Desolation (Daniel 9:27)

3582. Cyrus (Daniel 10:1)

3583. Three weeks (Daniel 10:2)

3584. The Tigris (Daniel 10:4)

3585. Linen (Daniel 10:5)

3586. Gold (Daniel 10:5)

3587. Twenty-one days (Daniel 10:13)

3588. Michael (Daniel 10:13)

3589. Greece (Daniel 10:20)

3590. Four kings (Daniel 11:2)

3591. Greece (Daniel 11:2)

3592. Four leaders (Daniel 11:4)

3593. The king of the South and the king of the North (Daniel 11:6)

3594. Michael (Daniel 12:1)

3595. A time, times and a half a time (Daniel 12:7)

3596. 1,290 days (Daniel 12:11)

Hosea

3597. Beeri (Hosea 1:1)

3598. Uzziah, Jotham, Ahaz, and Hezekiah (Hosea 1:1)

3599. Gomer (Hosea 1:3)

3600. Three (Hosea 1:4, 6, 9)

3601. Jezreel (Hosea 1:4)

3602. "Not loved" (Hosea 1:6)

3603. "Not my people" (Hosea 1:9)

3604. My husband (Hosea 2:16)

3605. Baal (Hosea 2:17)

3606. Silver and barley (Hosea 3:2)

3607. Prostitution (Hosea 4:12)

3608. Heifer (Hosea 4:16)

3609. Ephraim (Hosea 5:11, 13)

3610. Their love (Hosea 6:4)

3611. Sacrifice (Hosea 6:6)

3612. Ovens (Hosea 7:6)

3613. An eagle (Hosea 8:1)

3614. A calf (Hosea 8:6)

3615. Maniacs (Hosea 9:7)

3616. Grapes (Hosea 9:10)

3617. The calf idol of Beth Aven (Hosea 10:5–6)

3618. His son (Hosea 11:1)

3619. Doves (Hosea 11:11)

3620. Egypt (Hosea 12:9)

3621. A lion, leopard, and bear (Hosea 13:7–8)

3622. A king (Hosea 13:11)

3623. Paul in 1 Corinthians 15:55

3624. Cedar, olive, and juniper (Hosea 14:5, 6, 8)

Joel

3625. Pethuel (Joel 1:1)

3626. Locusts (Joel 1:4)

3627. The drunkards (Joel 1:5)

3628. The virgin and the priests (Joel 1:8, 13)

3629. The day of the Lord (Joel 1:15)

3630. The sun, moon, and stars (Joel 2:10)

3631. Judah (Joel 2:21)

3632. Locusts (Joel 2:25)

3633. Dream dreams (Joel 2:28)

3634. See visions (Joel 2:28)

3635. Turn to darkness (Joel 2:31)

3636. Turn to blood (Joel 2:31)

3637. They will be saved (Joel 2:32)

3638. The Greeks (Joel 3:4, 6)

3639. Swords (Joel 3:10)

3640. Wine, milk, and water (Joel 3:18)

Amos

3641. A shepherd (Amos 1:1)

3642. Tekoa (Amos 1:1)

3643. An earthquake (Amos 1:1)

3644. Uzziah (Amos 1:1)

3645. Jeroboam (Amos 1:1)

3646. Three, even for four (Amos 1:3, 6, 9, 11, 13)

3647. The gate (Amos 1:5)

3648. Damascus, Gaza, Tyre, Edom, Ammon, Moab, Judah, and Israel (Amos 1–2)

3649. The poor (Amos 2:7)

3650. Wine (Amos 2:12)

3651. The archer, the foot soldier, and the horseman (Amos 2:15)

3652. The prophets (Amos 3:7)

3653. Bethel (Amos 3:14)

3654. With hooks/fishhooks (Amos 4:2)

3655. Rain (Amos 4:7)

3656. Pleiades and Orion (Amos 5:8)

3657. A bear (Amos 5:19)

3658. Bed and couches (Amos 6:4)

3659. Locust (Amos 7:1)

3660. A plumb line (Amos 7:7)

3661. Amaziah (Amos 7:10)

3662. Jeroboam (Amos 7:10)

3663. A prophet (Amos 7:14)

3664. Sycamore-fig (Amos 7:14)

3665. Ripe fruit (Amos 8:2)

3666. Hearing the word of the Lord (Amos 8:11)

3667. Mount Carmel (Amos 9:3)

3668. Sword (Amos 9:10)

3669. Wine (Amos 9:13)

Obadiah

3670. Obadiah

3671. Edom (Obadiah 1)

3672. Esau (Obadiah 6)

3673. Jacob/Israel (Obadiah 10)

3674. Stubble (Obadiah 18)

Jonah

3675. Amittai (Jonah 1:1)

3676. Nineveh (Jonah 1:1)

3677. They were wicked (Jonah 1:2)

3678. Tarshish (Jonah 1:3)

3679. Joppa (Jonah 1:3)

3680. A storm (Jonah 1:4)

3681. Their own gods (Jonah 1:5)

3682. Cargo (Jonah 1:5)

3683. Sleeping (Jonah 1:5)

3684. They cast lots (Jonah 1:7)

3685. Throw him into the sea (Jonah 1:12)

3686. Row back to land (Jonah 1:13)

3687. Three days and nights (Jonah 1:17)

3688. Seaweed (Jonah 2:5)

3689. He vomited him up (Jonah 2:10)

3690. Three days (Jonah 3:3)

3691. Forty days (Jonah 3:4)

3692. Sackcloth (Jonah 3:5)

3693. A fast (Jonah 3:7)

3694. East of the city (Jonah 4:5)

3695. A shelter (Jonah 4:5)

3696. A leafy plant/vine (Jonah 4:6)

3697. Worm (Jonah 4:7)

3698. 120,000 people (Jonah 4:11)

Micah

3699. Jotham, Ahaz, and Hezekiah (Micah 1:1)

3700. Judah (Micah 1:1)

3701. Samaria and Jerusalem (Micah 1:1)

3702. Jackal and owl (Micah 1:8)

3703. A vulture (Micah 1:16)

3704. Wine and beer (Micah 2:11)

3705. Zion and Jerusalem (Micah 3:12)

3706. The mountain of the Lord's temple (Micah 4:1)

3707. Plowshares (Micah 4:3)

3708. Babylon (Micah 4:10)

3709. Bethlehem (Micah 5:2)

3710. A ruler over Israel (Micah 5:2)

3711. Old ancient times (Micah 5:2)

3712. Balak and Balaam (Micah 6:5)

3713. Rams and oil (Micah 6:7)

3714. Ahab (Micah 6:16)

3715. His own household (Micah 7:6)

3716. Into the depths of the sea (Micah 7:19)

Nahum

3717. An Elkoshite (Nahum 1:11)

3718. Anger (Nahum 1:3)

3719. The sea/rivers (Nahum 1:4)

3720. Nineveh (Nahum 1:8)

3721. The yoke on Judah (Nahum 1:13)

3722. Female slaves (Nahum 2:7)

3723. Chariots (Nahum 2:13)

3724. Her shirt (Nahum 3:5)

3725. Locusts/grasshoppers (Nahum 3:17)

Habakkuk

3726. The Babylonians (Habakkuk 1:6)

3727. Leopards (Habakkuk 1:8)

3728. Hooks and nets (Habakkuk 1:15)

3729. Bloodshed (Habakkuk 2:12)

3730. God's glory (Habakkuk 2:14)

3731. Shigionoth and selah (Habakkuk 3:1, 13)

3732. Deer (Habakkuk 3:19)

Zephaniah

3733. Josiah (Zephaniah 1:1)

3734. Baal and Molek (Zephaniah 1:4–5)

3735. The blind (Zephaniah 1:17)

3736. Dust (Zephaniah 1:17)

3737. Nineveh (Zephaniah 2:13)

3738. Desert owl and screech owl (Zephaniah 2:14)

3739. Officials, prophets, and priests (Zephaniah 3:3–4)

Haggai

3740. Darius (Haggai 1:1)

3741. The second year of his reign (Haggai 1:1; 2:10)

3742. Four times (Haggai 1:1; 2:1, 10, 20)

3743. Zerubabbel and Joshua (Haggai 1:1)

3744. The temple/God's house (Haggai 1:9)

3745. Their own houses (Haggai 1:9)

3746. Governor (Haggai 1:14)

3747. High priest (Haggai 1:14)

3748. Two—during the sixth and seventh months (Haggai 1:1; 2:10, 20)

3749. A signet ring (Haggai 2:23)

Zechariah

3750. Darius (Zechariah 1:1)

3751. Red, brown, and white (Zechariah 1:8)

3752. Myrtle (Zechariah 1:11)

3753. Judah, Israel, and Jerusalem (Zechariah 1:19)

3754. Jerusalem (Zechariah 2:2)

3755. Joshua the high priest (Zechariah 3:1–3)

3756. Satan (Zechariah 3:1)

3757. A turban (Zechariah 3:5)

3758. Seven (Zechariah 3:9)

3759. Sin (Zechariah 3:9)

3760. A lampstand (Zechariah 4:2)

3761. Zerubbabel (Zechariah 4:9)

3762. Olive trees (Zechariah 4:11)

3763. A scroll (Zechariah 5:1)

3764. A woman (Zechariah 5:7)

3765. The sin/wickedness of the people (Zechariah 5:6)

3766. Babylonia (Zechariah 5:11)

3767. Red, black, white, and dappled (Zechariah 6:2)

3768. Four spirits of heaven (Zechariah 6:5)

3769. Joshua the high priest (Zechariah 6:11)

3770. Branch (Zechariah 6:12)

3771. Flint (Zechariah 7:12)

3772. Faithful City (Zechariah 8:3)

3773. Fasts (Zechariah 8:19)

3774. Ten (Zechariah 8:23)

3775. Donkey and a colt/foal of a donkey (Zechariah 9:9)

3776. The shepherds/leaders (Zechariah 10:3)

3777. Judah (Zechariah 10:4)

3778. Lebanon (Zechariah 11:1)

3779. Bashan (Zechariah 11:2)

3780. Favor and Union (Zechariah 11:7)

3781. One month (Zechariah 11:8)

3782. Thirty pieces of silver (Zechariah 11:12)

3783. The potter (Zechariah 11:13)

3784. Judah and Israel (Zechariah 11:14)

3785. Their hooves (Zechariah 11:16)

3786. The right eye (Zechariah 11:17)

3787. A rock (Zechariah 12:3)

3788. Pierced (Zechariah 12:10)

3789. Hair (Zechariah 13:4)

3790. The sheep scatter (Zechariah 13:7)

3791. Mount of Olives (Zechariah 14:4)

3792. Uzziah (Zechariah 14:5)

3793. Living water (Zechariah 14:8)

3794. Festival of Tabernacles (Zechariah 14:18)

3795. Cooking pots (Zechariah 14:20)

Malachi

3796. Malachi

3797. Esau (Malachi 1:2–3)

3798. Edom (Malachi 1:4)

3799. Blind, crippled, and diseased (Malachi 1:8)

3800. Offal/dung (Malachi 2:3)

3801. Levi (Malachi 2:4–6)

3802. Divorce (Malachi 2:16)

3803. Refiner's fire and launderer's soap (Malachi 3:2)

3804. The Levites (Malachi 3:3)

3805. In tithes and offerings (Malachi 3:8)

3806. Heaven (Malachi 3:10)

3807. Elijah (Malachi 4:5)

3808. Fathers/parents and children (Malachi 4:6)

Keep Score

Which questions did you answer correctly?
Make copies and challenge your friends!

Question #	✔	Question #	✔	Question #	✔	Question #	✔	Question #	✔
Genesis		28		56		84		112	
1		29		57		85		113	
2		30		58		86		114	
3		31		59		87		115	
4		32		60		88		116	
5		33		61		89		117	
6		34		62		90		118	
7		35		63		91		119	
8		36		64		92		120	
9		37		65		93		121	
10		38		66		94		122	
11		39		67		95		123	
12		40		68		96		124	
13		41		69		97		125	
14		42		70		98		126	
15		43		71		99		127	
16		44		72		100		128	
17		45		73		101		129	
18		46		74		102		130	
19		47		75		103		131	
20		48		76		104		132	
21		49		77		105		133	
22		50		78		106		134	
23		51		79		107		135	
24		52		80		108		136	
25		53		81		109		137	
26		54		82		110		138	
27		55		83		111		139	

Question #	✔	Question #	✔	Question #	✔	Question #	✔	Question #	✔
140		174		208		242		276	
141		175		209		243		277	
142		176		210		244		278	
143		177		211		245		279	
144		178		212		246		280	
145		179		213		247		281	
146		180		214		248		282	
147		181		215		249		283	
148		182		216		250		284	
149		183		217		251		285	
150		184		218		252		286	
151		185		219		253		287	
152		186		220		254		288	
153		187		221		255		289	
154		188		222		256		290	
155		189		223		257		291	
156		190		224		258		292	
157		191		225		259		293	
158		192		226		260		294	
159		193		227		261		295	
160		194		228		262		296	
161		195		229		263		297	
162		196		230		264		298	
163		197		231		265		299	
164		198		232		266		300	
165		199		233		267		301	
166		200		234		268		302	
167		201		235		269		303	
168		202		236		270		304	
169		203		237		271		305	
170		204		238		272		306	
171		205		239		273		307	
172		206		240		274		308	
173		207		241		275		309	

Question #	✔
310	
311	
312	
313	
314	
315	
316	
317	
318	
319	
320	
321	
322	
323	
324	
325	
326	
327	
328	
329	
330	
331	
332	
333	
334	
335	
336	
337	
338	
339	
340	
341	
342	
343	

Question #	✔
344	
345	
346	
347	
348	
349	
350	
351	
352	
353	
354	
355	
356	
357	
358	
359	
360	
361	
362	
363	
364	
365	
366	
367	
368	
369	
370	
371	
372	
373	
374	
375	
376	
377	

Question #	✔
378	
379	
380	
381	
382	
383	
384	
385	
386	
387	
388	
389	
390	
391	
392	
393	
394	
395	
396	
397	
398	
399	
400	
401	
402	
403	
404	
405	
406	
407	
408	
409	
410	
411	

Question #	✔
412	
413	
414	
415	
416	
417	
418	
419	
420	
421	
422	
423	
424	
425	
426	
427	
428	
429	
430	
431	
432	
433	
434	
435	
436	
437	
438	
439	
440	
441	
442	
443	
444	
445	

Question #	✔
446	
447	
448	
449	
450	
451	
452	
453	
454	
Exodus	
455	
456	
457	
458	
459	
460	
461	
462	
463	
464	
465	
466	
467	
468	
469	
470	
471	
472	
473	
474	
475	
476	
477	
478	

Question #	✔
479	
480	
481	
482	
483	
484	
485	
486	
487	
488	
489	
490	
491	
492	
493	
494	
495	
496	
497	
498	
499	
500	
501	
502	
503	
504	
505	
506	
507	
508	
509	
510	
511	
512	

Question #	✔
513	
514	
515	
516	
517	
518	
519	
520	
521	
522	
523	
524	
525	
526	
527	
528	
529	
530	
531	
532	
533	
534	
535	
536	
537	
538	
539	
540	
541	
542	
543	
544	
545	
546	

Question #	✔
547	
548	
549	
550	
551	
552	
553	
554	
555	
556	
557	
558	
559	
560	
561	
562	
563	
564	
565	
566	
567	
568	
569	
570	
571	
572	
573	
574	
575	
576	
577	
578	
579	
580	

Question #	✔
581	
582	
583	
584	
585	
586	
587	
588	
589	
590	
591	
592	
593	
594	
595	
596	
597	
598	
599	
600	
601	
602	
603	
604	
605	
606	
607	
608	
609	
610	
611	
612	
613	
614	

Question #	✔
615	
616	
617	
618	
619	
620	
621	
622	
623	
624	
625	
626	
627	
628	
629	
630	
631	
632	
633	
634	
635	
636	
637	
638	
639	
640	
641	
642	
643	
644	
645	
646	
647	
648	

Question #	✔	Question #	✔	Question #	✔	Question #	✔	Question #	✔
649		683		717		750		784	
650		684		718		751		785	
651		685		719		752		786	
652		686		720		753		787	
653		687		*Leviticus*		754		788	
654		688		721		755		789	
655		689		722		756		790	
656		690		723		757		791	
657		691		724		758		792	
658		692		725		759		793	
659		693		726		760		794	
660		694		727		761		795	
661		695		728		762		796	
662		696		729		763		797	
663		697		730		764		798	
664		698		731		765		799	
665		699		732		766		800	
666		700		733		767		801	
667		701		734		768		*Numbers*	
668		702		735		769		802	
669		703		736		770		803	
670		704		737		771		804	
671		705		738		772		805	
672		706		739		773		806	
673		707		740		774		807	
674		708		741		775		808	
675		709		742		776		809	
676		710		743		777		810	
677		711		744		778		811	
678		712		745		779		812	
679		713		746		780		813	
680		714		747		781		814	
681		715		748		782		815	
682		716		749		783		816	

Question #	✔
817	
818	
819	
820	
821	
822	
823	
824	
825	
826	
827	
828	
829	
830	
831	
832	
833	
834	
835	
836	
837	
838	
839	
840	
841	
842	
843	
844	
845	
846	
847	
848	
849	
850	

Question #	✔
851	
852	
853	
854	
855	
856	
857	
858	
859	
860	
861	
862	
863	
864	
865	
866	
867	
868	
869	
870	
871	
872	
873	
874	
875	
876	
877	
878	
879	
880	
881	
882	
883	
884	

Question #	✔
885	
886	
887	
888	
889	
890	
891	
892	
893	
894	
895	
896	
897	
898	
899	
900	
901	
902	
903	
904	
905	
906	
907	
908	
909	
910	
911	
912	
913	
914	
915	
916	
917	
918	

Question #	✔
919	
920	
921	
922	
923	
924	
925	
926	
927	
928	
929	
930	
931	
932	
933	
934	
935	
936	
937	
938	
939	
940	
941	
942	
943	
944	
945	
946	
947	
Deuteronomy	
948	
949	
950	
951	

Question #	✔
952	
953	
954	
955	
956	
957	
958	
959	
960	
961	
962	
963	
964	
965	
966	
967	
968	
969	
970	
971	
972	
973	
974	
975	
976	
977	
978	
979	
980	
981	
982	
983	
984	
985	

Question #	✔
986	
987	
988	
989	
990	
991	
992	
993	
994	
995	
996	
997	
998	
999	
1000	
1001	
1002	
1003	
1004	
1005	
1006	
1007	
1008	
1009	
1010	
1011	
1012	
1013	
1014	
1015	
1016	
1017	
1018	
1019	

Question #	✔
1020	
1021	
1022	
1023	
1024	
1025	
1026	
1027	
1028	
1029	
1030	
1031	
1032	
1033	
1034	
1035	
1036	
1037	
1038	
1039	
1040	
1041	
1042	
1043	
1044	
1045	
1046	
1047	
1048	
1049	
1050	
1051	
1052	
1053	

Question #	✔
1054	
1055	
Joshua	
1056	
1057	
1058	
1059	
1060	
1061	
1062	
1063	
1064	
1065	
1066	
1067	
1068	
1069	
1070	
1071	
1072	
1073	
1074	
1075	
1076	
1077	
1078	
1079	
1080	
1081	
1082	
1083	
1084	
1085	
1086	

Question #	✔
1087	
1088	
1089	
1090	
1091	
1092	
1093	
1094	
1095	
1096	
1097	
1098	
1099	
1100	
1101	
1102	
1103	
1104	
1105	
1106	
1107	
1108	
1109	
1110	
1111	
1112	
1113	
1114	
1115	
1116	
1117	
1118	
1119	
1120	

Question #	✔
1121	
1122	
1123	
1124	
1125	
1126	
1127	
1128	
1129	
1130	
1131	
1132	
1133	
1134	
1135	
1136	
1137	
1138	
1139	
1140	
1141	
1142	
1143	
1144	
1145	
1146	
Judges	
1147	
1148	
1149	
1150	
1151	
1152	
1153	

Question #	✔
1154	
1155	
1156	
1157	
1158	
1159	
1160	
1161	
1162	
1163	
1164	
1165	
1166	
1167	
1168	
1169	
1170	
1171	
1172	
1173	
1174	
1175	
1176	
1177	
1178	
1179	
1180	
1181	
1182	
1183	
1184	
1185	
1186	
1187	

Question #	✔
1188	
1189	
1190	
1191	
1192	
1193	
1194	
1195	
1196	
1197	
1198	
1199	
1200	
1201	
1202	
1203	
1204	
1205	
1206	
1207	
1208	
1209	
1210	
1211	
1212	
1213	
1214	
1215	
1216	
1217	
1218	
1219	
1220	
1221	

Question #	✔
1222	
1223	
1224	
1225	
1226	
1227	
1228	
1229	
1230	
1231	
1232	
1233	
1234	
1235	
1236	
1237	
1238	
1239	
1240	
1241	
1242	
1243	
1244	
1245	
1246	
1247	
1248	
1249	
1250	
1251	
1252	
1253	
1254	
1255	

Question #	✔
1256	
1257	
1258	
1259	
1260	
1261	
1262	
1263	
1264	
1265	
1266	
1267	
1268	
1269	
1270	
1271	
1272	
1273	
1274	
1275	
1276	
1277	
1278	
1279	
1280	
1281	
1282	
1283	
1284	
1285	
1286	
1287	
1288	
1289	

Question #	✔
1290	
1291	
1292	
1293	
1294	
1295	
1296	
1297	
1298	
Ruth	
1299	
1300	
1301	
1302	
1303	
1304	
1305	
1306	
1307	
1308	
1309	
1310	
1311	
1312	
1313	
1314	
1315	
1316	
1317	
1318	
1319	
1320	
1321	
1322	

Question #	✔	Question #	✔	Question #	✔	Question #	✔	Question #	✔
1323		1356		1390		1424		1458	
1324		1357		1391		1425		1459	
1 Samuel		1358		1392		1426		1460	
1325		1359		1393		1427		1461	
1326		1360		1394		1428		1462	
1327		1361		1395		1429		1463	
1328		1362		1396		1430		1464	
1329		1363		1397		1431		1465	
1330		1364		1398		1432		1466	
1331		1365		1399		1433		1467	
1332		1366		1400		1434		1468	
1333		1367		1401		1435		1469	
1334		1368		1402		1436		1470	
1335		1369		1403		1437		1471	
1336		1370		1404		1438		1472	
1337		1371		1405		1439		1473	
1338		1372		1406		1440		1474	
1339		1373		1407		1441		1475	
1340		1374		1408		1442		1476	
1341		1375		1409		1443		1477	
1342		1376		1410		1444		1478	
1343		1377		1411		1445		1479	
1344		1378		1412		1446		1480	
1345		1379		1413		1447		1481	
1346		1380		1414		1448		1482	
1347		1381		1415		1449		1483	
1348		1382		1416		1450		1484	
1349		1383		1417		1451		1485	
1350		1384		1418		1452		1486	
1351		1385		1419		1453		1487	
1352		1386		1420		1454		1488	
1353		1387		1421		1455		1489	
1354		1388		1422		1456		1490	
1355		1389		1423		1457		1491	

Question #	✔
1492	
1493	
1494	
1495	
1496	
1497	
1498	
1499	
1500	
1501	
1502	
1503	
1504	
1505	
1506	
1507	
1508	
2 Samuel	
1509	
1510	
1511	
1512	
1513	
1514	
1515	
1516	
1517	
1518	
1519	
1520	
1521	
1522	
1523	
1524	

Question #	✔
1525	
1526	
1527	
1528	
1529	
1530	
1531	
1532	
1533	
1534	
1535	
1536	
1537	
1538	
1539	
1540	
1541	
1542	
1543	
1544	
1545	
1546	
1547	
1548	
1549	
1550	
1551	
1552	
1553	
1554	
1555	
1556	
1557	
1558	

Question #	✔
1559	
1560	
1561	
1562	
1563	
1564	
1565	
1566	
1567	
1568	
1569	
1570	
1571	
1572	
1573	
1574	
1575	
1576	
1577	
1578	
1579	
1580	
1581	
1582	
1583	
1584	
1585	
1586	
1587	
1588	
1589	
1590	
1591	
1592	

Question #	✔
1593	
1594	
1595	
1596	
1597	
1598	
1599	
1600	
1601	
1602	
1603	
1604	
1605	
1606	
1607	
1608	
1609	
1610	
1611	
1612	
1613	
1614	
1615	
1616	
1617	
1618	
1619	
1620	
1621	
1622	
1623	
1624	
1625	
1626	

Question #	✔
1627	
1628	
1629	
1630	
1631	
1632	
1633	
1634	
1635	
1636	
1637	
1638	
1639	
1640	
1641	
1642	
1643	
1644	
1645	
1646	
1647	
1648	
1649	
1650	
1651	
1652	
1653	
1654	
1655	
1656	
1657	
1 Kings	
1658	
1659	

Question #	✔
1660	
1661	
1662	
1663	
1664	
1665	
1666	
1667	
1668	
1669	
1670	
1671	
1672	
1673	
1674	
1675	
1676	
1677	
1678	
1679	
1680	
1681	
1682	
1683	
1684	
1685	
1686	
1687	
1688	
1689	
1690	
1691	
1692	
1693	

Question #	✔
1694	
1695	
1696	
1697	
1698	
1699	
1700	
1701	
1702	
1703	
1704	
1705	
1706	
1707	
1708	
1709	
1710	
1711	
1712	
1713	
1714	
1715	
1716	
1717	
1718	
1719	
1720	
1721	
1722	
1723	
1724	
1725	
1726	
1727	

Question #	✔
1728	
1729	
1730	
1731	
1732	
1733	
1734	
1735	
1736	
1737	
1738	
1739	
1740	
1741	
1742	
1743	
1744	
1745	
1746	
1747	
1748	
1749	
1750	
1751	
1752	
1753	
1754	
1755	
1756	
1757	
1758	
1759	
1760	
1761	

Question #	✔
1762	
1763	
1764	
1765	
1766	
1767	
1768	
1769	
1770	
1771	
1772	
1773	
1774	
1775	
1776	
1777	
1778	
1779	
1780	
1781	
1782	
1783	
1784	
1785	
1786	
1787	
1788	
1789	
1790	
1791	
1792	
1793	
1794	
1795	

Question #	✔
1796	
1797	
1798	
1799	
1800	
1801	
1802	
1803	
1804	
1805	
1806	
1807	
1808	
1809	
1810	
1811	
1812	
1813	
1814	
1815	
1816	
1817	
1818	
1819	
1820	
1821	
1822	
1823	
1824	
1825	
1826	
1827	
1828	
1829	

Question #	✔	Question #	✔	Question #	✔	Question #	✔	Question #	✔
1830		1863		1897		1931		1965	
1831		1864		1898		1932		1966	
1832		1865		1899		1933		1967	
1833		1866		1900		1934		1968	
1834		1867		1901		1935		1969	
1835		1868		1902		1936		1970	
1836		1869		1903		1937		1971	
1837		1870		1904		1938		1972	
1838		1871		1905		1939		1973	
1839		1872		1906		1940		1974	
1840		1873		1907		1941		1975	
1841		1874		1908		1942		1976	
1842		1875		1909		1943		1977	
1843		1876		1910		1944		1978	
1844		1877		1911		1945		1979	
1845		1878		1912		1946		1980	
1846		1879		1913		1947		1981	
2 Kings		1880		1914		1948		1982	
1847		1881		1915		1949		1983	
1848		1882		1916		1950		1984	
1849		1883		1917		1951		1985	
1850		1884		1918		1952		1986	
1851		1885		1919		1953		1987	
1852		1886		1920		1954		1988	
1853		1887		1921		1955		1989	
1854		1888		1922		1956		1990	
1855		1889		1923		1957		1991	
1856		1890		1924		1958		1992	
1857		1891		1925		1959		1993	
1858		1892		1926		1960		1994	
1859		1893		1927		1961		1995	
1860		1894		1928		1962		1996	
1861		1895		1929		1963		1997	
1862		1896		1930		1964		1998	

Question #	✔
1999	
2000	
2001	
2002	
2003	
2004	
2005	
2006	
2007	
2008	
2009	
2010	
2011	
2012	
2013	
2014	
2015	
2016	
2017	
2018	
2019	
2020	
2021	
2022	
2023	
2024	
2025	
2026	
2027	
2028	
1 Chronicles	
2029	
2030	
2031	

Question #	✔
2032	
2033	
2034	
2035	
2036	
2037	
2038	
2039	
2040	
2041	
2042	
2043	
2044	
2045	
2046	
2047	
2048	
2049	
2050	
2051	
2052	
2053	
2054	
2055	
2056	
2057	
2058	
2059	
2060	
2061	
2062	
2063	
2064	
2065	

Question #	✔
2066	
2067	
2068	
2069	
2070	
2071	
2072	
2073	
2074	
2075	
2076	
2077	
2078	
2079	
2080	
2081	
2082	
2083	
2084	
2085	
2086	
2087	
2088	
2089	
2090	
2091	
2092	
2093	
2094	
2095	
2096	
2097	
2098	
2099	

Question #	✔
2100	
2101	
2102	
2103	
2104	
2105	
2106	
2107	
2108	
2109	
2110	
2111	
2112	
2113	
2114	
2115	
2116	
2117	
2118	
2119	
2120	
2121	
2122	
2 Chronicles	
2123	
2124	
2125	
2126	
2127	
2128	
2129	
2130	
2131	
2132	

Question #	✔
2133	
2134	
2135	
2136	
2137	
2138	
2139	
2140	
2141	
2142	
2143	
2144	
2145	
2146	
2147	
2148	
2149	
2150	
2151	
2152	
2153	
2154	
2155	
2156	
2157	
2158	
2159	
2160	
2161	
2162	
2163	
2164	
2165	
2166	

KEEP SCORE

Question #	✔
2167	
2168	
2169	
2170	
2171	
2172	
2173	
2174	
2175	
2176	
2177	
2178	
2179	
2180	
2181	
2182	
2183	
2184	
2185	
2186	
2187	
2188	
2189	
2190	
2191	
2192	
2193	
2194	
2195	
2196	
2197	
2198	
2199	
2200	

Question #	✔
2201	
2202	
2203	
2204	
2205	
2206	
2207	
2208	
2209	
2210	
2211	
2212	
2213	
2214	
2215	
2216	
2217	
2218	
2219	
2220	
2221	
2222	
2223	
2224	
2225	
2226	
2227	
2228	
2229	
2230	
2231	
2232	
2233	
2234	

Question #	✔
2235	
2236	
2237	
2238	
2239	
2240	
2241	
2242	
2243	
2244	
2245	
2246	
2247	
2248	
2249	
2250	
2251	
2252	
2253	
2254	
2255	
2256	
2257	
2258	
2259	
2260	
2261	
2262	
2263	
2264	
2265	
2266	
2267	
2268	

Question #	✔
2269	
2270	
2271	
2272	
2273	
Ezra	
2274	
2275	
2276	
2277	
2278	
2279	
2280	
2281	
2282	
2283	
2284	
2285	
2286	
2287	
2288	
2289	
2290	
2291	
2292	
2293	
2294	
2295	
2296	
2297	
2298	
2299	
2300	
2301	

Question #	✔
2302	
2303	
2304	
2305	
Nehemiah	
2306	
2307	
2308	
2309	
2310	
2311	
2312	
2313	
2314	
2315	
2316	
2317	
2318	
2319	
2320	
2321	
2322	
2323	
2324	
2325	
2326	
2327	
2328	
2329	
2330	
2331	
2332	
2333	
2334	

Question #	✔
2335	
2336	
2337	
2338	
2339	
2340	
2341	
2342	
2343	
2344	
2345	
2346	
2347	
Esther	
2348	
2349	
2350	
2351	
2352	
2353	
2354	
2355	
2356	
2357	
2358	
2359	
2360	
2361	
2362	
2363	
2364	
2365	
2366	
2367	

Question #	✔
2368	
2369	
2370	
2371	
2372	
2373	
2374	
2375	
2376	
2377	
2378	
2379	
2380	
2381	
2382	
2383	
2384	
2385	
2386	
2387	
2388	
2389	
2390	
2391	
2392	
2393	
2394	
2395	
2396	
2397	
2398	
2399	
2400	
2401	

Question #	✔
2402	
2403	
2404	
2405	
2406	
Job	
2407	
2408	
2409	
2410	
2411	
2412	
2413	
2414	
2415	
2416	
2417	
2418	
2419	
2420	
2421	
2422	
2423	
2424	
2425	
2426	
2427	
2428	
2429	
2430	
2431	
2432	
2433	
2434	

Question #	✔
2435	
2436	
2437	
2438	
2439	
2440	
2441	
2442	
2443	
2444	
2445	
2446	
2447	
2448	
2449	
2450	
2451	
2452	
2453	
2454	
2455	
2456	
2457	
2458	
2459	
2460	
2461	
2462	
2463	
2464	
2465	
2466	
2467	
2468	

Question #	✔
2469	
2470	
2471	
2472	
2473	
2474	
2475	
2476	
2477	
2478	
2479	
2480	
2481	
2482	
2483	
2484	
2485	
2486	
2487	
2488	
2489	
2490	
2491	
2492	
2493	
2494	
2495	
2496	
2497	
2498	
2499	
2500	
2501	
2502	

Question #	✔
2503	
2504	
2505	
2506	
2507	
2508	
2509	
2510	
2511	
2512	
2513	
2514	
2515	
2516	
2517	
Psalms	
2518	
2519	
2520	
2521	
2522	
2523	
2524	
2525	
2526	
2527	
2528	
2529	
2530	
2531	
2532	
2533	
2534	
2535	

Question #	✔
2536	
2537	
2538	
2539	
2540	
2541	
2542	
2543	
2544	
2545	
2546	
2547	
2548	
2549	
2550	
2551	
2552	
2553	
2554	
2555	
2556	
2557	
2558	
2559	
2560	
2561	
2562	
2563	
2564	
2565	
2566	
2567	
2568	
2569	

Question #	✔
2570	
2571	
2572	
2573	
2574	
2575	
2576	
2577	
2578	
2579	
2580	
2581	
2582	
2583	
2584	
2585	
2586	
2587	
2588	
2589	
2590	
2591	
2592	
2593	
2594	
2595	
2596	
2597	
2598	
2599	
2600	
2601	
2602	
2603	

Question #	✔
2604	
2605	
2606	
2607	
2608	
2609	
2610	
2611	
2612	
2613	
2614	
2615	
2616	
2617	
2618	
2619	
2620	
2621	
2622	
2623	
2624	
2625	
2626	
2627	
2628	
2629	
2630	
2631	
2632	
2633	
2634	
2635	
2636	
2637	

Question #	✔
2638	
2639	
2640	
2641	
2642	
2643	
2644	
2645	
2646	
2647	
2648	
2649	
2650	
2651	
2652	
2653	
2654	
2655	
2656	
2657	
2658	
2659	
2660	
2661	
2662	
2663	
2664	
2665	
2666	
2667	
2668	
2669	
2670	
2671	

Question #	✔	Question #	✔	Question #	✔	Question #	✔	Question #	✔
2672		2706		2740		2773		2807	
2673		2707		2741		2774		2808	
2674		2708		2742		2775		2809	
2675		2709		2743		2776		2810	
2676		2710		2744		2777		2811	
2677		2711		2745		2778		2812	
2678		2712		2746		2779		2813	
2679		2713		2747		2780		2814	
2680		2714		2748		2781		2815	
2681		2715		2749		2782		2816	
2682		2716		2750		2783		2817	
2683		2717		2751		2784		2818	
2684		2718		2752		2785		2819	
2685		2719		2753		2786		2820	
2686		2720		2754		2787		2821	
2687		2721		2755		2788		2822	
2688		2722		2756		2789		2823	
2689		2723		2757		2790		2824	
2690		2724		2758		2791		2825	
2691		2725		2759		2792		2826	
2692		2726		2760		2793		2827	
2693		2727		2761		2794		2828	
2694		2728		*Proverbs*		2795		2829	
2695		2729		2762		2796		2830	
2696		2730		2763		2797		2831	
2697		2731		2764		2798		2832	
2698		2732		2765		2799		2833	
2699		2733		2766		2800		2834	
2700		2734		2767		2801		2835	
2701		2735		2768		2802		2836	
2702		2736		2769		2803		2837	
2703		2737		2770		2804		2838	
2704		2738		2771		2805		2839	
2705		2739		2772		2806		2840	

Question #	✔
2841	
2842	
2843	
2844	
2845	
2846	
2847	
2848	
2849	
2850	
2851	
2852	
2853	
2854	
2855	
2856	
2857	
2858	
2859	
2860	
2861	
2862	
2863	
2864	
2865	
2866	
2867	
2868	
2869	
2870	
2871	
2872	
2873	
2874	

Question #	✔
2875	
2876	
2877	
2878	
2879	
2880	
2881	
2882	
2883	
2884	
2885	
2886	
2887	
2888	
2889	
2890	
2891	
2892	
2893	
2894	
2895	
2896	
2897	
2898	
2899	
2900	
2901	
2902	
2903	
2904	
2905	
2906	
2907	
2908	

Question #	✔
2909	
2910	
2911	
2912	
2913	
2914	
2915	
2916	
2917	
2918	
2919	
2920	
2921	
2922	
2923	
2924	
2925	
2926	
2927	
2928	
2929	
2930	
2931	
2932	
2933	
2934	
2935	
2936	
Ecclesiastes	
2937	
2938	
2939	
2940	
2941	

Question #	✔
2942	
2943	
2944	
2945	
2946	
2947	
2948	
2949	
2950	
2951	
2952	
2953	
2954	
2955	
2956	
2957	
2958	
2959	
2960	
2961	
2962	
2963	
2964	
2965	
2966	
2967	
2968	
2969	
2970	
2971	
2972	
2973	
2974	
2975	

Question #	✔
2976	
2977	
2978	
2979	
2980	
2981	
2982	
2983	
2984	
2985	
2986	
2987	
2988	
2989	
2990	
Song of Songs	
2991	
2992	
2993	
2994	
2995	
2996	
2997	
2998	
2999	
3000	
3001	
3002	
3003	
3004	
3005	
3006	
3007	
3008	

Question #	✔
3009	
3010	
3011	
3012	
3013	
3014	
3015	
3016	
3017	
3018	
3019	
3020	
3021	
3022	
3023	
3024	
3025	
3026	
3027	
3028	
3029	
3030	
3031	
Isaiah	
3032	
3033	
3034	
3035	
3036	
3037	
3038	
3039	
3040	
3041	

Question #	✔
3042	
3043	
3044	
3045	
3046	
3047	
3048	
3049	
3050	
3051	
3052	
3053	
3054	
3055	
3056	
3057	
3058	
3059	
3060	
3061	
3062	
3063	
3064	
3065	
3066	
3067	
3068	
3069	
3070	
3071	
3072	
3073	
3074	
3075	

Question #	✔
3076	
3077	
3078	
3079	
3080	
3081	
3082	
3083	
3084	
3085	
3086	
3087	
3088	
3089	
3090	
3091	
3092	
3093	
3094	
3095	
3096	
3097	
3098	
3099	
3100	
3101	
3102	
3103	
3104	
3105	
3106	
3107	
3108	
3109	

Question #	✔
3110	
3111	
3112	
3113	
3114	
3115	
3116	
3117	
3118	
3119	
3120	
3121	
3122	
3123	
3124	
3125	
3126	
3127	
3128	
3129	
3130	
3131	
3132	
3133	
3134	
3135	
3136	
3137	
3138	
3139	
3140	
3141	
3142	
3143	

Question #	✔
3144	
3145	
3146	
3147	
3148	
3149	
3150	
3151	
3152	
3153	
3154	
3155	
3156	
3157	
3158	
3159	
3160	
3161	
3162	
3163	
3164	
3165	
3166	
3167	
3168	
3169	
3170	
3171	
3172	
3173	
3174	
3175	
3176	
3177	

Question #	✔	Question #	✔	Question #	✔	Question #	✔	Question #	✔
3178		*Jeremiah*		3244		3278		3312	
3179		3211		3245		3279		3313	
3180		3212		3246		3280		3314	
3181		3213		3247		3281		3315	
3182		3214		3248		3282		3316	
3183		3215		3249		3283		3317	
3184		3216		3250		3284		3318	
3185		3217		3251		3285		3319	
3186		3218		3252		3286		3320	
3187		3219		3253		3287		3321	
3188		3220		3254		3288		3322	
3189		3221		3255		3289		3323	
3190		3222		3256		3290		3324	
3191		3223		3257		3291		3325	
3192		3224		3258		3292		3326	
3193		3225		3259		3293		3327	
3194		3226		3260		3294		3328	
3195		3227		3261		3295		3329	
3196		3228		3262		3296		3330	
3197		3229		3263		3297		3331	
3198		3230		3264		3298		3332	
3199		3231		3265		3299		3333	
3200		3232		3266		3300		3334	
3201		3233		3267		3301		3335	
3202		3234		3268		3302		3336	
3203		3235		3269		3303		3337	
3204		3236		3270		3304		3338	
3205		3237		3271		3305		3339	
3206		3238		3272		3306		3340	
3207		3239		3273		3307		3341	
3208		3240		3274		3308		3342	
3209		3241		3275		3309		3343	
3210		3242		3276		3310		3344	
		3243		3277		3311		3345	

Question #	✔	Question #	✔	Question #	✔	Question #	✔	Question #	✔
3346		3378		3412		3446		3480	
3347		3379		3413		3447		3481	
3348		3380		3414		3448		3482	
3349		3381		3415		3449		3483	
3350		3382		3416		3450		3484	
3351		3383		3417		3451		3485	
3352		3384		3418		3452		3486	
3353		3385		3419		3453		3487	
3354		3386		3420		3454		3488	
3355		3387		3421		3455		3489	
Lamentations		3388		3422		3456		3490	
3356		3389		3423		3457		3491	
3357		3390		3424		3458		3492	
3358		3391		3425		3459		3493	
3359		3392		3426		3460		3494	
3360		3393		3427		3461		3495	
3361		3394		3428		3462		*Daniel*	
3362		3395		3429		3463		3496	
3363		3396		3430		3464		3497	
3364		3397		3431		3465		3498	
3365		3398		3432		3466		3499	
3366		3399		3433		3467		3500	
3367		3400		3434		3468		3501	
3368		3401		3435		3469		3502	
Ezekiel		3402		3436		3470		3503	
3369		3403		3437		3471		3504	
3370		3404		3438		3472		3505	
3371		3405		3439		3473		3506	
3372		3406		3440		3474		3507	
3373		3407		3441		3475		3508	
3374		3408		3442		3476		3509	
3375		3409		3443		3477		3510	
3376		3410		3444		3478		3511	
3377		3411		3445		3479		3512	

Question #	✔
3513	
3514	
3515	
3516	
3517	
3518	
3519	
3520	
3521	
3522	
3523	
3524	
3525	
3526	
3527	
3528	
3529	
3530	
3531	
3532	
3533	
3534	
3535	
3536	
3537	
3538	
3539	
3540	
3541	
3542	
3543	
3544	
3545	

Question #	✔
3546	
3547	
3548	
3549	
3550	
3551	
3552	
3553	
3554	
3555	
3556	
3557	
3558	
3559	
3560	
3561	
3562	
3563	
3564	
3565	
3566	
3567	
3568	
3569	
3570	
3571	
3572	
3573	
3574	
3575	
3576	
3577	
3578	

Question #	✔
3579	
3580	
3581	
3582	
3583	
3584	
3585	
3586	
3587	
3588	
3589	
3590	
3591	
3592	
3593	
3594	
3595	
3596	
Hosea	
3597	
3598	
3599	
3600	
3601	
3602	
3603	
3604	
3605	
3606	
3607	
3608	
3609	
3610	

Question #	✔
3611	
3612	
3613	
3614	
3615	
3616	
3617	
3618	
3619	
3620	
3621	
3622	
3623	
3624	
Joel	
3625	
3626	
3627	
3628	
3629	
3630	
3631	
3632	
3633	
3634	
3635	
3636	
3637	
3638	
3639	
3640	
Amos	
3641	

Question #	✔
3642	
3643	
3644	
3645	
3646	
3647	
3648	
3649	
3650	
3651	
3652	
3653	
3654	
3655	
3656	
3657	
3658	
3659	
3660	
3661	
3662	
3663	
3664	
3665	
3666	
3667	
3668	
3669	
Obadiah	
3670	
3671	
3672	
3673	

Question #	✔
3674	
Jonah	
3675	
3676	
3677	
3678	
3679	
3680	
3681	
3682	
3683	
3684	
3685	
3686	
3687	
3688	
3689	
3690	
3691	
3692	
3693	
3694	
3695	
3696	
3697	
3698	
Micah	
3699	
3700	
3701	
3702	
3703	
3704	

Question #	✔
3705	
3706	
3707	
3708	
3709	
3710	
3711	
3712	
3713	
3714	
3715	
3716	
Nahum	
3717	
3718	
3719	
3720	
3721	
3722	
3723	
3724	
3725	
Habakuk	
3726	
3727	
3728	
3729	
3730	
3731	
3732	
Zephaniah	
3733	
3734	

Question #	✔
3735	
3736	
3737	
3738	
3739	
Haggai	
3740	
3741	
3742	
3743	
3744	
3745	
3746	
3747	
3748	
3749	
Zechariah	
3750	
3751	
3752	
3753	
3754	
3755	
3756	
3757	
3758	
3759	
3760	
3761	
3762	
3763	
3764	
3765	

Question #	✔
3766	
3767	
3768	
3769	
3770	
3771	
3772	
3773	
3774	
3775	
3776	
3777	
3778	
3779	
3780	
3781	
3782	
3783	
3784	
3785	
3786	
3787	
3788	
3789	
3790	
3791	
3792	
3793	
3794	
3795	
Malachi	
3796	
3797	

Question #	✔
3798	
3799	
3800	
3801	
3802	
3803	
3804	
3805	
3806	
3807	
3808	

Group Quiz Score Card

Here's 150 spaces for you to choose your own questions.
Make copies and set up a group challenge!

QUESTION #	CORRECT	INCORRECT	QUESTION #	CORRECT	INCORRECT	QUESTION #	CORRECT	INCORRECT	QUESTION #	CORRECT	INCORRECT	QUESTION #	CORRECT	INCORRECT

																QUESTION #
																CORRECT
																INCORRECT
																QUESTION #
																CORRECT
																INCORRECT
																QUESTION #
																CORRECT
																INCORRECT
																QUESTION #
																CORRECT
																INCORRECT
																QUESTION #
																CORRECT
																INCORRECT

Group Quiz Score Card

QUESTION #	CORRECT	INCORRECT	QUESTION #	CORRECT	INCORRECT	QUESTION #	CORRECT	INCORRECT	QUESTION #	CORRECT	INCORRECT	QUESTION #	CORRECT	INCORRECT

																QUESTION #
																CORRECT
																INCORRECT
																QUESTION #
																CORRECT
																INCORRECT
																QUESTION #
																CORRECT
																INCORRECT
																QUESTION #
																CORRECT
																INCORRECT
																QUESTION #
																CORRECT
																INCORRECT

About the Author

Troy is a writer with credits in publishing, television, and video. Some of the highlights of his career include: the producer for the GSN game show *The American Bible Challenge*, writer of the popular Max Lucado series Hermie & Friends, host and writer of the GLO documentary *In His Shoes*, and writer for three seasons of *The Mickey Mouse Club*.

Troy is also a campus pastor at First Baptist Church of Windermere, Florida, where he has worked since 1997. He has written a number of books for children and inspirational books for adults.